For more information,
contact publishing@burningman.org
First paperback edition October 2021
Published by Burning Man Project, San Francisco USA

Cover art by Louise Jarmilowicz
Cover design by Dominic "DA" Tinio
Book design by David Marr
Edited by Stuart Mangrum

ISBN 978-1-7349659-2-6 (paperback)
ISBN 978-1-7349659-3-3 (ebook)
www.fascinatingstranger.com
www.burningman.org

TURN YOUR LIFE INTO ART

LESSONS IN PSYCHOMAGIC
FROM THE SAN FRANCISCO UNDERGROUND

By Caveat Magister aka Benjamin Wachs
© 2021 Benjamin Wachs

Published by Burning Man Project, San Francisco USA

THIS BOOK IS DEDICATED:

To Sondra Carr,
the extraordinary artist with whom I first explored
these techniques.

To Misa Rygrova,
my bodyguard, who first encouraged me to write this book.

To Nicole Marie Johnson,
for everything else.

TABLE OF CONTENTS

INTRODUCTION

I'm sorry to have to tell you this, America, but you don't know what you missed.

That goes doubly for the world.

If you didn't live in the San Francisco Bay Area at some point between approximately 1983 and 2015, you missed one of the most extraordinary underground scenes in the history of art and culture – one that was so different, so unique, that most cultural observers still have no idea what it was they didn't understand, or didn't even see.

I grant you that every significant art scene can lay a claim to being both unique and unappreciated in its time – the Harlem Renaissance was quite the thing, too, and America still hasn't given it its credit, either. I'm quite partial to the Vienna coffee house scene in the period after WWI. But at least when we look at these periods, we understand what we're missing. Something fundamentally different was happening in the SF Bay Area across 30-odd years, and because it was not understood, the lessons learned from it are unintelligible to many of the people who need them most. Which is a pity, because they are lessons that everyone from giant Fortune 500 companies to small art colonies are struggling to figure out.

That lesson? How to create profound, some would even say "transformative" experiences. The underground artists and practitioners of this movement reached a peak of what is now called "experience design" that not only has no one else climbed, but most people are still staring at, trying to figure out how high it goes.

San Francisco didn't invent it – every culture has had people creating amazing experiences for one another in some form (Masses in cathedrals are pretty cool, right? And I heard ancient Greek bacchanals were great) – but San Francisco underground artists were able to refine the practice into something that often seems like magic. That indeed appears to create magical experiences. Miracles without religion.

The way in which most of the world figured out that something weird and new was happening in San Francisco was the development of Burning Man, which by now most people have heard of and is a global media darling, with exhibits of its art appearing around the world, including in the Smithsonian, and academic conferences being held about it, and recognition from the White House, and jokes about it appearing on The Simpsons (which was a terrible episode), Malcolm in the Middle (which was a great episode), South Park (in which the elder god Cthullu destroyed Burning Man, and was actually pretty true to life), 30 Rock, and a thousand stand-up routines looking for a lazy punchline. Most people still don't really understand Burning Man, but they know it's a thing, it's a movement, and they can point at it, and laugh at how stupid people look without their clothes on.

Corporations are now paying big money to try to capture

the flame of that Burning Man "experience" – but the closest they've come is "music festivals" with "branded content" and "big name DJs." Which is actually less fun than a really good board game night and far less profound a human experience than a junior prom.

People who have studied Burning Man more closely know that it wasn't *sui generis* – it didn't come out of nowhere. Nothing ever does. It emerged out of a scene of blue collar philosophers, a group of surreal pranksters called "The Cacophony Society," and a collection of existential daredevils known as "the Suicide Club."

What's even less well known, a history struggling to be told, is the degree to which other daring groups of inspired madmen were also profoundly influential. The Diggers, from the 60s; Survival Research Labs, a group whose events were so dangerous that they have been blacklisted by the San Francisco Fire Department; Cyclecide, the world's first punk rock bicycle troupe, and many more.

And then – and this is what almost nobody knows – there are the groups that came later, who didn't build Burning Man (though they are often composed of people who had helped) but who operated in its shadow, pushing the envelope of what was possible. Very few of them were public facing, the most open being the San Francisco Institute of Possibility (the SFIOP), which was entirely above ground and open to anyone who wanted to join. Groups like the Mystic Midway and Hoax put on shows, and thus were "open" to the extent you could get a ticket or a job. The Jejune Institute and the Latitude Society both played at being secret organizations; they were difficult to get into, but they were in fact open to the public if you could stumble or work your way in. But most of these groups were either ad hoc ... there was nothing to join if you weren't already in the scene ... or they had strict rules about when someone could or couldn't acknowledge their existence, and anyone who violated them was forever banned from their presence. Even writing this book, I'm not going to tell you who they are because I'd like to keep attending some of their events.

Put all this together, and you have over 30 years of an extraordinary counter-cultural record, a rich set of heroes to be cheered and stories to be told, of parties and art events that were psychology experiments, and magical rituals attempting to connect the profane with the ineffable. It's a history that must be recorded.

This book is not that history.

This book is an explanation of *what they learned.* How they did it.

This book is the theory of experience design that came out of their practice. A how-to manual for creating breakthrough experiences, as individuals and communities. For living a life that connects the profane with the ineffable. To turn your life into art.

It is a practical how-to manual, but it will not cover a lot of the superficial aspects of what is now increasingly referred to as "experience design." Go to an Immersive Design Summit (the first of which was held in San Francisco in 2017, because the scene was so active), and you'll hear a lot about narrative structure and how to branch decisions and creating experiences for political action and acquiring funding, and related things. And these are all useful, and worth talking about if you want to design a conference ice-breaker; but they are what you talk about when you're not talking about the real thing. The experiences that fundamentally change lives. That touch souls. That feel like impossible magic, rather than merely good design.

This book is about how the San Francisco scene did what made it special, and then never wrote it down because everybody who "needed to know" already knew. It's what geniuses talked about over drinks as they planned impossible things - not what they talked to prospective employers about after they professionalized.

At the end, it will be a manifesto explaining why rag-tag groups of weirdo artists have been so good at this, and why big money corporations filled with equally talented people have been so bad. We can help big corporations and political activists and municipal theater troupes alike get better at it, but experience design at this level, at these heights, will always require freaks and monks devoted to their craft above all else. It's not just about talent, it's about what you're willing to risk.

Me and My Sources

This is as close as we're going to get to a history lesson in this book. You can skip this part if you just want to get right to the bit about how to create experiences that lead to psychological breakthroughs that change the lives of everyone you know.

Take a moment and decide if you're in a hurry.

Okay? Great.

This scene, as I said, has many cultural heroes. I am not one of them.

But I am the guy who many of the cultural heroes of this scene talked to and who some of them turned to, to synthesize their ideas into words.

In 2007 I met John Law, one of the key founders of Burning Man, one of the founders of the Cacophony Society, a member of the Suicide Club, and a legendary urban explorer to this day. We became friends and began a series of conversations about that cultural history that continued through 2017.

In 2007 I also met "Chicken John" Rinaldi, a former protégé of Law's, a member of the Cacophony Society, an early pioneer of Burning Man's Department of Public Works, and a brilliant reprobate whose "criminal mind" would go on to create some of the most bizarrely magical urban events in San Francisco's modern history. We became close friends. When Chicken wanted to write books about living your life as art and the challenges art organizations face in the 21st century, he turned to me to be his official editor and unofficial ghost writer. Those books were fairly successful within the scene, but so far as we can tell never really traveled out of it; their secrets are still secret. When he created a non-profit to serve as a hub and training ground for this scene, I helped him organize it, and I served as the chair of its board from 2013 – 2018.

In 2013, Burning Man's primary founder, Larry Harvey, reached out to me: He said he had been influenced by my writings on Burning Man, and wanted to meet. We instantly struck up a friendship, and would remain close friends through his death in 2018, talking not just about Burning Man, but about culture, constantly.

These friendships put me in an unusual position: at this point John, Chicken, and Larry all loathed each other. Don't be surprised: it was a scene. People have falling outs. Drama happens. But by the time I met Larry, John and Chicken had said so many terrible things about him that I was expecting to be ushered into the presence of Satan himself. I got over it, and was one of very few people to be on good terms with all of them, and was perhaps the only confidant on cultural matters that they had in common during that decade.

The scene, meanwhile, was beginning a new growth spurt, as organizations I am committed to not naming began deliberately picking up the mantle of a generation of earlier experience artists and public pranksters. It was a period of creative destruction, and exiles from collapsed groups like the Latitude Society would, in a few years, start to found businesses that would bring experiences descended from this tradition to corporate events and conferences.

Today I have a strange place in this world: I came to San Francisco in 2006, arriving at the closing decade of the period we're talking about. But I got so deeply in it that people who had been involved much longer started putting me back in time – describing me as "a Burning Man elder," or claiming that I was a regular at a legendary bar that closed in 2004. That's still pretty weird to me, and it is important that I not claim false glory. While we'll hear plenty of my stories, all of the really important work we're going to talk about in this book was done by other people.

This is also still a movement without a manifesto – it mostly has oral traditions and lineages. There are no schools of thought, but there are tight lines delineating who worked with whom, and arguments between them. People clearly align with one group or another, both on the basis of the kind of experiences they create and the personalities involved, but there is no common vocabulary to explain these differences. A few books have emerged out of the scene, but they are mostly picture books specifically about Burning Man or the

Cacophony Society, rather than the scene and its techniques as a whole. Chicken was attempting to write unifying texts and create a common vocabulary in the books I wrote with him in 2011 and 2015, and Larry was attempting in a roundabout way to develop a common vocabulary through the writing I worked with him on about Burning Man's themes in the last years of his life, but ... as in many scenes ... these works were taken more as referendums on what you thought about Chicken and Larry themselves, rather than something that was engaged with on substance.

Perhaps not surprisingly, most of what a scene about experience design has to say about itself was best said through the experiences it created, not the words written about us.

So to describe what this scene teaches us, I'll be telling a lot of stories about events, I'll be leaning on the work of Chicken, Larry, John, and others where I can. Where I can't I'll be leaning on sources from outside of the scene – thinkers and theorists who I believe have had their insights validated by what the scene achieved and how it was done. In particular I'll be turning to the insights of existential-humanistic psychology (with an emphasis on the work of Rollo May, Carl Rogers, and Kirk Schneider), Carl Jung's depth psychology, and Alejandro Jodorowsky's critical notion of "psychomagic."

Indeed, to the extent that a single word needs to be found to encapsulate the specific kind of experiences that the San Francisco underground experience design scene created and honed, I think it is that term: psychomagic. We created psychomagical experiences, and we did it better than anyone.

These thinkers and ideas were not unknown to the San Francisco scene – on the contrary, it was possible to get into long, long, talks about them – and in fact much of the development of humanistic and existential psychology was done in San Francisco, some of it contemporaneous with the development of this scene. There are meaningful links. But they also didn't represent a common vocabulary for the scene the way Burning Man terms, the work of Gary Warne, and (to a lesser extent) Chicken's conceptual framework did. This is my attempt at a synthesis, and I think these outside concepts are often the best way to describe what this scene actually achieved.

Got it? Okay.

The first section of this book will talk about what psychomagical experiences are, and why they have such a powerful effect – it's a guided tour of the unconscious psyche and what happens when you reach it.

The second section is the "how" – how to design experiences, large and small, that get this process going and turn the world we live in into a magical garden and infinite game for people to play in.

The third and final section will take a step back and look at the implications of all this – what we'll want to keep in mind about artists and society, about businesses and civic groups, now that we know how this works.

There we go. Now let's talk about how to build experiences that are actually magic rituals that will change your soul forever.

SECTION 1

Who We Are and What We're Looking For

I want to tell you a story about two different bars. Here's the first one.

Not too long ago I was in Prague, and I went to an alchemy themed bar. It was part of a building where real alchemists, of historical note, had lived and worked in the 16th century. It was decorated to the nines to represent a modern version of an alchemist's lab combined with a bar. Formulas and diagrams were written on all the walls. Glass laboratory jars were on each table holding liquids of weird colors – we weren't sure if they were candles or drinks or what. A series of tubes forming a large chemistry apparatus hung from the ceiling, and ran the length of it. When you walked inside, you really walked into something. It was impressive.

But the menus were standard bar menus, just with alchemy themed drinks. And the process of ordering was exactly the same as bars everywhere, and the process of getting the drinks was exactly the same as bars everywhere, and at the end of the night all the decoration was really just a façade. You were in a standard bar where the experience you had was exactly the same one as you would have everyplace else, and would mostly hang not on anything that the bar did, but on whether you and your friends were enjoying yourselves.

Which we did. We totally did, my friends and I. But after the first moment of "wow, cool," we really could have been at any bar, anywhere.

You see what I'm saying? That's the first story.

Here's the second story.

One night, two strangers from Los Angeles, a couple, walked into what I like to euphemistically call the "Magical Bar." It has a real name, but I have others I like to use. When people ask me about it, I tell them: "San Francisco has many good bars, and several great bars, but this is the only bar that matters."

For the record, I am only telling you absolutely true stories in this book.

It's a small room attached to a much larger bar. That much larger bar is louder, with seating. The magical bar has no seating, just a small L-shaped counter with a man standing behind it and a few people standing around it.

Sometimes, I am one of those people.

Seeing their puzzled looks, the bartender, Aaron, asked them "is this your first time here?"

Yes, they said.

"Well," Aaron said, gesturing at me, "we actually like to have him introduce you to all this, if that's all right."

Now they gave me a puzzled look. "Sure," the man said.

"Oh, great!" I said, gesturing for them to stand next to me. "It's really important to have somebody explain the experience you're about to have, because it's easy to misunderstand it at first. In fact, a lot of people come in here under the very mistaken impression ... and maybe you have too ... that they are in a bar. Is that something you think? That you're in a bar? It's okay if you do, there's no shame, a lot of people do that."

"Yes," the man said. The woman nodded. They looked around again.

"Sure," I said. "Happens all the time, and it's completely understandable. You walk in, there's a counter, there's a guy behind it, there are shelves of liquor behind him ... and you think, 'this is a bar. I'm about to have a bar experience.' Completely understandable. Absolutely. But ..."

My tone darkened. "It is a mistake." I let the gravity of that fact sink in.

"This ... is not a bar. This ... bears only a passing resemblance to a bar. This ... has the same resemblance to a bar that absolute reality bears to the shadows on the wall in Plato's cave! THIS, in other words, is the Platonic ideal of a bar! Its perfect form! The state to which all bars aspire!"

They gaped at me, shocked. But also eagerly anticipating.

Tonight was nothing like they'd expected.

"And it turns out that the perfect form of a bar is not a bar at all. It is, in fact, a church. You are in a church. A place of prayer, and miracles, and fellowship."

They considered this. "Okay," the woman said. "Okay." The man looked around again.

"And the way most people first connect to this," I said, "the way they first realize that something different is happening, is when they see that here, in this place, there are no drink menus. Here, there is no prescribed list of ingredients that are shuffled around mechanistically, or even algorithmically, to put us all on the same conveyor belt or assembly line towards mediocrity. NO! The only way to get a drink here ..." my tone was strident now, filled with holy fervor, " ... is to walk up to this structure," I ran my hand along the bar, "which is an altar. And offer up across it a prayer from your heart. It can be ANYTHING, as long as it is truly from your heart. A wish, a desire, a memory, a sense impression, a fictional character, a fragment of poetry, a personal problem, an abstract concept, a historical event ... ANYTHING, as long as it is from your heart. And THIS MAN!"

I slammed my hand upon the bar.

"... this purple Pope in our church! Will answer that prayer, in drink form!"

The bartender, stunned at the thunder in my voice, jumped and pretended to nearly drop a glass.

"A unique, never before created cocktail will be made expressly to address the wishes of your heart, and then never be made again. A perfect miracle encapsulating the truth that in this place every drink order is a prayer and every prayer is answered with a drink, and IT IS GOOD! And that is the experience that you are about to have here tonight, and friends I welcome you to our congregation!"

They gaped. They laughed. They clapped. And then, hesitantly, they stepped up to the bar ... and spoke from their hearts. She talked about a challenge she was facing in life. He described a childhood memory. Each of them received a strange elixir in a baroque glass, took a sip ... and gaped again. Yes, they said. This is it! Somehow, this was my thought, my wish, my need, in drink form.

"Can I get an amen!" I called out. "AMEN!" they both called back.

The room cheered. I raised up my hands. "HALLELUJAH, BROTHERS AND SISTERS! A MIRACLE HAS OCCURRED!"

As they sipped their drinks, they asked about what everyone else in the room was drinking: what had we prayed for? Whenever someone ordered another drink, the room hushed to listen, and all eyes followed Aaron as he worked his magic.

A few hours later, they were ready to go. They stopped to see me on their way out. "Thank you," they said, "for the most amazing night of drinking we've ever had."

"You're welcome, but ..." I waved the compliment away and pointed at Aaron. "Really, he did all the work."

"No, you don't understand," the woman said to me. "It could have just been you and a glass of water, and it still would have been the most amazing drinking experience of my life."

That is one of the best compliments I've ever received. But of course it's not true: it really mattered that the bartender here could actually live up to the story I told about him. Indeed, the patter I'd developed for this place, with which I'd introduced hundreds of people to this bar over the years, was based on the bartender's skills: I hadn't created a story and then found the bartenders who could live up to it, I'd found bartenders who were doing this and then found a way to describe it that enhanced the truth of the moment, honed it, but never lied about it.

Still ... the fact that they were thanking me and not Aaron is indicative of something very important: what mattered to them wasn't really the quality of the drinks, even if they were amazing and unique. What mattered to them was the experience they had, and the connections they made with other people through it.

Chapter 1:
Nightlife as a Spiritual Pursuit

Why do people go to bars and clubs?

This may seem like a stupidly basic question with an obvious answer: "to have fun!" But that's the kind of answer that hides more than it explains.

I mean, what recreational activity, what personal endeavor that isn't done because the person you work for tells you to do it or a loved one guilts you into trying it with them, isn't at some level done "for fun?" The question isn't "why do anything at all" (for FUN!) but why do *this* instead of *that.* Why go to bars and clubs instead of going to a movie or playing with your cat?

Not that there's anything wrong with staying home watching a movie while you snuggle with your cat. Or (even better) sneaking your cat into a movie theater. (Actually, that's a great idea – hold that thought.) But why are there times when people who have access to very good movies and very good cats will still decide to go out to a bar or a club? What kind of experience are they looking for?

I've had this conversation a lot, beginning when I was a freelance nightlife reporter for Playboy.com back in the 90s, and the answer that people most reach for first is the booze: they go out to have a drink. But outside of very high end cocktails that really do require a professional hand with an extensive shelf of obscure ingredients, bars are actually an incredibly inefficient alcohol delivery system. It is simpler, more efficient, and cheaper, to drink at home.

Another common answer is to hang out with friends. Which, sure, okay, that's a thing; but again, if the goal is really just to hang out with friends, there are a lot of other ways to do it. You can hang out at somebody's home. You can hang out in a park. On a street corner. Have dinner together at a restaurant. Drink coffee at a Starbucks. Protest outside a Star- bucks. There are so many choices. Yet a lot of people want to go to the bar or the club, even though the easiest thing in the world is to get some friends together and to drink at home, which will probably save you a shit-ton of money and possibly aggravation.

What about meeting new people? We're closer now – except that a lot of people, even most people, will go to a bar or a club and only end up talking to their friends. Or drinking alone. This answer also used to be a better one before the digital revolution. We used to go to bars and clubs to meet people, sort of, but now we meet the people we might later go to bars with on the internet. Going to bars specifically to meet people is going the way of the flip phone.

To find sex partners? Yeah, sure, kind of ... but again there are lots of other ways to do that, and, once again, going to bars and clubs is actually a pretty inefficient means of doing that. The possibility is always there, but, the vast majority of people who go to bars and clubs don't get laid. Plus ... once again ... internet ...

Don't discount these things entirely. They all play some kind of role. What I'm pointing out is that something else is happening here. Something fundamental that these explanations touch on but largely miss. Of course people go to bars to drink, but if their real desire was to drink, they'd drink at home. Of course people go to bars to see their friends, but if seeing their friends was the underlying goal, they'd visit someplace less noisy and expensive. So why do people go to bars?

They go to bars because they want to have an experience, and more than just an experience of pleasure or friendship or dancing ... they want an experience in which _something unexpected can happen, and they can play a role in it._

What bars and clubs introduce that you can't have drinking at home or snuggling with your cat or playing board games with friends is a cast of unknown characters together in an environment in which social rules are looser and social lubricants are present. You are more likely to have a _memorable encounter with something unknown._ People are more likely to behave in unexpected ways, and by being present for that _you are more likely to behave in unexpected ways._ You can have an encounter, with unexpected people, and behave in new ways.

You *can*. That doesn't mean you *will*. It doesn't happen to the extent people want every time. Or even most times. But bars offer the potential for such encounters, a path for such encounters, in ways that most other things people have easy access to do not. (Or so they think.) When it's not just done lazily, out of habit (and let's be honest – the reason most people do almost anything is out of habit, a default, because they can't think of anything better to do), going out drinking at a bar alone, or telling a friend "let's go to the bar," is a way of expressing the hope that *something will happen.* That there will be a memorable, even amazing, encounter, that you can be part of.

That wish for an encounter is the underlying hope. The underlying desire. The exact experience people are looking for is different from person to person, of course, but there is a kind of experience we're craving. Something that, even if we don't understand it, we're willing to go out of the house for, and spend money on, and take risks for. Something we dream of. And we generally don't think we can find it at home, with our friends, watching movies. No matter how amazing our home, how good our friends, or how great the movies.

At its most basic, its most unintrusive, it is the wish not even to have something happening to you, but to be in a place where such encounters are happening. To sit at the periphery and witness, and absorb that energy, that activity, that sense that anything is possible.

Over time, I've come to see nightlife as being a kind of spiritual pilgrimage: the quest for a bar experience is a quest for the holy grail. We go to the club hoping to have a miraculous encounter, to be part of moments that cannot be recreated.

I get shocked looks when I say I found dancing with prostitutes in a Russian nightclub to be as spiritual an experience as singing Latin plainchant in a Swiss cathedral; partying at a tequila bar just outside Jerusalem's Old City to be as religious as kissing the Wailing Wall; and running away from the Verona police with two Dutch girls and a Croatian woman to be as holy as living in a Buddhist monastery in India.

The surprise is understandable — but these experiences were all part and parcel of a single tapestry to me, because I entered them all in a state of pilgrimage.

Nor did I invent the connection between spirituality and nightlife. The Sufi poet Rumi beat me to it by over 700 years, comparing a mystical union with God to drinking wine and dancing with his beloved.

When I came to San Francisco, I discovered that this kind of language was actually common among people trying to create experiences that were *different* from going out to a bar because they were *better*. Experiences that got you closer to the miraculous encounter you really wanted. Drinking and dancing are great, but they're low hanging fruit.

We're going to talk about the nature of these experiences a lot more across this book, a lot more, but for the moment let's take a 10,000 foot view and say that there are three different kinds of this experience we can talk about. Later, this picture is going to get a lot more expansive. But for the moment let's think about it three ways.

The first is the "bar" experience in "bars and clubs." Because in fact the two really aren't the same. While there's a great deal of overlap in practice ... the real world never conforms to easy categories, which is why it's so damn interesting ... the prototypical experience that people go to a "bar" to have involves the kinds of encounters that happen in a place where you sit with strangers and talk, while the prototypical experience that people go to a "club" to have involves the kinds of encounters that happen in a place where you dance with strangers and can barely hear each other.

The "bar" experience is one in which you meet a stranger and have a conversation and it leads to something you never predicted happening and, despite drinking, you can remember every detail and tell your friends the story and it is meaningful in its particulars – they ignite your mind and open your soul. The "club" experience is one in which the story takes second place to the sensations: the dancing, the music, the connection between yourself and your environment. There might be some great details – you met a celebrity or a rich guy bought your drinks – but the essence of the experience is something you can't really describe to people, only how amazing and overwhelming it was. The bar experience is often verbal and conceptual and particular, the club experience is often an attempt to leave the verbal and conceptual behind.

The third kind of experience is more akin to falling in love, or at least infatuation. Nothing in particular "happens," but an encounter with someone touches you on a deep level in a place that was tender or raw, and as a result you feel changed – or the potential for change – although you can't really explain why. Obviously this can overlap with either the "bar" or "club" experience, the one turning into the other.

This isn't an exact taxonomy of these experiences, and honestly I'm dubious that an exact taxonomy is even possible, though we'll be looking at them in more detail. But hopefully you see the larger point: none of these are kinds of experiences we can have by ourselves. And they're extremely difficult to have when you just get your friends together in a living room. (Doable – absolutely – but you have to know what you're doing.) They're experiences that, like the Holy Grail, you probably have to go on a quest to find, leaving your comfort zone and entering new environments filled with mysterious and strange people.

Most of this book will be about how you create such quests for others. But we're going to spend the next chapters talking more about that want, that yearning, for these experiences, and what it says about us. Without understanding what we are looking for, and why, it's very easy to create grandiose and exotic experiences that are as impactful as a trip to the mall food court. On the other hand, when you understand what drives people, you can turn a trip to the mall food court into a life changing magical moment.

Chapter 2:
The Unexamined Psyche

This isn't actually a story from the San Francisco scene, but it's the story that always comes to my mind when I think about the things we're going to talk about in this chapter. It hasn't gotten less interesting in 20 years.

Back in the day, in Indiana, a brilliant friend of mine who I knew from high school started a game of D&D with some people he had known since childhood.

This wasn't an ordinary campaign. Instead of making their own characters, instead of reading who they were off of their character sheets, the players never got to look at the full character sheets of the characters they were playing. The characters woke up in a dark box, with no memories, and had to discover who they were through the course of play. And they weren't first level characters – they were established, powerful, high level characters with histories and backstories, all of which they had to discover for themselves.

And that's where it gets really interesting. The DM – who, remember, had known the players since elementary school – had secretly designed these characters to be the kinds of heroes that the people playing them had always dreamed of being. Their personal heroic archetypes, handed to them on a platter, to discover and play.

The campaign was an excuse for this psychology experiment. He wondered what would happen.

What do you think happened?

Of the five players, two dropped out. They just weren't interested, they had better things to do. The remaining three stayed in, they stayed attached for a long time. And ... it was a disaster.

On every level.

It turned out that they could not – or would not let themselves – play these characters well.

It wasn't just that the paladin got into stupid arguments with his god, or that the deadly swordsman couldn't figure out how he wanted to fight people, or that their tactics were a self-destructive mess. They were incapable of even making basic game decisions. They were experienced gamers, they'd been playing together competently for years: but trying to play these characters, they'd waste an entire afternoon's gameplay arguing about which direction to go in. About how to pack equipment. It was absurd, and soul-deadening, to watch. The DM and I stared at each other across the table (by that point I'd been brought in to replace one of the players who'd left), our eyes asking "how is this POSSIBLE?"

They could play any generic set of characters competently, even well. But given these particular characters, characters who actually represented some version of their hopes and aspirations for their real selves, something in them rebelled. Something deep in their unconscious was responding: "I am NOT this person!" and so was not letting them be this person. They were sabotaging themselves at every turn.

The game eventually faded away. What else could it do?

Now here's another story, in San Francisco, about the same thing from a different direction.

My friend Robin Ziiro, an artist in the scene, had invited me over to the warehouse where she lived for the first time, and we got into a conversation about what makes people become assholes. Robin admitted that she did not understand this, that she struggled with this, and in-between developing a "taxonomy of assholes" to help her recognize different kinds of assholes and figure out how to deal with them, we decided that it would be good if she could access her own "inner asshole" for a while, have the experience of being a "type 1" asshole from our taxonomy – the kind who isn't actually cruel or mean for its own sake, but who cares so passionately about doing something difficult that he runs over people to do it the way he thinks it needs to be done. Robin wanted to experience what that was like, instead of feeling like other people's needs were her responsibility to take care of.

So I created a ritual for her, there on the spot. To bring her inner asshole up and give it power for 48 hours.

We gathered up a bunch of oranges, and I had her hold each one and as she held it, think of an experience she'd had in which someone had been an asshole, and it had pissed her off, but she'd also been secretly jealous of their ability to be that. To feel that feeling again, and then, when she was absolutely filled with it, to throw the orange against the wall with all her strength. And then not pick it up. Just leave it there, broken, where it lay.

Then to take another orange, and think of another instance, and fill herself with it, and throw the orange. And leave it there.

Again and again.

Until, when she had gone through all the oranges, and relived all these experiences, and filled herself with them, I handed her a dessert fork, and told her to stab me in the arm with it.

Which she did.

The ritual worked. The next day, at work, Robin organized collective action against abusive management. The company office ground to a standstill as headquarters sent a representative to negotiate with her to get work moving again by addressing long-standing grievances.

I got a message from her a day later. "I need an extension," she'd said. "I can't just stop being an asshole in the middle of this."

Of course I gave her one.

Now the point isn't why this ritual worked, or what made it work – those are all things we'll get to later. The point right now is that *this kind of thing happens.* That for whatever reason, there are things happening in our unconscious mind, and they impact what it is we can do in the world, and who we can be. We've seen one example in which this can stop you from doing something, and one example in which it can be harnessed to help you achieve something.

This happens. All the time, in fact.

What we think of as our conscious minds are in fact only a small portion of our psyches. Much of what we do, much of the way we see the world, is influenced by subconscious, even unconscious, factors.

Different cultures – and different thinkers within cultures – have had different explanations for what the "subconscious" and the "unconscious" are. The ancient Greeks thought of it as a connection to the gods. The Muses inspired you, the Furies tormented you, gods and goddesses could give you ideas or drive you mad with desire, change you into a bestial state or elevate you to the stars. You can take that literally (if you want), but you can also see it as metaphors for psychological states that we all go through. What caused them? It was the divine acting through us. Our connection to the transcendent in the universe.

I have to admit I kind of like that explanation. And there's a reason that when Freud pioneered the idea of the psychological unconscious in Western culture, he cribbed Greek myth.

Hindu and Buddhist philosophers came up with other explanations, which we'll (radically) shorthand to "karma." We experience the things we do, including subtle mental states, because we are conditioned by previous events – some of them decisions we made, some of them decisions other people made that affected the environment we're in, some of them decisions made in previous lives that endure. Whatever their origins, those causes must be played out through effects, and in responding to them we create more causes, which create more effects ... we're never just in the present moment, we're always unwittingly playing out the results of things that have happened before.

Enlightenment, Nirvana, is what happens when you actually break that cycle and are free from the conditioning of past events.

Physicians in the Middle Ages located the unconscious in bodily processes – "the four humors," blood, phlegm, and two colors of bile. Having an imbalance in these humors ... too much of one, two little of another ... could cause melancholy and depression, or mania.

And of course they were perfectly comfortable with the idea of divine revelation, demonic possession, or angelic conversation – these things happened – but on a casual, day-to-day basis, they identified the forces beneath our conscious minds that shape our moods and behaviors with biology. That's a tradition which has continued down to the present day, now seen in hormones like testosterone and neurotransmitters like serotonin.

But of course unconscious motivations are most commonly associated with Freud, and his analysis of the human mind as a creature divided against itself. And however literally accurate it may be, his approach, descended from the Greeks and expanded by Jung, has endured so long and its metaphors become so central because it most potently stirs the imagination and "feels" most true to our lived experience. And not just "feels" – it is useful. It helps us to grapple with what we're living. People asking "what are my unconscious motivations" can gain more insight into their intentions and actions.

The Delphic maxim to "know thyself" is necessary precisely because we can't see everything important in a single glance.

It's not a simple process. We don't always know how to do it – and ironically our unconscious frames may be exactly what block us from examining our unconscious motivations.

To the extent that one wants to describe this process in its most literal form, I'm partial to a model developed in San Francisco in 2007 by psychologists Kirk Schneider and Orah Krug, which they call "existential-integrative psychology."

The idea is to find whatever is impacting your behavior and conscious thought by going through a list of possible causes from the "outside in," going deeper and deeper. You start with the broadest, most physical possible causes and work through the psychological towards the soulful.

The first level you examine is the **physiological** – factors like genes, illness or injury, diet, exercise, and substance use can all impact your behavior and perceptions without your conscious knowledge.

The second level is the **environmental** – consistent positive or negative reinforcement, workplace culture, the stress of poverty, can all impact your behavior and perceptions without your conscious knowledge.

The third level is the **cognitive** – one's habits of thought, the ability to engage in clear and rational thinking. Problems at this level are generally addressed by Cognitive Behavioral Therapy, schema restructuring, and the like – changing the way you habitually think about things, without even knowing it.

The fourth level is the **psychosexual** – and here we're in traditional Freudian territory. How one handles the intersections of one's drives and social prohibitions. Are you engaged in compulsive gratification? Are you too repressed? Obviously this can create patterns that fly underneath your conscious awareness even as you live them out, over and over again.

The fifth level is interpersonal – one's ability to be both connected and independent from others. To form authentic and healthy relationships beyond just the sexual. This is addressed through psychodynamic therapy as it is generally understood today: looking over your life choices and your past, finding patterns and re-examining issues you've been living with, uncovering hidden motivations and assumptions.

Finally, we come to the experiential level, the core of our being – the existential condition that we always live in. Embracing the mystery of your full humanity, with its attendant limitations. You are a body, and you will die, and you have only so long in which to make meaningful choices, but you are here, physically present, right now.

To the extent that one wants to be reasonable and practical about where the unconscious mind is located and what causes unconscious drives, this is a very good and very practical and very reasonable approach. My favorite, for those things.

But we're not really going to do that.

Oh, we may come back to the practical and reasonable, from time to time. And certainly if somebody is having an experience of the world as an enchanted place, you want to consider the various parts of that checklist – is this physiological (are they dehydrated)? Is it environmental (do they belong to a cult)? Is it cognitive (do they have a habit of ascribing everything to magical experiences)? It's important that we not lose sight of the fact that an awful lot of experiences people have can be explained on just those levels, and that's not what we're talking about here.

But mostly, going forward, we're going to focus on a way of looking at our unconscious, and self-knowledge, that doesn't entirely rule out being touched by the gods. Or the movements of the soul.

Why? Because fairly often, surprisingly often, and at our most profound moments, that is what we actually experience in our lives. Even if it's not the least bit true (and hey, it might be), we *experience* magic, and destiny, and the divine. We live the unconscious as a connection to those things. And amazing things happen if we are able to work at that level of lived enchantment, instead of constantly trying to reduce our lives down to small, rational, and orderly boxes.

This matters. It matters a lot. We only feel truly alive, and behave at our most soulful, when we are stepping outside of our small, rational, and orderly boxes.

Chapter 3:
The World As We Live it is a Magical Place

I'm not sure I should tell you this story. It could get me in trouble; this is one of those events that everyone involved in pledges never to talk about. But hell, by the time this is published it will have been years ago.

That's no excuse, of course, and if anything gets me excommunicated from part of the San Francisco art scene, it'll be telling you that one of the events in this story happened. But you know what? It's too damn good.

One year, a bunch of us dressed up in formal costumes and broke into a private park at night. The advance team set up nocturnal stations, with glowing lights and surreal decorations and small art experiences you could discover and musical instruments that could be played, and we all wandered through the dark gardens, in our finery, coming upon these places, and it was utterly otherworldly. Extraordinary.

A small group of people among those attending had said they'd wanted to do something secret with me while we were in the park, and I'd said sure, because I trusted them. But in the process of breaking into the park, I'd gotten separated, and instead of trying to find them (this was a strict "no phones out" event), I'd just wandered on my own. And by midnight, I hadn't seen any of them again.

But they were still together, standing around a piano in a grove, and it was getting late, and they had plans to keep. They debated whether to fan out and search for me and then meet back in 20 minutes, or if they should just give up and catch me in more mundane circumstances.

"No," said Robin Ziiro. "We're going to perform a magic ritual, and summon him. Henry just learned to play 'Hallelujah' on the piano today: he's going to play it on this keyboard, and we're going to get everyone to sing it as loud as they can, and Benjamin's just going to show up."

That wasn't a random choice. The night before, there had been a tribute event to Burning Man founder Larry Harvey, who had died a few months before. As part of that event, in the Castro Theater, I had sung Hallelujah, backed up by a men's choir that only performs Leonard Cohen songs (It's hard to believe San Francisco is a real place, sometimes), to a packed house of 1,500 people. The experience had been intense, and cathartic – one of the greatest musical experiences of my life – and I've been associated with that song to many people in the San Francisco underground scene ever since.

The very next night, Robin was saying that the symbolic connection would have a real world effect – singing the song would have the power to bring me forth.

They tried it.

At that moment, far across the park, I was walking through the botanical display, lost in my head. And then, faintly, I heard the beginning of the song. And, swear to God, my neck snapped in the direction of the music as a tingle went down my spine and I felt a compulsion to rush over and join in the singing. I was – this is the right word – compelled.

But I said no.

No. I mean, come on, I told myself: just because someone's singing this song doesn't mean I have to rush over and sing it too. What is that? It's nonsense. Irrational. No, I'm going to slowly finish the rest of my ancient plant walk, and then leave like I was going to go anyway.

The thing was, I didn't know where the music was actually coming from, and as I finished my walk and headed towards the garden's exit … I realized I was moving closer to it. The song was on my way out.

Well, now I had to do it! Didn't I? Once again, I felt that strange compulsion, a clear sense that that's where I had to be. And once again, I mentally kicked myself until I knew better. Because really now: I didn't write the song. I don't own it. Other people get to sing it. Leave it alone. It's time to go home.

I walked around a bend, and I realized that the path I was on was literally taking me right past the grove in which the large group of people were all standing around the piano singing the song.

And now I wondered: had I really just coincidentally walked right up to this, or had I subconsciously led myself over to it, not even consciously knowing where it was, because I wanted to join in?

That was ridiculous: it was on the way I would have gone even if there hadn't been music. Even so, in that moment I really didn't know.

But I was still not going to do it. I wanted to, but I wouldn't. At this point this was sheer cussedness, a refusal to even consider that this song could possibly have anything to do with me. It seemed prideful, egoistic, to think that the people singing it could want me there as much as I wanted to be there. So I walked down the path, passing the clearing, and because it was dark on the path and only vaguely lit around the piano, nobody even noticed me.

The piano kept playing as I passed, but now nobody was singing. "Okay," the piano player said, still playing. "I know this song has more words. There are more verses. Does anybody know them?" Quiet. "Does ANYBODY here know the rest of the verses?"

I stopped in my tracks. Oh, the hell with it. This was too much.

I walked into the clearing and took up one of the verses that I didn't think they'd done. The crowd went wild – I didn't recognize anyone yet, my eyes hadn't adjusted, but a lot of them had apparently been at my performance of the song the other night. I was instantly not only singing the song, but leading it, and we were all in this together.

It was, on its own terms, a wonderful moment for me.

And then, when it was all over and we'd all cheered and we'd all clapped, I felt a hand on my shoulder, and turned to find Robin, and everyone I'd been supposed to see, all right here.

"Wow," I said. "This is quite a coincidence."

"No," she said, "it's not." She explained that they had done this on purpose: cast this song as a spell specifically to summon me.

And I have never known what exactly I was feeling in those moments – was I really compelled? Why was I resisting? What the hell was actually going on? But it felt, it really felt, exactly like I had been summoned, and that no matter how much I resisted I was gradually, irresistibly, pulled in, led by either an external force that genuinely summoned me, or my subconscious mind, which tossed me in the direction of that singing, no matter what my conscious mind told me to do.

And they'd done it on purpose.

* * *

Am I seriously saying we are touched by the gods, that our souls have destinies they want us to fulfill? That the world is an enchanted place?

No, but I'm saying we experience it this way. We experience it this way at the very core of our being. There's no use denying it.

What should we make of this? Does this mean we have to take gods and souls and destinies seriously? Or that, because of its siren call, we must reject enchantment all the harder in order to support rationalism?

In his 1969 book *Love and Will*, legendary existential-humanistic psychologist Rollo May (a teacher and mentor of Kirk Schneider, the San Francisco psychologist whose work I cited in the last chapter), gave what I think is probably the best description I've ever seen of what we are to make of the gods and demons and enchantments that our (psychological) world is full of.

We cannot take them literally, May said, because to do that is to return to superstition and lose our ability to think carefully about them.

But ...

We also cannot think of them as wholly symbolic, because to do that renders them bloodless and powerless, and thus stops describing the experience of them that we actually have – wherein they are tremendously powerful, tremendously vital and alive, and tremendously real.

We have to treat them as neither literal events nor entirely psychological ones. To understand these experiences, we have to understand them as operating on multiple, sometimes contradictory, levels. Levels that come together to create an experience that is extremely powerful, even magical, offering catharsis and insight we need.

Many people have come to think that the advance of science has tamed the unconscious – that the more we've secularized, the more we can design our lives around rational principles that are easy and make sense and so we can do away with the enchanted nonsense of the unconscious.

The evidence suggests that this is not how things work. The secular world is not so secular – it has just learned not to talk about its superstitions in polite company. Silicon Valley and Wall Street types who disdain the very idea of visiting a church use psychics, consult astrologers, and spend obscene amounts of money on New Age health products that have no more scientific validity than the health potions in a video game. And that's not even including "scientific" replacements for superstition like "uploading our consciousness to the cloud," or "the world is a simulation," which are little more than Christian eschatology transferred over to the latest technology.

Have you been to a transhumanist party? They are filled with people talking about the singularity in exactly the same way that kids at the YMCA summer camp I attended as a teenager talked about God. Which, not coincidentally, is how hipster atheists will also talk about the power of "art" at their parties.

However rational we get, however much we learn about the world, we do not "outgrow" the unconscious, or the way that it speaks to us in ways that seem – and perhaps even are – enchanted.

This is a given. Awe and wonder are fundamental to being human. They don't come to everyone from the same sources, but the experience is basic to us all.

We may use scientific terms, or art school terms, or religious terms ... but all of our lives are oriented in some way towards experiences of the soulful, and the enchanted.

How that plays out, not whether, is the most important question. But we start from this point: we're not talking about magic and enchantment and the soul as literally true in the superstitious sense, but we are also not talking about them as purely symbolic metaphors. Our experience of them is very concrete and specific.

52

This is also the level that, over and over again, we'll see the kind of experiences people learned to design in San Francisco operating on. Shockingly real for something so magical.

Chapter 4:
The Psyche Moves in Mysterious Ways,
its Wonders to Perform

In 2010, San Francisco event producer and counter-cultural OG Scott Levkoff created an experience called the "Mystic Midway" which would last for years at various locations. It's part surrealistic carnival, part mythological Hero's Journey. Like many of the creations of this scene, it felt to the artist like a personal necessity as much as a creative opportunity.

"I was couchbound from a herniated disc, high on Tramadol, prevented from attending Burning Man with all my community," Scott remembers. "I was ready to exit my life at Mission Control as the sexy party guy and my 10 year relationship was coming to an end. It was a tumultuous, painful time. Mystic Midway was a vehicle of permission I crafted for myself to move forward with my love of all things mystical, carnival, alchemical, and immersive."

To walk through the Mystic Midway was to meet all manner of creatures in the role of carnival barkers and hustlers, who invited people to play games that guided you to reveal uncomfortable truths or intimate secrets. They would give you tokens, depending on the kind of experience you had, and over time the combination of tokens you got could influence the outcome of the experience for everyone.

One of those creatures was "Mr. Nobody," a man in a suit

with a giant skull for a head, inspired by the Gede Loa of Voudou, who would ask you to tell him your greatest fear, and would then devour it.

Many people felt trapped in that moment, and didn't know what to say. Some of them laughed it off and went on to other games.

"The default answer for people who just wanted to say something was 'spiders,'" said Henry Andrews, a performer and co-producer of the Mystic Midway. "Pretty much every time, if they just wanted to name a plausible fear without really exposing anything about themselves, they'd say 'spiders.'"

And that was fine – not every game was for everyone, just like not every religion is for everyone. Just as often people would play along in a way that was real but not especially deep: they'd talk about a fear of dying, or of being alone, or of a particular failure. This was real, and they were serious, and they were engaged - but it's an open question whether they really got something important out of the experience.

But sometimes, sometimes, "Mr. Nobody," the fear-seeking giant skull, was exactly what someone needed.

"You give people permission, and they'll drop amazing things on you. Things they need to tell you," Henry said.

One moment in particular stands out in his memory. "We were doing a corporate event, of all things," Henry told me, "and you never expect corporate events to be very interesting. It's the kiddie pool of this kind of thing, because nobody actually wants to take a risk, they never want to be a real person in front of their co-workers. But that was the day that someone came to Mr. Nobody, and told us the fear that we still talk about to this day, the one that made us ask afterwards – should we have tried to hook him up with mental health services for survivors? Should we have called the police about what happened to him? Should we have taken him aside and talked with him more? And we've gone back and forth on that, because no, ethically we're not counselors, and for all we know he's tried professionals already. But what we can definitely say is that this was something he desperately needed to talk to someone about, and he didn't have anyone else in his life who he could do it with. And then, out of nowhere, there's a 'spirit' in a suit with a giant skull walking around his office, and the spirit asks him to speak his greatest fear aloud, and he does. And it's a deep and powerful moment that he's been wanting to have for years, and this was the time he could have it. Talking to Mr. Nobody the fear spirit. That's what got him able to do it."

That was the most extreme case Henry remembers, but many of the interactions during the Mystic Midway's run were like that. "We weren't really functioning as actors, and we weren't really performers, and we weren't therapists or counselors," Henry said. "But when we put on the costumes and took on the identities, it was like we were channeling something, and that's what people responded to. Not our performances, but the connection to something larger. Something that they wanted to have witness, and listen, and be present with them."

* * *

The enchantment we experience when we are being spoken to by our unconscious isn't random, and it isn't haphazard. Quite the contrary: it creates a sense of deep and profound meaning and purpose. It doesn't follow rational laws, but it does follow poetic ones. It's not a rule-bound experience, but it does tend to follow certain patterns.

We're going to start by looking at the more basic ones as building blocks. And it's no accident that for the next few chapters we're going to sound a lot more like therapists than event producers.

* * *

There are, it should be noted, a lot of different ways people who do the work describe what they're working with. In the introduction to this book I described the San Francisco experience design scene as one fundamentally lacking a manifesto – but that doesn't mean that people are silent. On the contrary, in the absence of a unified way of describing the phenomenon, each person often comes up with their own description based on the references that speak most to them, leading to a jargony Tower of Babel. Open the tower door and you'll hear people talk about transactional analysis, game theory, Ericsonian stages of development, Lakoffian "framing" … Larry, who founded Burning Man, was a pretty serious Freudian …

And a crucial thing to realize is that, generally speaking, their theoretical understanding of what they were doing had very little relationship to the caliber of experiences they created. It did – and we'll discuss this at length later – have a big impact on the *kinds of experiences* they tried to create. But how good at it are they? Eh, not so much. Use whatever metaphors work best for you.

To the extent that there is any kind of consensus in the scene about what was actually happening, I'd say that it tended towards what we could call "neo-Jungian." So those are the terms I'm going to proceed from, and hone and sharpen until they serve the purpose of explaining what is best experienced. Not everyone in the scene will agree with these terms, or even like them. But I think this is the most useful synthesis.

We'll start with the fact that most of us are on auto-pilot most of the time. We are simply not paying full, conscious, attention to much of what we do. If we were, would so many people be trying to sell us on "mindfulness?"

Being on auto-pilot serves to put us in boxes of our own making, where we don't really feel alive. But most of the time it's still a pretty good idea. I mean, if you had to carefully think through the sequence of events every time you got up in the morning, you'd never get to work on time. So you develop a morning routine. You habituate the techniques of driving a car because it's actually much smoother and safer to be on "auto-pilot" when you're driving, and let your habits run the show, than it is to think through every lane change and blind-spot check. Much of the time it's okay, even really useful, to be creatures of habit.

But this is also where we get into trouble. Especially when we develop habits we don't actually know we have. The Jungian term for a series of significant habitual behaviors that we don't even know we have is a "complex." Charged reactions we don't realize we're having to events that we don't realize are triggers. And we repeat these charged response patterns over and over again, thinking we're making a unique and rational decision every time, when in fact we're being guided by unconscious scripts and habits. We find ourselves repeating the same relationship over and over again, no matter how many times we tell ourselves we're going to do something different this time; we fall into the same social role with our friends, no matter how much we try to break out of it; we sabotage ourselves at work in the same ways over and over again; we start projects and never finish them because of an escalating anxiety we do not understand ... we suspect, sometimes, that there's something going on under the surface, some underlying cause for these repetitions, but no matter how hard we look, we can't see it. Often we're the only ones who can't see it: it's so obvious to everyone else, but their pointing it out rarely helps.

When we can see what's happening – view one of our own complexes for what it is, and then step out of it? Oh, that feels like an adrenaline shot of pure magic. Suddenly the world is filled with wonder and anything seems possible, because indeed you literally have just created new possibilities. That's an amazing feeling of magic.

And while it may seem grandiose to say right now, one of the most common goals of great experience design that has developed in the San Francisco scene is to do just that – to liberate people from their habitual ways of looking at the world, and free them from their complexes.

This is hardly a goal unique to San Francisco. A number of modern art movements, from Dada to the Surrealists to the Situationists, had this basic goal: to awaken something slumbering in the mind and bring it to full consciousness. What's original and interesting about what the San Francisco scene pioneered are the techniques they adopted to do this, and just how good they got at it, not the goal itself.

One of the key mechanisms of complexes are "projections." Most of the time we are not actually seeing other people as they are: we are instead projecting our hopes, fears and expectations onto them and responding to that. Jung went so far as to say that we are projecting the unacknowledged parts of ourselves onto other people, and that doing this stands in the way of our personal development. In that sense, liberating someone from their projections has the same effect as freeing someone from their complexes. Sure.

But that's not actually how projections are used in magical experience design, most of the time. Quite the opposite, in fact: far from eliminating projections, we tend to use them to create more intense experiences. Look at the story that started this chapter: one in which a grown man is asked by a skeletal figure to admit to his greatest fear ... and he DOES! He opens up an emotional vein to tell a complete stranger, someone who he knows – come on, he HAS TO KNOW – is just a random guy in a mask with no formal training or doctor-patient confidentiality rules, about something so terrible that maybe the police should have been called.

And then he FEELS GOOD ABOUT IT! Honestly now, how is that possible?

It's possible because, in a very important way, he wasn't in his right mind. He was projecting an unacknowledged part of himself onto the performer. But whereas doing this in daily life usually leads to disaster, because people don't know they're being projected on, and aren't prepared to handle it, this is a case where the experience was designed to court this kind of encounter, and was ready for it, and able to respond in a way that acknowledged what was previously hidden.

Once again, this is an experience that feels utterly mystical when you go through it. And why wouldn't it? Something deep within you, often taboo, often locked away, is suddenly summoned to the conscious world, and when you express it, it is acknowledged, and accepted, in a way you feared could never happen. How else could it feel but miraculous?

But why did the performer have to wear the skull mask, and be called "Mr. Nobody?" Costuming is, frankly, a pain in the ass. Why go through all the rigmarole?

Before we look at the psychological mechanisms involved, let's look at a word I've used in this description: "performer." Because while it's a useful shorthand for someone playing a role in an art experience (you knew exactly what I meant), it's not actually an accurate description of what is really happening here. At least not from the perspective of someone inside that experience.

Scott and Henry and others have been very clear about this: they've found that the people who were most successful in these roles are not "actors," not "performers," not people who are attempting to act a part, but people who are open to channeling the role. I know that sounds odd, maybe even off, but there's a meaningful distinction here: it's the difference between someone whose focus is trying to use talent and technique to convince someone that they are, in fact, an archetypical creature of the psyche ("performing") and someone whose focus is listening to the person they're talking to, being receptive to what that person is projecting onto them, and then following their lead to play the role their psyche needs you to play ("channeling").

"A key thing I look for in folks I work with is a desire to be of service to others, as facilitators," Scott told me. "This is ESSENTIAL. Actors who long for the lights and applause never worked out. Learning to listen and find the openings with folks was key, almost an 'oracular orientation' if you will that was needed to find and assist guests with those 'moments of realization' and ideally, Healing & Grace."

The key skill here isn't to perform: it's to be present for another person.

All the performance skill in the world actually does very little good if you cannot acknowledge what it is that the participant in the experience is projecting onto you. If you can't do that, you're just a guy in a mask being entertaining. On the other hand, someone with no performance skill at all who can understand what is being projected onto them and respond in a way that acknowledges it, brings everything important to the role.

This isn't to say that performance skills aren't valuable to people trying to create experiences – on the contrary, there are times when you simply need somebody acting at a professional level if you're going to pull something off. But there are also, and this will become absolutely critical later, certain kinds of experiences you simply cannot create if all you are relying on is performance.

But this brings us back to the question: why have the costumes? Why bother with all that rigmarole?

Well, you don't always need it. Think back to the "magical bar," my church ... where I initiated people into the experience without any costumes. I was wearing whatever I happened to be wearing that day. There were no masks, no robes, no swords, no hats. The bartender was wearing whatever he'd worn to work. There were no props. No lighting effects. It was all done simply by talking. Just by telling a story.

Except ... wait ... there was a prop, wasn't there. Of course there was: the drink. The woman in the story I told you said that it didn't need to be much, even a glass of water would have done it, but there had to be *something*. Something that actually happened, that can be referenced, pointed at, engaged with.

Otherwise you're just telling a story. And there's nothing wrong with that: a good story can be an incredibly powerful experience. But it's a very different kind of experience than the one we're talking about. We'll discuss why in more detail as we go, but I think you can understand pretty easily that there is a difference. It's one thing to be told a story about the

Italian Renaissance in a classroom, or from a friend, it's quite another to be told the exact same story while in Italy and to have someone point at a building and say "And that was the workshop where the statue was made 400 years ago, and it's still displayed in the town square we're walking to."

How good does the prop have to be? Could I really have pulled the "magical bar" effect off with just a glass of water? I doubt it. I think it mattered that they were in fact getting incredibly high quality cocktails, made in the spur of the moment, in answer to the prayer of their hearts. Production value helps. But it's shocking how little production value the "something" needs to display to still have the desired psychological impact. The people who summoned me by singing "Hallelujah" weren't singing especially well. The dessert fork that Robin stabbed me with was a shitty piece of tin. But then, maybe this shouldn't surprise us: no one going through a Eucharist ceremony is really concerned about the quality of the wafer or the vintage of the wine.

So there has to be a "something," but the quality of the "something" doesn't necessarily matter. What's going on?

Answering that brings us to Jung's most famous concept, the "archetype," and his less famous but equally relevant concept of the "imago."

Everybody thinks they know what an archetype is, and nobody ever does. I'm pretty sure not even Jung did, honestly:

the concept is vague and slippery and seems to change all the time to fit the need of the moment, and I don't think I have ever heard two people use the term to mean the exact same thing. But the concept has lasted so long because, for all its vagueness, it is also a tremendously useful reference point. A powerful symbol, lodged in our collective unconscious, that we all at some level just get. Whether it is really universal or not (in practice, it's really not), it seems to represent something universal: a smallest fundamental particle of symbolism. Something whose meaning is both expansive, full of creative energy ("numinous" was Jung's term), and undeniable. It is fundamentally itself, and also more than itself, at once.

Yeah, you see? That's not really clear at all.

Jung sorta-kinda noted this problem in *The Archetypes and the Collective Unconscious* when he wrote "The fact is that archetypal images are so packed with meaning in themselves that people never think of asking what they really do mean."

But much in the same way that, as I noted earlier, the theoretical frameworks that people develop to do this kind of work actually have very little relationship with how good they are at it. The point of the archetypes isn't so much what they mean, or even how they are defined, but that they are numinous – that they carry this energy, and charge, that fundamentally means something to us just because they do. Archetypes represent something that has *unconditional value*

(Larry Harvey's phrase), and carry that with them. Jung's definitions are not precise, but they are very clear on this point: what makes archetypes relevant is specifically that they have this impact:

"Archetypes are, by definition, factors and motifs that arrange the psychic elements into certain images, characterized as archetypal, but in such a way that they can be recognized only from the effects they produce." (from *A Psychological Approach to the Trinity*)

Useless from a classification standpoint, but very clear from a use standpoint: an archetype is a symbol that has a certain kind of effect. "They are meant to attract, to convince, to fascinate, and to overpower. They are created out of the primal stuff of revelation and reflect the ever-unique experience of divinity." (from *The Archetypes and the Collective Unconscious*)

So speaking practically here, archetypes are symbols that most people have some version of swimming around in their unconscious psyches. And because they represent something unconditional, and the possibility of experiencing it, they have energy, they are numinous.

Much in the way that everybody has an unconscious, and it's running much of our lives in ways we don't even notice, every unconscious has archetypes. Has a personal mythology. And it's when you can reach that level of the unconscious where the archetypes dwell, or summon them into the level of your consciousness, that you get this magical, numinous, effect.

Does that make sense? When you can reach someone's personal mythology, you're reaching them on a level where magical things happen. That's the point. And personal mythologies are made up of archetypes, which are symbols that are at once personal and universal.

Right. So that's archetypes.

Imagos are the visual manifestations of archetypal symbols. Charged images, numinous in their own right, that when you see them, reference the archetypes. Imagos tap archetypes on the shoulder. Even summon them up. An image that brings what is below our conscious minds to the surface.

Having something like that in an experience changes it profoundly: when a random ordinary stranger on a street says "tell me something you fear," you're probably not going to take it seriously. But when a human skull tells you to do it … even if it's not a very convincing representation of a skull or a skeleton man … something stirs. There's a connection made with your unconscious, and now you're experiencing that question in a whole different way.

It's one thing if you were to meet me in a bar and I were to just ask you to tell me the prayer of your heart. It's quite another thing for me to say "this man - right here - will create a drink that answers your prayer." We all have some idea of what a magic potion is ... and that element not only makes the question more solid, more real, but when you finally get the drink, and indeed it's not water, it's unique and different from anything else anyone has or can order, it evokes your unconscious. It gives it a channel into the conscious moment, and a place to go where you can see it.

These things reinforce each other – if the conditions under which the imago appears are powerful, then a mediocre imago, or even a silly one, can activate someone's unconscious, get their personal mythologies engaged. Maybe I really could have pulled off the experience of the magical bar with a glass of water. Maybe. On the other hand, a profoundly powerful imago will activate the personal unconscious of someone whatever they do; at that point the personal unconscious will be looking for some way to express itself, for something to connect to. You just have to give it an opening.

Okay, let's stop here for a moment. Why have we been going through all this again?

We're talking about this because to no small degree the "experience" being created in this kind of "experience design" isn't what's happening in the bar, or the garden, or the warehouse, or the conference room – it's what's happening inside the unconscious of the participants. This kind of experience works, and works brilliantly when – but only when – the personal mythology of the participants can be reached, so that it emerges and engages with what's happening in the world around it, and even becomes visible. If that's not happening, you might as well be producing a freshman orientation or a game night with your neighbors. Whatever happens, it won't be memorable.

Understanding how to "channel," becoming a vessel someone projects the unacknowledged parts of their psyche onto; knowing how to interrupt people's complexes in a way that makes them visible; understanding how to create situations that are compelling to the archetypes in someone's personal mythology; figuring out how to create imagos, and deploy them – these are basic tools of the trade. Whether or not you use these terms, or use this specific framework, the unconscious is where the most important aspect of the psychology of San Francisco experience design happens. If you can reach all this effectively, then you can create the most amazing experiences people will have in their lives with a little speech and a glass of water. If you can't, then no amount of technical wizardry or production values will even get you close.

Odyssey Works, a fascinating San Francisco/New York art collective founded in 2001 that creates art experiences for one person at a time - experiences that can last days, weeks, or even months - likes to say "design starts with empathy."

But this is only the first level of what it means to reach

someone's personal unconscious and engage it with a designed experience. We've been talking about the "what" – to go deeper, we need to talk about the "why." Only then can we get to the "how."

Chapter 5:
Meet the Daimon

The impact of an experience like this can be incredibly powerful. It can change your life. To really get what we're talking about here, you need to see just how much impact it can have.

I love this story so much. This is one of my most favorite stories of all. I had nothing to do with it, it's a Chicken John story, and if I could go back in time and be involved in one San Francisco art experience I missed the first time around, it would probably be this one.

Which ... as you'll see ... would have been a terrible decision. Just awful. A very bad life choice.

And yet ...

In the mid-1990s, Chicken John started a traveling circus, and took it on a national tour in a bus that couldn't go more than 30 miles per hour. Called the "Circus Redickuless," it was a circus unlike any other you've seen. It was stupider. It was amateur. Its premise, deceptively simple, was that none of the acts you would see that night would require any actual talent. At all.

This made some of the acts stupid puns: the "man eating chicken" was in fact a man, eating chicken. The "temporarily tattooed man" was ... well, you've already figured it out. The vegan geek would bite the heads off broccoli. Other acts were brilliantly conceptual: the reverse stripper would come out naked, make the audience chant "Put it on! Put it on!" and then seductively wear an article of clothing. Over and over again, until she was fully dressed. Chicken would try to get his dog, Dammit, to jump through a hoop ... two inches off the ground. The dog wouldn't do it, and a battle of wits ensued.

And then there were a few performers who, in violation of the concept, had "talent" in the strangest sense of the word: David Apocalypse, a genuine circus geek who had actually been institutionalized, would show you how he'd learned to break out of a straightjacket. Dannygirl would tap dance to speed metal.

Watching it was like spinning an emotional wheel over and over again: at first it was impossible to believe that this ... THIS ... was actually a real show that was happening. You kept waiting for the other shoe to drop. Then the realization came over you that yes, this really was happening, and it was ON PURPOSE! You were stunned. Then you got angry: how could someone waste your time with this shit? Why? The awfulness of the experience washed over you. Then ... then ... it came full circle. It was so bad it was hilarious; it was amazing because it was really happening. Then it became so bad that it was awful again, and then hilarious ... round and round.

But it was when the show ended that the most amazing

thing happened.

Chicken would tell the crowd that since this was a circus with no talent, anybody could join. They had the opportunity, tonight, before the bus left in the wee hours of the morning, to run away and join the circus. This was really happening. They could really do that, if they wanted.

And across three national tours over five years, hundreds of people did.

They'd have woken up that morning never having heard of the Circus Redickuless. At 11 a.m., a friend would have shown them a flyer or a listing for this bizarre event, and asked if they wanted to go. At 8 p.m., the show started. At 10, they were invited to run away and join the circus. At midnight, they'd be desperately selling their furniture to their roommates. And at 2 a.m., they'd get on the bus and be driven away, trying to come up with an act that fit their particular lack of talent.

Hundreds of people.

That, as Chicken would say, was the real show. That moment when someone was inspired by what everybody acknowledged was pure bullshit to walk away from their life and do something completely different.

I've always wondered, if I'd seen the Circus back then, if I'd have had the guts to do that. I like to think so, but I doubt it.

It would have been a terrible decision. The Circus never made money. The performers were starving. But ... but ... they traveled across America, from the smallest, most insular towns to the big cities, and learned how to turn bullshit into bizarre and profound experiences. Into magic. Impossible to look away from. Life changing. They learned how to be the circus you run away to join. And however miserable it was, none of them really regret it.

What the hell was that? Why would somebody do that?

Why would they look back on it fondly?

Well, among other reasons, they learned a set of skills that most people don't even know exists. It's not easy to turn bull-shit into magic – it's the psychological equivalent of turning straw into gold. The Circus Redickuless was an extreme boot camp for people who wanted that magic in their lives, and once they learned these skills, they could take them anywhere. As Chicken liked to say: "We who have done so much with so little for so long are now completely qualified to do anything and everything with absolutely nothing at all."

It's the truth. And it turned them into different people. You're never the same after you run away to join the circus.

That's an extreme example, and a harsh one – pushing

things too far was Chicken's stock in trade. It doesn't have to be that harsh.

Here's another one, no less extreme, but much gentler. Bay Area artist David Best is best known for making temples at Burning Man, but from those beginnings he has taken the practice to troubled places all around the world.

The first temple was dedicated to the victims and survivors of suicide. Many of the people who built it with their own hands had suffered the loss of a loved one who had killed themselves. They built that structure to address the loss, and then let anyone who had lost leave a message inside it, or write on the walls. And then they burned it down. A simple act, one that provided an immense sense of catharsis and release.

The process has been the same wherever it's gone: To a conflict zone in Ireland; to a city decimated by an earthquake in New Zealand; to an American school devastated by gun violence. In each location no professional builders are hired, no professional staff are brought in from the outside: the people who want to grieve build the temple themselves, however immense it is, with their own hands. If they don't have a skill that they need to build the temple, they learn it. When it is finished, it stands as a community resource. Anyone can enter, and anyone who grieves – for any reason – can leave a message or a memento behind. At the end of its life, the temple is burned with everything left in it. Gone.

Vanishing in front of your eyes.

It is one of the most powerful experiences people have. It can change the course of lives. For those who visit it, but especially for those who built it. Because you did that. You took your grief, and your pain, and created something out of legends and poetry with it, then gave it to your community, and let it go. And sometimes, nothing is the same after that.

Here's one more: another story about a very different experience but with a very similar result.

One night, in a very dark San Francisco bar, "Melissa" told me that the only thing her parents let her watch as a kid were very old time cartoons.

"I think they thought that this would shield me from the weirdness and the problems of the world. But ... have you watched many old time cartoons? Have you SEEN prohibition era Betty Boop?"

"I ... don't know, actually ... nothing comes to mind."

"It gets really surreal. Whoever was animating those ... I don't know what it is, but, they definitely didn't protect me from the world. Instead they focused my attention on this bizarre fantasy world, and I love it so much. It made me want to be a cartoon character, you know? Because they were so wild and transgressive and uninhibited, and that's what I was comparing myself to."

Talk about imagos – this image of the transgressive cartoon figure was imprinted on her early, and carried an enormous energy. It sat in the back of her head, lurking in her subconscious, all her life, until she moved to San Francisco and discovered a chaotic burlesque clown troupe. She saw one of their shows, and her jaw dropped. Time seemed to slow down. Everything clicked.

She auditioned for the troupe, and got in. And discovered that being a risqué clown with boundless energy and no inhibitions is about as close to being a living cartoon character as you can get in this world. It allows her creative unconscious to come to life.

"It's not that it takes over or anything," she told me. "But it's so freeing. And authentic. It doesn't feel like I'm putting on a costume, it feels like I'm taking one off." And that person, psychically naked, knows how to talk to a crowd and make people feel good even as she lampoons them. And sometimes, when it really works, she is able to give people the same kind of experience she had – to access what she accessed.

She has organized her life around this experience.

"I say I'll stay in the Bay Area as long as it keeps feeding me like this," Melissa said. "For all the housing problems, money problems, all the techies, all the drama ... I can't imagine working a 9-5 job anymore. I know that this, accessing this spirit, having these incredible, magical, experiences, and helping other people have them, is what I'm here to do. So I'll stay as long as it feeds me these opportunities, and if it stops, then I'll leave, and it will be pretty easy."

* * *

The highest achievement of an art experience in the San Francisco style is not to get someone to say "it was beautiful," or "it was amazing," or even "it moved me." But "it changed my life." That's how success is measured. Breakthroughs that lead to significant personal change.

The phenomenon of changing your life after having this kind of art experience is common enough that it's spawned a warning aphorism: "Don't marry your parakeet." (There's also a "don't divorce your parakeet" version, which is functionally the same.)

It means that right after you get back from Burning Man, don't make any sudden life changes. Don't change careers, move cities, adopt a child, sell all your possessions and join a monastery, abandon your friends, join the military, or get a major tattoo. In short, don't marry your parakeet ... for at least three weeks. Give it at least that much time to see if what you're experiencing is a state of euphoria you will come down from, or in fact a fundamental change that, after waiting a month, you'll still want to act on. People who are euphoric

78

make stupid decisions, to be sure. But people who have breakthrough experiences … from building a temple, from becoming a clown, from confessing one's darkest secrets to a visiting spirit … usually find that the decisions they make are good ones. Melissa's decision to live her life in pursuit of her art has made her life so much more difficult, but it's not a decision she regrets at all: it's filled her with purpose and drive. The people who ran away to join the Circus Redickuless had an even more intense version of that experience, with all its highs and lows.

We've touched on what it means to create an experience in which you enlist someone's personal mythology to co-create it with you. Now we need to recognize just how life-altering, in the best sense, these experiences can be, and ask why. Why do the most dizzying and intense experiences of our lives not leave us dazed and confused, but rather infused with a new sense of purpose, resolve, and a higher sense of self?

Let's talk some more about the psyche, shall we?

Notions of personal fate and destiny exist in cultures around the world. Often it's seen in religious terms – the will of the gods, God's plan for us, karma. But it doesn't have to be: Abraham Maslow described it as "self-actualization," and said that it is the highest human need. We can't get to it until we've handled the basics – safety, shelter, food, community – but there is a drive in us all to grow into ourselves – to become what we are capable of. And it doesn't go away. So long as our basic needs are met – and often even when they're not – the need to self-actualize, to grow into our destiny, the self we were "meant to be," is present. And grows stronger and stronger.

Jung called this "individuation," and I'm going to quote noted Jungian psychologist James Hollis on this concept, because I think his description is so apt:

Individuation is

"(T)he lifelong project of becoming more nearly the whole person you were meant to be – what the gods intended, not the parents, or the tribe, or, especially, the easily intimidated or inflated ego. While revering the mystery of others, our individuation summons each of us to stand in the presence of our own mystery, and become more fully responsible for who we are in this journey we call our life. So often the idea of individuation has been confused with self-indulgence or mere individualism, but what individuation more often asks of us is the surrender of the ego's agenda of security and emotional reinforcement, in favor of humbling service to the soul's intent. This is quite the opposite of self-indulgence; it is the service of the ego to the higher order manifested to us through the Self."

Individuation involves not just growing in what we'd normally regard as "positive" ways, but addressing the "shadow" side of one's self: assimilating the parts that you normally keep buried in the unconscious into your whole, conscious self. It is also never finished: because you are always growing and changing and developing as a person, you never reach a static point where you are done and a little bell goes off and now you're who you were always meant to be. You never reach the end, but you can get much closer.

Indeed, you are driven to it. Maslow calls self-actualization the highest human need, and Jung describes individuation as a fundamental calling, and to ignore either your needs or your calling is to court disaster. Anxiety, ennui, neurosis, depression, unhappiness ... these are Furies which afflict you for ignoring the calling of your gods and not becoming who you are meant to be.

And they're not the only thing.

Because the truth is that most of us resist individuation much of the time. It's not really convenient for the lives we live, or the world we live them in. We stay in jobs that don't engage us because we need the money; we stay in relationships that don't fulfill us because we're stuck in a rut, or we don't get into relationships we want because we're frightened; we stay in places we've outgrown because we're lazy or afraid of change; we hold on to habits that make us unhappy because they also make us feel secure; we avoid confrontations and conflict that we need to have because they make us feel uncomfortable; we refuse to connect with something greater than ourselves because we don't know how to be humble. Sometimes we feel the yearning for change deeply, but we really have no idea *what to do*: We're stumped. There are hundreds of good reasons to stay in place and refuse to grow in the way individuation demands.

And there is something within us that does not care. That lashes out at us when we stall. That is going to knock down every wall we put up and kick through every door we lock, until we're moving again.

Rollo May, appropriating a term from the ancient Greeks, calls that part of us the "daimonic."

To the ancient Greeks, a "daimon" was the force that connected you here in the mortal world to your destiny, the person the gods had planned for you to become. It assisted you when you were heading in the right path, and it afflicted you when you weren't. In Plato's dialogues, Socrates told the judges of Athens that he knew he was doing the right thing by standing against them because his daimon, which had argued with him so many times about so many smaller decisions, was supporting him in this one. It wasn't good for him personally – he died as a result of that decision – but to truly "be Socrates," he had to follow this path.

Happiness, Aristotle wrote, is to live in harmony with one's daimon. "Eudaimonia" is to achieve happiness through living up to one's potential, achieving excellence in your virtues, and being who you are meant to be.

Once again, you can take that as literally or metaphorically as you like, but when you are in the grip of it, it is subjectively real – stunningly real. Yeats called the daimonic "the other will," and in his book *Love and Will*, May describes the way in which it can seem as though it takes us over during moments when we stop acting like the character we are trying to play and instead act in accordance with our honest impulses. It shares an etymology with "demonic" precisely because it is so often experienced as a compulsion, and even a possession.

When we have set up a life that gives us no more room to grow, or to grow in ways that are intrinsically meaningful to us, the daimonic acts out against it. The more we repress our potential to be authentic, the more extreme the daimon's reaction eventually becomes.

"When inward life dries up," May wrote, "when feeling decreases and apathy increases, when one cannot affect or even genuinely touch another person, violence flares up as a daimonic necessity for contact, a mad drive forcing touch in the most direct way possible."

But this isn't random aggression, it's not tearing our lives down or lashing out at what we've built for no reason. The daimonic isn't evil, but rather amoral: it is our drive towards individuation. And it will not take "no" for an answer, or "not yet," or "when it's convenient." If we are suppressing our own growth into who we authentically wish to become, if we are surrendering ourselves to an agenda we do not really care about, then the daimonic will not listen to reason. It will be as irrational as it needs to be to get us on track.

Perhaps the most difficult thing about living in harmony with this inner drive is that it is not usually experienced as a push towards self-aggrandizement. Rather, it generally involves greater vulnerability – admitting what you really want, opening yourself up to others, even putting your personal needs aside in support of a higher calling that you find more meaningful. To be guided by the daimonic, however violent or irrational it initially appears after being repressed for so long, is to move towards greater humility – which is also a characteristic, Jung said, of successful individuation.

And when we are actively pursuing individuation, when we are trying to become our true selves, the daimonic can support us in unexpected ways.

"The destructive activities of the daimonic are only the reverse side of its constructive motivation," May wrote. "The daimonic (unlike the demonic, which is merely destructive) is as much concerned with creativity as with negative reactions. That is, constructiveness and destructiveness have the same source in human personality. The source is simply human potential."

It is the daimonic in its creative aspects that we are most interested in, in experience design – although you can't always separate them out.

Now for those among us not comfortable with the degree of spiritualism implied here, that's okay: we can surely all agree at least that intrinsic motivations do exist, that they are real, and that denying them can cause psychological issues. This has been repeatedly demonstrated through scientific research. (For reference, I'm particularly fond of the research done by psychologists Richard Ryan and Edward Deci on these points.) May, in fact, explicitly thought that the daimonic originated in basic physical impulses for things like sex and violence. It was, in his mind, a wholly physical phenomenon. But it can't be *dismissed* as a purely physical phenomenon because it is experienced psychologically, and because it can best – even only – be addressed at a psycho-spiritual level. To reduce it to chemical interactions is to ignore what it actually says about your life, which is real and important. Emotions are, in fact, an objective phenomenon, and learning to interpret them isn't irrationality but wisdom.

Larry Harvey understood that, too: though an ardent materialist who did not believe there was anything remotely like a "spiritual substance," he nevertheless understood that people have experiences that are best described as "soul" and "spirit" – and that trying to ignore them by saying "oh, that's just a brain chemical reaction" is like telling someone to ignore their sense of sight because it's just a brain chemical reaction. John Law, interestingly, was also a hard materialist back in the day. One of the few things that he and Larry ever agreed on was that human beings have real spiritual needs, even though the spirit isn't real. And that these needs are best addressed on their own level.

(Today John says his stance on the spiritual has "softened with time." "I was an atheist-existentialist when younger. Now not at all. I am an agnostic and a skeptic. NOT an atheist, nihilist or intractable materialist. I concede I know nothing and consequently assume nothing.")

So it's fine if you think that's what's happening here – nothing spiritual, just the weirdness of what happens when matter starts to experience psychology.

And, indeed, if you want some more quantitative explanation for what's happening here, I suggest you'll find it in the work of psychologists Art Bohart and Karen Tallman, whose 1999 book *How Clients Make Therapy Work*, published by the American Psychological Association, illustrates the point.

Looking at research on the effectiveness of different psychodynamic therapeutic modalities (types of talk therapy), Bohart and Tallman conclude that outside of certain very clear cases, the type of therapy applied actually has little-to-no impact on whether a patient improves. Instead, what mat ters is whether or not *they feel they have an authentic connection with their therapist.*

How can that possibly be? Well, consider: most of us don't need a therapist most of the time, any more than most of us need a doctor most of the time. We don't go to a doctor for ordinary cuts and bruises and aches and pains, or even colds or flus, because our bodies can heal themselves. We have the capacity to recover on our own. We only go to a doctor when our capacity for self-healing is overwhelmed, or turned off, or some truly horrific damage is done that's beyond its capacity.

Same thing with mental health. We encounter so many setbacks, mental bruises, minor traumas and depressions, in our day-to-day life, and we generally don't need a therapist for them. That's because we have a capacity for self-healing and growth. We don't need a professional's advice, we've got this.

But when our capacity for self-healing is somehow stalled, or is overwhelmed, or we suffer a truly traumatic psychological injury that is too much ... then we see a therapist. And what the therapist does, Bohart and Tallman show, isn't to "cure" the patient, but to jumpstart the patient's capacity for self-healing. When that happens, patients get better, and when that doesn't happen, patients don't.

And outside of certain very mechanistic problems (think of the outermost rings of the Existential-Integrative model we talked about before, physiological and environmental factors) it doesn't really matter what kind of therapy they're getting. Because it turns out that the thing that most jumpstarts someone's capacity to self-heal isn't the wisdom of Freud or the latest affirmations of positive psychology, but an authentic connection with another human being, who is paying attention to your wellbeing. That's what really matters. That's the factor that gets statistically significant improvements, which last over time, in therapy.

The daimonic is focused on authentic growth, rather than self-healing, but the principle is very similar and there's a lot of overlap there. If the "daimonic" is too poetic or fanciful a reference for you, then think of it as the human capacity for self-actualization, and the intrinsic motivation we have to grow and develop – both of which are objectively provable things. I think "the daimonic's" poetic aspects actually make it more explanatory for the psyche, not less, but you do you. The point is that there is a force here, a process, that needs to be taken into account.

However you describe it, something along these lines happens. And now that we've had this quick tour through the psyche, we can put it all together to talk about what kind of experiences we're designing, and how they work.

Chapter 6:
An Introduction to Psychomagic

The playa was rough, and even with my flashlight it was too dark to see the bumps in front of my wheels. Every jolt was a surprise, and instead of relaxing into the ride it made me stare at the ground even harder, as though I could pierce the darkness by concentrating.

That's how I almost missed the flaming altar, and the cluster of people around it. I nearly biked right into them. They were whispering to each other and nearly missed me too: one of a million near-collisions that happen at Burning Man every day, averted at the last minute as I veered off to the east and hit my brakes, coming to a bumpy stop.

I turned and shone my flashlight on their backs. There were maybe seven people huddled around an altar with a small flame, and behind them were three large towers. Maybe climbable. Either they'd appeared out of nowhere, or I had.

I love the deep playa, the empty space far out beyond the inhabited areas of Black Rock City. I love it when something appears there, like a dream. I was going deeper tonight. All the way in. But first ... I wanted to see what I'd nearly knocked over, concentrating on the darkness so much I'd missed the light.

The sign on the towers said this was the "Pillars of Wisdom."

Okay. I remember something about this. There was an early Christian hermit. Saint ... saint ... St. Somebody, who built pillars through the Middle East as spots for contemplation. These are probably not what his pillars looked like, but it's a nice conceit. There is writing on the pillars – graffiti in markers of every size and shape. I can either get closer to read it or cluster around the first, hear what they're whispering at the altar.

I decide to listen before I look.

The altar is filled with little glass or plastic beads, and the flame hovers around them ... it's a neat effect. Four people there are having a conversation about something their campmates did wrong today. One person at the altar is explaining what this place is about to two others.

"First," he says, "you take this paper," and he hands each of them an onion thin sheet of paper and a pen. When he sees me there, he hands me one too. "And then you write something down on it, something you want to tell the divine. And then you toss it on the flame. Then you open your mind and climb into one of the towers, or walk around them if they're full, until you hear what God has to say to you. And when you hear that, you take a marker and write it on the tower."

They take their papers and stare at them. What do any of us have to say to God, anyway? It's funny, we go through our lives wishing we could give the creator of the universe a piece of our mind ... but when asked to put it in a bullet point, we blank. We don't so much want to talk to God as we want to howl at him, to hold up our lives to the creator and wail.

My two companions on this journey are hesitating. They have no idea. Leaning down over the paper, so no one else can see, I write the confession of failure that has haunted me for most of my life ... the standard I have never lived up to. "I'm sorry," I begin, and end two sentences later. I fold the paper up. I hold it over the fire. It catches immediately, and is gone in an instant.

The facilitator nods to me and I turn and begin walking clockwise around the towers. I know this is supposed to be quiet contemplation, but I can't help holding my flashlight out and seeing what other people have written: what they thought the divine was saying to them in the dark.

It reads:

"Love everyone!"

"Don't be afraid to try new things!" "It will be alright!"

"Forgiveness is good for the soul."

Really? We listen for the voice of God, and we think he speaks in clichés? Is God supposed to be writing a self-help book? Is this honestly the best we can do? If it is, we're in trouble. If we think this is how the voice of the universe speaks, we're a community that doesn't understand the first thing about spirituality no matter how much yoga we do in the morning. I walk around the three pillars of wisdom, shaking my head.

Having had these thoughts, there's no way I'm going to be open to the divine voice now. I chose to be a critic rather than a prophet. I step back to the fire, and see that one of the people who got paper with me is finally writing something down. She's a tall, thin, brunette, and when she holds her paper out to the fire it, too, disappears with a flash.

But instead of walking towards the pillars, she walks away from them, back towards Black Rock City. I watch her go until she stops, almost out of sight, to fiddle with her pack; then I turn back to the fire. I run my hand through it. I wish someone here had had something profound to say.

Next to me, a monster with a swirling black and white face steps up to the fire.

I jolt. The small crowd jumps, half-shouts. The monster looks around at us, and then back at the fire. It takes us all a moment, in the darkness, to realize that this is a mask. A very good mask that fits perfectly on a costume. It was ... shocking. It was ... I can see now ... the girl who just walked away. She stepped out in the darkness and took a mask out of her pack, put it on, and came back. I don't think she meant to scare the hell out of us – but my God she did.

Slowly, people go back to their whispered conversations. Suddenly, I get an idea. I slip away from the altar, back to my bike. I've left my own pack next to it. In the darkness ... working without a flashlight ... I pull out my own mask, the one I was given just this morning. It's an old, beaten up, rubber thing, a skeleton face in a helmet. It fits perfectly. I slip it on. Count to 10, and walk back to the fire, standing next to the girl in her mask.

Nothing happens.

Apparently one mask was shocking and terrifying. A second is old hat.

Except that she ... mask girl ... is paying attention. She leans closer. "Are you supposed to be a demon?" she whispers.

"I don't know. This face was a gift."

She nods, thinking that over. "I worked on mine for months," she says. I nod back. The fire is eerie on our false eyes.

I get an idea. An inspiration. "I'm headed out to deep playa," I say. "Come with me. I'll bet you ... I'm absolutely certain... that we'll bump into somebody else with a mask.

There's a horde of demons out there, waiting for us. I can feel it. We'll walk away from the Pillars of Wisdom, head out into deep playa, and find a whole city of the damned."

The fire crackles.

"Wow," she says. "That's awesome." She looks ahead, as though she could see into the darkness. "But ... I'm here with friends. They're over there," she points vaguely. "At that sculpture thing. And we really want to all be at the temple at midnight, to see the monkey chant. I don't think ..." She lets that trail off.

I nod. "Of course," I say. The wind picks up. We both shiver. The fire flickers. I won't be able to do it myself. If I go out to deep playa on my own, I won't find any more masks.

"You could come with us."

I shake my false head. I have to go deep tonight.

I put my hands over the fire and then turn around. Walk back to my bike. I aim it out towards 12 o'clock and pedal, thinking that the Pillars of Wisdom have it all wrong. The divine doesn't speak to us in words and sentences. It doesn't care about prayers and poetry. The only words it knows are "yes" and "no." It speaks to us in dreams and comets, in calls to action and faces suddenly appearing out of the darkness.

My friend Eric Myers, who founded Burning Man's official radio station and produced avant-garde theater in San Francisco and Columbus, Ohio, once received advice from legendary artist, filmmaker, and tarot card reader Alejandro Jodorowsky.

He told Jodorowsky that he was suffering from creative fatigue, that he found it hard to keep writing, and some days exhaustion overtook him.

Jodorowsky responded that he was suffering from a sense of himself growing thinner as he worked, and that in these moments he needed to re-infuse himself with his own essence. So, he said, have a sample of your blood taken, and place the blood into empty pill capsules. Place those blood capsules in the freezer. And whenever you are feeling creatively exhausted and empty, go to the freezer, take one of these pills, and swallow it. Your problem will resolve.

Eric never did it – he chickened out, his wife was a nurse, this was totally doable – but he's never forgotten the moment. And he's always wondered: what would have happened?

It's a story that has a lot in common with the other stories you've been reading here. Creating rituals to access your inner asshole, complete with stabbing, or to summon a friend; building temples to create spaces where grief can be accessed and expressed on a whole new level, or absurd circuses that people can run away and join; telling your greatest fear to a skeletal spirit at a corporate mixer, or writing it down on flash paper at a dark tower of wisdom in the middle of the desert, or ordering the wishes of your heart in a bar with no menus.

Jodorowsky's term for these kinds of things is "Psychomagic," and it contains a crucial insight that ties everything we've been talking about together.

Let's summarize and synthesize:

Our conscious minds are not the entirety of our psyches, our selves – just the parts we're aware of (literally that we're "conscious" of), moment to moment. Beneath that is an unconscious realm that, though we're not routinely aware of it, has a tremendous impact on the way we see the world, and the way we see ourselves. It influences our assumptions, our choices, and our sense of what's possible, in ways we're not aware of. And each of us, as we go through life, develops a personal mythology within our unconscious – stories and symbols emerging out of our lives that represent what our unconscious, and therefore we, make of the world and ourselves.

Within that unconscious is a drive to individuate, to grow and become our full selves, and it's a powerful urge. But in most people it is routinely thwarted by the lives we live. That thwarting doesn't just happen with the decisions we consciously make: it happens at the unconscious level, too, which is why despite our explicit desires to break out of old patterns, lift ourselves out of ruts, and take new kinds of risks to get new kinds of outcomes, we so often find ourselves repeating the same behaviors, and mistakes, again and again and again.

Our need to individuate is thwarted by the complexes we develop, and the way in which we project the parts of ourselves we're unwilling to acknowledge onto other people, who have no idea that they're part of our psychodrama. We want to change, we want to grow, we want to be authentic in the world ... but much of that work has to be done on the unconscious level, and we don't have direct access to it.

Why don't we have direct access to it? Because the unconscious and conscious minds *speak different languages.* We try to convince ourselves to do things using language, and logic, and reason, and abstract thoughts. But the unconscious speaks in experiences, in dreams, in archetypes, in symbolism, in mythology, and in images. We're trying to talk to it one way, it's trying to communicate with us another way, and the result is that nothing happens.

Psychomagic, Jodorowsky proposed, is the art of consciously creating symbolically significant actions and events that the psyche can understand and process. Why magic? Because, as I hope has been made abundantly clear by now, when this works it doesn't just feel like magic, it seems even to your rational mind and critical faculties that something magical has just happened.

The techniques of psychomagic don't seem like they ought to work. I mean, come on, it's kind of ridiculous, right? Robin threw oranges and stabbed me with a dessert fork, and that's somehow supposed to change her whole outlook on the world for 48 hours? Somebody sees an incredibly stupid circus show – bafflingly, impossibly stupid – and then throws their whole life away to join it?

This makes no sense. How can this possibly work? How can it possibly be effective?

It works because we have an ally in the daimonic. Create the conditions under which a complex that is holding someone back can be seen for what it is, or a projection can be repurposed to facilitate growth, and the creative aspect of the daimonic awakens. Connect with someone's personal unconscious, and the daimonic within them will assist you in helping them be present in the experience. The part of their psyche that is always seeking an opportunity to further individuation recognizes psychomagical experiences as an opportunity, and takes you up on it.

You have an ally on the inside, doing the work for you. Much in the same way that Bohart and Tallman demonstrated that a therapist doesn't "heal" a patient, but rather stimulates the patient's ability to heal themselves when they're stuck, a psychomagical experience stimulates the part of the recipient's psyche that is trying to be more authentic, but has encountered obstacles.

Which means, of course, that this is not precision work. It's very difficult to predict exactly how someone you know very well is going to react to psychomagic – it's impossible with strangers. General predictions? Yeah, you can design for those. But specific predictions? No, the unconscious is a complicated and irrational place, and personal mythologies rarely move in straight lines. You have to be capable of paying attention, improvising, rolling with the punches.

Which is why "channeling" is so much more useful a skill here than "performing." When you're performing, you're assuming you know what's going on in the person's unconscious, and trying to lead it. When you're channeling, you're paying attention to how they're reacting, and following their lead. To perform is to follow the script in your head, rather than going where their daimon leads, and it knows better than you do what it needs. Much in the way that Bohart and Tallman discovered that an authentic connection with a therapist was the most important factor in successful therapy, an authentic "channel" to the person undergoing psychomagic is the single most important factor to a successful experience. If you don't have that, then this isn't going to work, no matter how good the performance or production values.

So, to sum up: over 30 years, San Francisco's artistic underground developed a series of tools to create psychomagical experiences, which speak directly to the unconscious minds and personal mythologies of people going through them, thereby supporting their process of individuation and having an effect that is, often, life changing.

I frankly wouldn't have believed it if I hadn't seen it, over and over again, and then helped create these experiences myself.

Chapter 7:
Success Looks Like Serendipity

One year, at Burning Man, I gave my friend Mao a piece of writing, and he wanted me to sign it.

"Sure," I said, getting out a pen.

"No," he said. "Not with that. We need a marker or a highlighter or something."

It's hard to just come up with supplies like that at Burning Man, in the middle of the desert, but we were at the BMIR radio station, where Mao was a manager, and so we figured we might be able to find a highlighter or a marker somewhere. We looked, and then asked around.

No luck.

There wasn't anything like that in the station's supplies, and nobody we could find had brought one.

"Oh well," he said. And then I said goodbye.

I walked out of the station onto the road that serves as the boundary between the camps at Burning Man and the open playa, turned right, and walked maybe 200 feet to a road that leads back into the city. (5:30, if you know anything about Black Rock City's geography). I started walking that road for maybe another 200 feet and then a crowd of people walked out of a camp to my right, laughing.

One of them, a man I'd never met before, ran up to me. "Hey!" he said. "I want to give you a gift!"

He put something into my hand, and ran off. It was a green highlighter.

I gaped. Stunned.

Even for Burning Man, a place famous for being so filled with moments of synchronicity that it seems like magic, this was bizarre.

But it actually happens there all the time.

And not just there. On the contrary – this is a case where Burning Man is a very large example of something that the San Francisco art underground did all the time on a smaller scale.

Here's another example. More baroque but just as baffling.

The Lost Horizons Night Market is an event that was actually developed in New York City, but quickly immigrated to San Francisco. It's an elegantly unpermitted event in a city where it's almost impossible to get significant space on the cheap. Here's how it works:

A bunch of artists each rent a box truck, the length is up to them. They each turn the back of the box truck into an experience – I've seen people turn their trucks into bowling alleys, 50s diners, dance clubs, bars, libraries, cinemas, storytelling venues, reverse ball pits, petting zoos, lecture halls, fortune telling booths, virtual reality playgrounds, massage parlors ... and places far more strange and unique.

The box truck artists and their crews then all meet late at night in a commercial parking lot or along the perimeter of vacant buildings, and people arrive and wander around the space, in and out of box trucks, having bizarre and surprising experiences until the night ends or the cops come – in which case the trucks all leave separately and then rendezvous at another location, which is texted back to the network of people attending.

It's a DIY wonderland of infinite possibility. You wander through a dark space at night, going from truck to truck, things that shouldn't be there, that will be chased away if they're discovered, and literally anything could be inside. Anything.

At one of these events, my friends Noona and Paul had prepared a box truck that advertised as a beating service. A couple of big, threatening, men in old style gangster costumes were standing outside, and when anyone asked what this was, they said that if you went in, you'd get the beating you deserved. People would walk in, the makeshift doors would close behind them, and people outside would hear the sounds of punching and shouting. The door would open again, and the person would walk out with bruises and a black eye.

It was a trick, of course. When you got inside, they sat you down in a chair, made noises, and had a makeup artist do quick work. Then they sent you back outside to talk about how much it had hurt. And people laughed and said it couldn't possibly really be what it said it was – and they were right – but, they still had to wonder ...

Noona and I had arranged in advance that I'd show up, make a big fuss about how this was no big deal, maybe even bullshit, and then go inside. I'd worn clothes that I didn't mind being ripped, and they went to town on my makeup. A few moments after I'd walked in, I screamed my head off and then limped out with ripped clothes and terrible bruises and an "open wound" on my head.

I pretended to be delirious, and in pain, and limped around from box truck to box truck, waving to people I didn't know and "hallucinating" that they were my friends, calling them by the names of my actual friends, asking where they'd been and whether we were going to hang out after the night market. And people cringed and kinda-laughed and wondered "what the hell HAPPENED to him? Was ... was that really the beating truck?"

There was one truck that had an exceptionally long line of

people waiting to get in. I never really found out what was in there. From outside, it looked like they were sitting people down on reclining chairs and putting some sort of apparatus over their eyes that made them see a light show ... or something. I was too in character to really find out.

For some reason I zoomed in on three of the people waiting near the front of the line – two men and a woman.

"Eric!" I said to one of the men. "Scott!" I said to the other. "Karen!" I said to the woman. "Hi, Karen! Where'd you all go? I didn't ... I ... I got confused ... I haven't seen you in a while, have I?"

The guys just laughed this off but the woman engaged. When was the last time I'd seen her?

Well, I said, making it up as I went, and basing it loosely off of an actual friend of mine, I hadn't seen her since before she'd left for her trip to Ecuador, right?

"Right," she'd said, "right," playing along. Then she gave me a cool look. "Do I ... actually know you?"

"Yeah, of course you do, Karen!" I'd said, not dropping character. "We've known each other for years I ... I ... I can't ..." I swayed in place, due to my injuries.

"Hey," one of the guys asked. "What did she do on her trip

to Ecuador?"

"Well," I said, righting myself, "I heard you went to an ayahuasca ceremony, with a shaman ..." and I went on, making up details. Sometimes she'd ask me questions, sometimes the guys did, but between the three of us we had a surreal and mildly funny conversation about my long history with "Karen" and the details I supplied about her "trip to Ecuador."

It was going pretty well, I thought.

Then the line moved forward, and the three of them could get in. The guys immediately rushed in, this was what they'd been waiting for, after all, but she stood in place, and gave me a glowering look.

"Okay," she said. "Okay, I don't know you. I'm sure of it. So WHO THE HELL told you about my trip to Ecuador?"

It turned out I'd gotten most of the details right. The country, the trip to see the shaman, the kind of family she'd lived with ... most of it.

And her name actually was Karen.

Up until that point, I'd been pretending to be dazed and confused ... now I wasn't pretending. I considered dropping character, but, to say what? How do you explain this?

The member of the truck's staff who was monitoring the line came over. If she didn't go in now, she'd lose her spot and have to go to the back of the line. She hesitated, weighing her options.

"Who told you?" she asked again. "Some of those things ... I didn't tell ANYBODY when I got back!"

My genuine confusion looked so much like my fake confusion that it seemed to her that I was withholding information, rather than trying to figure this out too. She made a disappointed noise, turned, and walked into the truck.

Once she was out of sight, I limped away, wondering every bit as much as she was: what just happened?

* * *

This is weird, I know it is, but it's true: moments like those happen *all the time* at these kinds of events. When they are going well, they are full of serendipity. To a degree that is baffling and sometimes frightening. It's such a phenomenon that Bishop Joey, of the San Francisco based First Church of the Last Laugh, started referring to it as "serentypical," because it happens just that often.

Go ahead and explain that to yourself with whatever explanation is most convincing to you. I've got nothing. A lot of people, even people who don't believe in magic, just say "yeah, something magic is happening," and leave it at that. A lot of people pull out the old standby that, look, coincidences are actually a statistically probable event, and they're going to happen somewhere, sometime, so it might as well be here. I tried that one for a while, but it didn't last. Even if that's true, something is happening to cluster these coincidences at these events. So you could say, okay, that's a selection bias, but now you have to propose some kind of mass selection bias effect and ... I don't know, it could be true. It could be. It just ...

... look, when this actually happens to you? You can't help but wonder: WHAT KIND OF WORLD AM I LIVING IN?

And when it keeps happening? You eventually start to think that maybe things you didn't think were possible are, in fact, possible. Which, of course, is kind of the whole point.

Despite its impossibility, this is a recognizable, and recognized, metric: success in these kinds of events creates serendipity. Unleash enough people's daimonic unconsciouses, turn enough space into a playground for people's personal mythologies, and shit gets weird. Reality buckles.

"Anyone can design and execute synchronicity-inducing scenarios that look and feel exactly like magic," Robin Ziiro tells her collaborators. "But it really is synchronicity. You don't make it happen, you let it happen."

When you're playing at a high level, you come to expect it. It becomes a kind of virtuous cycle: success creates moments of synchronicity, which in turn makes the event more powerful and successful, which in turn creates more synchronicity. And it still surprises you. I'm not going to go into much more detail about this because I honestly don't have much more to say, only that it is a thing, a very real aspect of these kinds of events, and a sign of success.

But we can talk in more detail about what other signs of success look like, and what happens when things are going well.

Chapter 8:
Awe and Vulnerability

The further we go into this book, the more we're going to move from stories about very simple experiences to stories about very complex ones. That shift has already begun: we've gone from one-on-one encounters and small groups that didn't need a lot of context, to describing the Circus Redickuless and the Lost Horizons Night Market. By the time we pass the Jejune Institute and the Latitude Society to reach The Fallen Cosmos, we're going to be talking about events that were absurdly baroque and ridiculously complicated.

There's a danger in that, though, one that the scene itself has fallen into: people mistake the baroque and the elaborate for the experience itself. And it's not. Veering into the baroque and elaborate is one of the ways you try to scale. The actual experiences, however, the ones that matter, are always those moments of connection and realization: "I'm going to run away and join the circus!" "You're here because we summoned you with a magic ritual." "How does this person know the secret details of my trip to Ecuador?" "I want to give you a green highlighter!"

Those are the moments that matter. Any elaborate set-up is just a way to get people there, and not something you do for its own sake.

So it's really important to point out, as often as we can,

just how simple these experiences can be. More complex is not always better, and can be counter-productive if it gets in the way.

Chicken used to do a bit, I've only seen it a couple of times, in which he'd get on stage and get two volunteers from the audience. Usually men, it worked best with guys who had been drinking a little. They'd stand on opposite sides of him, and then he'd get out a $20, and he'd explain that this bill was up for auction. They'd be bidding against each other for it, and whoever made the highest bid would get it. They could start as low as they wanted. BUT, if the bidding goes over $20, then they'll both have to pay however much more they bid over the actual dollar amount of the bill at the end. So if your final bid is, say, $24, then win or lose you owe $4 to Chicken.

So maybe one would bid a dollar, and the other would be two dollars, and on they'd go. And maybe they had the wherewithal to quit while somebody was ahead. That would happen, sometimes.

But sometimes they wouldn't, they'd get into a competitive guy thing, and they'd start pushing the bidding over $20 – bidding $21 for it, and then $22. And the more they bid, of course, the worse it gets, because they actually have to pay Chicken the excess. But now they're also locked in, because at least the winner will get the $20, so, even if he bids $30, at least he wins $10. But as the bidding gets higher and higher, even that prize starts to fade, and the smart thing to do is to just stop, just stop ... but they can't let go, and you can see them in pain as they understand just how bad this is getting, but they can't stop bidding against each other because they want to win the thing that is no longer actually a prize, and so winning has become losing and they can't stop and they don't understand why they're not stopping ...

I told you, Chicken plays rough. It's amazing when it works, though – you're in the crowd, gawking: is this REALLY happening? – and it's incredibly simple. All you need is a crowd and $20.

But by far the most extraordinarily simple-yet-powerful experience I think I've ever seen designed for a mass audience is the Decentralized Dance Party (DDP), which was conceived of and founded by Gary Lachance in Vancouver BC, and operated in San Francisco by artist Michael Ryan Garcia.

It takes a little technical doing, but it's brilliantly straight-forward. You get a low-powered portable FM transmitter, and put it in a backpack. You create a party mix that will play on it. You get a bunch of boom boxes (remember those?) and put them on the channel that the FM transmitter is playing on. You get a bunch of people to wear silly costumes, and all gather in a public place. You distribute the boom boxes, one guy wears the backpack with the transmitter, you press play, and then you all start dancing. And then you dance from one public place to the next, your own mobile dance party ... and just like the circus, anybody can join.

You dance down sidewalks, past restaurants, bus stops, subway stations ... you go down to the subway stations and dance on and off the trains. You go to public squares and statues and business plazas, and you pass hundreds of people. And there's something incredibly infectious about people just dancing ... no club scene, no cover, no fancy clothes. People smile, they laugh, they gaze in wonder. And some of them say, screw it, this is more fun than I'm having, and they join in, and they're dancing with you. And the crowd gets bigger, and bigger, and it can go on for hours.

It's pure, unbridled, totally inclusive, ecstatic joy, with no cover charge. It can get primal, people lose themselves in it. And once you've got the equipment, it's free to do. To change it up all you have to do is change your music mix and your route.

"There's always a feeling of working without a net when you decide to assemble a mob of strangers in public in the middle of the night," Michael told me. "But the payoff for that risk is creating the opportunity for a city full of strangers to stumble into an unexpected dance party (or have a dance party stumble into them), which is an environment rich in psychomagical potential. Importantly, the dance party itself is almost never the psychomagical moment: more often, it's just the canvas on which such moments are painted. But the beautiful thing about canvas is it's rough and it stretches - it doesn't have to be perfect or polished, it just has to be there."

This doesn't have to be hard. All too often, we make it much harder than it needs to be. And that's when the synchronicity, and the other signs of success, stop.

* * *

Outside of synchronicity, which is really both the most rarefied sign of success and also the least explicable, what does success look like? When things go right, what kind of experiences are people having as they go through these moments?

It will depend, of course, on the type of experience being designed – Chicken's $20 bill game and the DDP create vastly different kinds of feelings. And yet there are some similarities that, with success, you tend to see across the board.

The first is **Presence** – people become present, in the moment. (The Burning Man term for this is "Immediacy.") They are focused on what they are experiencing in this moment, and often connected to an unusual degree with their physical bodies. They tend to feel what they are feeling intensely, be- cause in this moment it's not competing for attention with a dozen other things. Instead they're here. Now.

One could argue, probably rightly, that any effective art has this impact upon its first encounter. When it comes to experience design, though, if you don't have this, you don't got 'nuthin. If people are present in the moment when they look at your painting, that's a sign of success, sure, but they don't have to be to think it's a good painting. But if your experience can't compel people to be present in the moment, it will likely fail.

The next is a greater sense of **vulnerability** – not in a "fear for my safety" way, though that can be a factor too (as the more L.A. based "extreme haunt" scene will attest), but in a psychological sense: that what they have hidden can now be seen, that what they have repressed can now express itself. This can feel incredibly good, but also frightening; it can bring up anger, and resentment. It can create any number of feelings, but these feelings all come from a sense of shared emotional vulnerability. Your defenses do not work here. Your walls are permeable. The moment people ask WHAT KIND OF WORLD AM I LIVING IN? they are absolutely certain to be present, and they are very likely to feel vulnerable, even if that vulnerability comes with a sense of expanded capacity: we are always vulnerable, for example, when we try doing new things, even if it's also very exciting.

People who go through such experiences together tend to bond afterwards. After all, vulnerability is tied to intimacy.

I would definitely say that these first two items are part of a step ladder – that people have to reach presence before they can reach vulnerability, and that they have to reach vulnerability before they can go any farther. But it isn't clear to me that any of the next experiences have to happen in any particular order – if you can get any of them, you are increasingly likely to have the rest of them.

Another sign of success is an awakening of awe – not in the shallow way we often use the term, where it's a synonym for "really great," "looks expensive," and "the YouTube clip of you doing that has gone viral," but in its deeper aspects. Psychologist Kirk Schneider (who came up with Existential-Integrative therapy, which we talked about earlier) has written extensively on the psychology of awe, and says that one of the key aspects is an overwhelming experience of the paradoxical nature of existence. We are simultaneously free and compelled, powerful and fragile, knowledgeable and ignorant, living and dying, loved and alone. Most of the time, we focus on just the aspects of life that make us feel secure and comfortable, and thus lose the experience of what existence actually is. An experience of awe brings us back to a full awareness of the paradoxical nature of our own lives.

This is where the use of "awe" as a synonym for "really good" breaks down, because while aspects of awe absolutely build us up – we are gods, in our way – other aspects break us down. Awe is every bit as associated with anxiety and discomfort and a feeling of powerlessness in the face of the majesty of existence as it is a sense of glory that we are part of the majesty of existence. This is awe's connection to vulnerability: to experience that which is so much greater than yourself, you have to be open to it, and to be open to it is to be vulnerable. But that connection is simultaneously a place of strength: there is so much more to the universe than is dreamt of in our philosophies, and we are connected to it. We are a part of it.

The experience of awe that frequently occurs in these events is not always serious and somber. That absolutely does happen, but just as often – more often, I'd say – it is experienced through laughter. What people experience is so bizarre, so unexpected, so paradoxical, that they can't help but laugh, and through that laughter experience the openness to possibility and paradox that awe represents.

When that guy came out of nowhere and handed me a green highlighter? After I stood, stunned, for a minute, I laughed. How could I not? Honestly, what other possible reaction could I have had? It was all so impossible, and yet it had really happened. When I tell people the story of how I somehow got most of the details right for Karen at the Night Market, they usually laugh – because again, what else is there to do? Laughter is one of the ways we reconcile paradox, and so is more closely connected to awe than we usually credit it.

Not surprisingly given everything that's been said so far, another sensation people often have when an experience like this is successful is that they are a **dynamic self** – that is to say, that change is possible in ways they had not realized before, and they can make that change happen We've discussed at some length already the intrapsychic mechanisms that make this possible (having your complexes interrupted and made visible, having a projection land on someone who can actually respond to it in a meaningful way ... all that stuff), so I'm not going to repeat it here. I'll just reiterate that the experience of dynamism where before there was a static self, the experience of new possibilities, is often experienced as a shot of magic. Our personal mythologies are as subjectively real to us as the laws of physics, and to the extent that they change, we're used to them changing very slowly, over time. To have a sudden change to your inner notions of what is possible is often the result of sudden trauma, and we know just how psychologically powerful trauma is. To have a sudden change to your inner notions of what is possible that is *not traumatic*, even if it makes you feel vulnerable and baffled, is equally powerful, but wondrous. When effective, experiences like this can leave you with the opposite of Post-Traumatic Stress Disorder (Post-Transcendence Serenity Discovery?), a sense of awe and wonder that infuses the rest of your life and that you cannot shake easily.

This doesn't necessarily mean anything will change. Only that you've had the recognition that change is possible. That you can still grow, and develop, and be more authentic.

Interestingly – paradoxically, which should not be a surprise at this point – people often feel a sense of **integration** as well. That is, a sense that they cannot be reduced to components.

And it's strange to say that, because actually we've

spent a lot of time here talking about people as aggregates of their different components – of their consciousness and unconsciousness, their archetypes and their daimons, their complexes. And there are lots of other ways in which people are frequently divided into component parts that we haven't really touched on: their bodies, their "brain chemicals," their neuronal firing patterns, pheromones, cultural backgrounds, medical histories, astrological signs, Myers-Briggs scores ... there are so many ways we can slice and dice people up to try and understand them better.

These can be useful approaches. But they are also, at some level, fictions. Of course I'm not saying that neurons and brain chemicals and cultures don't exist, but I am saying that, at the level of your personhood, you are not divisible by them. You are not reducible to them. In that context they are – like archetypes and daimons themselves – something that we cannot take too literally or entirely metaphorically. They are part of an integrated whole. And it is as that integrated whole, moment to moment, that we exist. So when having these kinds of experiences, people can simultaneously discover new aspects of themselves to play with and explore (Ranging from "I'm a unicorn!" to "I have a capacity to love and be loved that I never believed in") and also feel more integrated into a person not reducible to parts.

And if that's paradoxical, well ... yes.

Chapter 9:
Moving from "What" and "Why" to "How?"

I think it's true in many cases – I know it's true in some – that people who ended up in San Francisco devoting much of their lives to the creation of psychomagical experiences had a sense earlier in their lives that something like this was possible, even if they didn't have the concepts or the vocabulary to express it, let alone any idea how to do it. They figured it out as they started doing it together, and then other people (like me) came and learned how to do it from them. But we'd all been trying, certainly I had, to figure out how to do this – even as we wondered if it was really possible – earlier in our lives.

I think the first experience like this that I really created on purpose came almost a decade before I even thought of moving to San Francisco. I had no idea what I was doing, but I was desperate, and desperation creates accidental geniuses. In hindsight, it's a remarkable example of the form; at the time, I had no idea that it even could be an example of anything. I just needed it to work.

It wasn't for me, it was for the kids. Really.

I was a graduate student, studying linguistics at a University that we'll call ... oh, let's see ... "Purdue," a hypothetical land grant college founded in 1869, and best known today for its engineering and agricultural programs. It has programs in the liberal arts and social sciences, yes, but only in the sense that prisons have show choirs. However talented the people involved, Purdue is a gulag where such arts go to die.

I knew all this not only because I was enrolled in a social science program, but because I was teaching in a liberal arts one: I was a graduate teaching assistant in the composition program of the School of Liberal Arts. It was my job to allegedly teach classes in which students from all the various schools on campus were allegedly taught to read and write. This was a task that I cared about, but it was immediately clear that the university did not. Everything about their system was designed to avoid the messy process of actually teaching people how to be better (or even adequate) writers, and instead to simply shuffle them through a procedure that could be checked off on a transcript so that they could go to the state legislature and say "See! We're teaching them valuable on-the-job reading skills!" and then get more money.

It was a futile and Kafkaesque nightmare, but the worst part about it wasn't the administration but the classroom culture which the students were a part of. Composition classes were required courses, and so we were locked into a scenario in which all the students were only going to put in the minimum effort necessary to get the minimum grade they thought they needed, and absolutely nothing more. And the minimum effort was always to parrot back to me what they thought I wanted to hear. Absolutely no time would be spent really thinking about anything, because that was more effort than they needed to put in, given the way the system was designed, to get the minimum grade they wanted.

So we were stuck doing this dance together. And there was nothing that I could do about it.

Except ... except ... I discovered, quite by accident, that there was one scenario in which my students started really thinking for themselves. If they were confused about what kind of answer I was actually looking for ... so confused that they didn't actually know what to parrot back to me ... then their brains started warming up and turning on and they actually thought about what was going on and being said, while they figured out which way to set the auto-pilot.

During the times when my students were genuinely confused about what the "right answer" looked like, an actual education could take place.

Realizing this, I took action. I was teaching two units of English 102 the next semester, and designed my syllabus specifically to confuse the hell out of my students.

It was, I was advised at the time, the first laugh-out-loud funny syllabus in the history of the university. Not just funny, but surreal – the instructions for contacting the professor were biblical parodies (to see me during my office hours "first build an ark 40 cubits by 40 cubits, into which the instructor will place a copy of this syllabus, never again to be seen by mortal eyes." To see me out of my office hours "slaughter a fatted calf, and cook the meat so that the smoke billows up into the heavens, at which point the instructor will descend and either smite your enemies or help you with your home-work"); the rules for classroom decorum required students to refer to each other as "Jedis-in-training"; course outcomes including singing Scottish ballads; students were encouraged to bring livestock to the classroom. It was nonsense, written in black and white and handed out by their authority figure on the first day of class, and then gone over together with deadly earnestness.

The only part that was serious was the workload: it wasn't surreal at all when it made clear that students would be do-ing a lot more homework in my sections than in the average ones. By my rough calculation, they'd be doing ten times the number of papers as the students whose instructors were us-ing the pre-fab syllabus provided by the university. For all the surrealism, this wasn't an attempt to have a good time – it was an attempt to really educate them.

About a third of the students in each of my two sections immediately dropped the class. There were dozens of English 102 courses being taught each semester, and it became a running joke among the other TAs that my former students were walking up and down the halls, sticking their heads into classrooms, and saying "My professor is a crazy man, can I come here instead?"

But ... here's the thing ... the other 2/3rds of each class, that decided to stay. They made a deliberate decision to stay. They asked themselves, "do I want to drop?" And then decided, "no, no I want to stay and see where this goes. I **want** to be in this class and find out what happens."

In making that decision, in spite of a heavy workload and the fact that this could be an incredible disaster (or perhaps even because of it ...) they were engaged, every day. They were committed to figuring out what was signal and what was noise, what mattered and what didn't, and not just what I cared about and what I didn't but what they cared about and what they didn't. This became a challenge that they wanted to take up, were intrinsically motivated to take up, once they decided it was really an option. It was the greatest teaching experience of my life. Eventually, a few students asked if they could transfer *into* my courses: they were bored by their English classes, they'd heard that something interesting and intense was happening here, and they wanted to be part of it. I had 100% attendance the Friday of the Indy 500 race weekend, which was unheard of. One student showed up just after class had started, drunk off her ass. She walked to the back of the room, turned, pointed at me, said "This is the ONLY class I'm coming to, today!" sat down, and fell asleep.

But she showed up. Because she was invested. She gave a damn.

All this was enhanced by the fact that, once the students

did start to understand that the crazy rules were in fact just crazy, not rules, they were far more willing to trust me, and go out on limbs, than I'd ever seen students to be. That was because I had already taken a very big, very public, risk in creating this syllabus: they had hard evidence that I wasn't just pretending to be a different kind of teacher when it was easy and convenient for me. I'd gone out on a limb, and I'd done it first. Their response was to take chances in this classroom, rather than making sure they were always saying the safe thing.

The surrealist experiment in classroom pedagogy – a semester long designed experience – was a complete success. More than I'd ever imagined. Beyond just being exposed to better writing and practicing much more often, students told me it was inspiring, and changed their whole sense of what an education could be. It was something, they now understood, that they could actively engage in, rather than being passive receptacles of information they didn't care about.

Of course I was fired for it. You had to know that was coming.

I appealed the decision, and much to everyone's surprise I won, thus setting off a long and complicated back and forth with a department that desperately wanted to get rid of me. That is several other stories in its own right. But those stories don't have anything to do with experience design. And it turns out that this experience I amateurishly created in fact had all the hallmarks of what was, across the country, developing as a set of experience design principles and aesthetics in San Francisco. That resemblance might not be coincidental: the Suicide Club, decades earlier, had emerged out of a course taught at Communiversity, a university experiment in radical pedagogy.

The point I'm making is this: no amount of earnest entreaties to my students could ever have gotten them to be this enthusiastic. Getting up in front of them and giving a rousing speech about how education should work and how we were going to do it right this time, would have failed, and indeed always has. Appealing to their self-interest, trying to rationally convince them that what I had to say was so important that they should listen to me for the sake of their futures, would never have gotten me anywhere.

But creating enough funny confusion that they wanted to figure it out for themselves? That was an insight of uncommon clarity for me at that age. Some of them left, which was exactly the right thing for them to do under the circumstances, and was a potential outcome I had to not only accept but respect. If students couldn't have walked away they couldn't have chosen to stay, either. And it was that choice they made, far more than any antics I engaged in or wisdom that I had to impart, that made all the difference. They chose to stick around, and that mattered. They chose to trust me because I had made myself vulnerable first, and that mattered.

We had to go through all that to get to the kind of class-room experience it turned out we all really wanted to have, but didn't believe we could. Getting there was never going to be the shortest route from where we were.

Many years later I would have to re-learn all of that when I got to San Francisco. Or rather, learn it in a new context, one where it had generalizable principles that could be applied again, and examples of other people doing it masterfully.

* * *

Together, that list of things that we've discussed – presence, vulnerability, awe, personal dynamism, integration, synchronicity, and ultimately personal breakthroughs – represent the various characteristics of the psychomagical experiences that the San Francisco underground scene learned to design so well. All integrated together in ways that, when you live them, are seamless.

It's equally important, though, to notice what you don't see. "Fun." "Bliss." "Comfort." These events aren't even "parties" in the prosaic sense of the term.

Things like "fun" and "bliss" and "party" might or might not exist in any given event, but they are actually not central to the nature of the psychomagical experience being created. In fact, emphasizing them past a certain point is corrosive to such experiences. In the 21st century, religion isn't the opium of the masses – being entertained without being engaged and challenged is. This is a point that will come up over and over again as we look at how these kinds of experiences are created. The bottom line, for the moment, is that if fun or bliss or comfort is your highest virtue, you're never going to get to psychomagic. Remember that the goal of the daimonic is not for you to have the best time, but to fulfill your destiny by becoming the person you are meant to be.

Yet at the same time, however much we may value presence, vulnerability, synchronicity, and the like, these are not actually things that can be directly designed for. You can't insist that people be present – it doesn't work that way. You can't shout or make art at people until they feel a sense of integration – on the contrary, it's going to come across as preachy and superior and new age-y and basically awful.

You can tell people "okay, let's all be vulnerable ... right ... NOW!" I've actually done that event, I called it "Existentialists Anonymous," and it was pretty great. But that was done with a handful of people who had long experience in this kind of thing, and had a lot of context behind it which made it work. But that's sort of the point – the context matters as much as the actual imperative to "be vulnerable." Without context like a therapy session, or someone you love asking you to do this for them, an explicit request to be vulnerable is way more likely to backfire than to go anywhere useful.

And so on, across the board. I mean, contrived synchronicity isn't really synchronicity at all.

So in a very important way, if you want to design these kinds of experiences, you have to come at them sideways. If telling our unconscious "okay, we're going to do this now!" actually worked, we'd live in a very different world.

And, indeed, I think it's worth pointing out that the San Francisco underground experience design scene didn't begin with people on a mission to align themselves with people's personal mythologies in order to create a kind of magical impact through immersive experience. Nobody was thinking that. They discovered this worked by doing other things and starting to put the pieces together: they came at it sideways in pursuit of other passions, and paid attention to what was happening. This is the distinction between "performing" and "channeling" writ large, applied to a whole scene. Failure to understand that distinction is usually where people go wrong, imitating the surface of what they've seen without understanding the depths of why it worked.

Now that we have some sense of that, we have reached the point where good intentions can be usefully harnessed by skill and experience to create psychomagical experiences that can buckle reality and change lives. The first section of the book has been the "what" and the "why." The next section goes into the "how."

SECTION 2

How We Do It

Chapter 10:
Infinite Gardens vs. Finite Robots

By the early 2010s, the hot real estate trend among Silicon Valley billionaires was not just to buy a huge house in the most expensive real estate market in the world, but to buy up an entire block of houses and use them as a kind of privacy hedge to make sure that you didn't have any neighbors who could post opinions about you on social media.

One such billionaire, who I will not name because this part of the story I got second-hand from someone whose fact checking is less than scrupulous, was frustrated in their effort to buy up their block because the last house on on it wasn't a house at all, but a funeral home – a family business that had been running for almost 100 years, and they didn't want to sell.

The billionaire kept coming back with sweeter offers, and with mounting pressure, and eventually, after long wrangling, the family agreed. At which point the billionaire, frustrated by delays, paid them extra to vacate immediately and told their contractor to get to work NOW to make the building fit their vision.

"Okay," the contractor said. And then asked, "What do you want me to do with all the stuff?"

"What stuff?" the billionaire said.

"Well, it's a working funeral home. It's got all kinds of stuff … furniture, coffins, gurneys, TVs, coffee machines … what do you want me to do with that?"

And the billionaire said – and so much of the world we live in is explained in this remark – "I don't care! Just get rid of it and get to work!"

This put the contractor in a bind, because he couldn't get to work without clearing out all the stuff, and there was a lot of stuff – moving it was going to take time. So he needed to find a subcontractor who could get rid of everything fast.

Fortunately he knew a guy named Lightning who knew a guy named Chicken.

The contractor asked Chicken: "can you get everything moved NOW?" And Chicken said "Sure, I can get a couple trucks and some guys and we can clear this whole thing out."

Then Chicken asked: "Where do you want it to go?"

And the contractor said – and so much of the world we live in is explained in this remark – "I don't care! It's not my problem! Just get rid of it!"

"Okay," Chicken said. And so … and this is the part of the story where I was personally present and saw everything … that's how Chicken ended up with a warehouse full of stuff from a large funeral parlor. He took everything, and moved it right into his space.

Then, because this is what he did, Chicken decided to turn it into a show.

"The Funeral Show" was the San Francisco Institute of Possibility's attempt to reclaim the funeral from its dismal reputation. Because you know what? "Funeral" is actually a great format! You get everybody together in one place, everybody's all dressed up, you have a ritual where you think big thoughts about life and death, you tell a lot of stories about someone you know, maybe you have a choir or some music, maybe you have a big spread and you mingle and you talk … it's a great time! The problem is that we only throw these things when somebody dies, and everybody's all sad! That's no good!

So we threw a funeral without a body, in a warehouse decked out with the authentic gear of a working funeral home.

I sang some songs about death, Dr. Hal read an epic poem, we had some performance art, there was some stand-up comedy, an actual mortician came in and gave a lecture on how he prepared a body for burial, using red marker on a naked model to show all the places he'd make incisions … it was all weird and deep and creepy and wonderful.

Then came the best part. At the end, Chicken got up in front of everybody and told them that we'd all had our fun, but we still had a warehouse full of funeral home stuff, and it all had to go. So please, take whatever you want with you! The furniture? It's all from the funeral home – take it! The paintings on the walls? From the funeral home, so take it! All the creepy gurneys and medical instruments and urns and memento moris that you walked by ... they've gotta go! The coffins? We don't need them – well, except for this one here, which Chicken had decided to be buried in, so he's keeping that – so walk out with them!

The result was a mad scramble, and then a parade ... an absolute parade ... of people walking down Mission Street in San Francisco carrying all the instruments of death and grieving, holding them above their heads or lifting them together, laughing about what a great time they'd just had. Wheeling gurneys onto the subway, and comparing urns. Nobody had ever seen anything like it.

The kicker came a few days later. Andie Grace had gotten one of the paintings – the big, ugly, awful, oil paintings that we'd said could only possibly exist to be put on the walls of funeral homes and dentists' offices – and she put a picture of it up on Facebook, saying that she thought it would be improved if she added some aliens to it. Little flying saucers.

And someone wrote back not to do that, because it would ruin the value of the painting.

"Oh, come on," Andie said. "This terrible art isn't worth anything."

Her friend sent back a link. Apparently those paintings had all been part of a set of some minor repute, and as a set had all been worth about $35,000. And we'd let it just walk out the door as part of a spontaneous mad funeral parade.

We couldn't stop laughing. For weeks. It was the perfect, absolutely perfect, conclusion to that event.

* * *

In previous chapters we looked at what happens during these experiences in ways that told you *what was happening* without ever actually specifying *how to do it*. It's all very well and good to see that, "yes, okay, I guess I need to create conditions that engage someone's unconscious archetypes, so that when they project an unacknowledged part of their psyche onto me, I respond to it in a way that speaks to their personal mythology so that their complexes are interrupted and made visible, and their daimonic force helps them push through to create personal change. Right. That." But it's a little vague on the specifics.

That's because the only way to get from here to there is not the shortest distance between those points. On the contrary: when you're dealing with the unconscious, it's usually the scenic route. As I implied in the last chapter, this is one of those things that is happening, that you are causing to happen, but that you cannot *just do.* The whole point of psychomagic is that you need to convince the psyche to come out and play with you, rather than pushing button A to get response B. Some people, people who are really good at this, sometimes look like they are doing that – just spontaneously creating psychomagical experiences. I have a reputation in this scene for being able to do that kind of thing, and I guarantee you, that's not what's happening. After a great deal of practice and attention, some people are able to set conditions very quickly and to lead people into relatively short order experiences without them noticing until they're already in it. Some of us have psychomagical tools on hand, imagos that we are very practiced with, just in case the need arises. We know how to deploy them in ways that look spontaneous, when in fact we are biding our time, carefully waiting for the right opportunity. After a friend gave me a nylon unicorn horn at a party, I kept the damn thing in my pocket for a month until I was in a conversation where somebody actually used the word "unicorn," and then, the moment they looked away, I slipped it out of my pocket and onto my head while keeping the conversation going, so that when they looked back the change was sudden and abrupt – though I was acting as if nothing had happened. They freaked out; it was a fantastic moment (if psychologically trivial). But the point is that I couldn't just go around doing this to people whenever I wanted – for it to really create an effect, I had to wait a month for the right moments to present themselves. I had created the conditions under which, if the right thing happened, I could create a seemingly spontaneous moment of magical effect. But it was spontaneous on their part, not mine: it took me a month of waiting. I got two more people this way in the next few weeks before I stopped carrying the thing around. It wasn't worth it anymore.

And it's those words I just used, "I had created the condition under which" this could happen, that is the most important thing to realize here. Because that's what you're doing: you're not "doing psychomagic" to someone, you are *creating the conditions* under which psychomagic can happen. And those are two very different models.

In the second book I wrote with Chicken John, *The Book of the UN: Dissertations in Dystopia,* he presented an excellent metaphor for how to think of this. You're not creating something mechanistic, you're creating something organic.

A mechanism can be designed by a blueprint. A mechanism has clear inputs and outputs, it's supposed to work the same way every time, and if it doesn't, something's broken and can be repaired. An organism, on the other hand, at least once it reaches any level of complexity, can't be designed to that level of specification. It behaves and evolves in unpredictable ways. At its simplest levels it has clear inputs and outputs, but the more complex the organism becomes, and the more it cares about the outcomes, the less clear those factors are. An organism won't respond to the same stimuli the same way every time – context and motivation matter enormously –

and many organisms actually resist the attempt to get them to behave systematically. This doesn't mean they're broken, it's what they are.

This doesn't mean there aren't clear best practices and techniques you can use, but you're not building a robot, you're creating a garden. You're not trying to get predictable results, you're trying to create an environment in which beautiful and surprising things will happen. If you try to design these experiences mechanistically, either you'll end up creating very shallow experiences that may look pretty but have no real impact, or you'll end up crushing the very experiences you're trying to get people to have. On the other hand, if you design a garden that, for all its beauty, has a wild streak in it, elves and fairy creatures might come take up residence.

Indeed, one of the most important dynamics in psychomagical experience design is understanding when to use control and when to let it go. When do you curate the experience, saying "this is what's happening," and when do you let people make their own decisions and then follow through, however unexpected the direction they choose to take it.

That's something you mostly learn by practice, though I'll give you what advice I can. The important thing to understand is that you are creating a garden, not a machine. You are creating the conditions under which these psychomagical things can happen, and coaxing them in certain directions – not directing them or giving orders. You are a designer, but you are not in charge. You are creating conditions where things can occur, not mandating how they turn out.

I asked Robin to describe the night she'd "summoned" me by "magic" in the park, from her perspective. "We hoped to run into you at the park all night but we couldn't find you," she said.

"We couldn't go searching for you and insisting or we would have created a different kind of thing altogether than we'd intended. This kind of art falls apart fast when you force it. Sucks the life right out of it. When you insist, the spirit leaves the garden and the whole thing turns into a school play very quickly. So instead, we decided to give up, spending the rest of our time just having a blast with whoever was around. I made a joke that we'd create a laser beam of fun that would summon you. Henry started playing Hallelujah on a piano under a tree for us, and at the same time, across the garden inside your head, somehow, the ritual began."

Another useful distinction for experiences comes from James Carse's 1986 book *Finite and Infinite Games*, which is well known around the San Francisco scene.

Here's Carse's summary of the distinction:

"There are at least two kinds of games: finite and infinite.

Finite games are those instrumental activities - from sports to politics to wars - in which the participants obey rules, recognize boundaries and announce winners and losers. The infinite game - there is only one - includes any authentic interaction, from touching to culture, that changes rules, plays with boundaries and exists solely for the purpose of continuing the game. A finite player seeks power; the infinite one displays self-sufficient strength. Finite games are theatrical, necessitating an audience; infinite ones are dramatic, involving participants.

Now, a mechanistic system is always a finite game. A garden isn't always the same as the infinite game – as we'll see, in the majority of cases gardens are (as the metaphor implies) bound by time and space. Their impacts last, but they themselves don't continue on.

However, there are many characteristics of an infinite game which a garden aspires to, and that are key components of psychomagical experiences. The emphasis on participants rather than audiences, authentic interactions, playing with boundaries, changing rules, no way to "win," only to continue playing ... these are all characteristics that, done well, make experiences numinous, and primed for psychomagical engagement. An experience you design probably cannot be infinite, but you want it to have as many of the characteristics of an infinite game as you can. An infinite psychomagical garden is the holy grail of experience design, the ur-experience to which we all aspire.

So remember that: garden, not machine. Infinite game, not finite. Your guiding question should be how do I make this more interesting?" If things get interesting enough, that question will turn into "How do I most effectively clear the path for where these things are taking me." The question "How do I get people to do or feel what I want" is a very distant third.

This dynamic will be present in whatever kind of experience you try to create. The rest of the elements that we'll discuss won't always be there. The ideal psychomagical experience, the infinite garden, will have all of them, but in real life you have to work with the limitations you have, and so they come and go in varying degrees with varying events – hopefully being made up for by the intense presence of the others. You want as much as you can get of as many factors as you can get, and if something's really not working it's probably because you're in flagrant violation of one of these elements. Real life always has constraints. Working with the constraints to make them enhance the experience, rather than take away from it, is where things get especially engaging.

Which brings us to our first key point for designing conditions.

Chapter 11:
Create Non-Fiction

Danielle Baskin is a latecomer to the San Francisco scene, but since arriving she's become a legendary art prankster. Her work mostly occurs online, but spills into the real world with remarkable frequency. Here are some recent examples:

- She created the world's first "decruiting" service, reaching out to people who want to quit their jobs. The website offers one free consultation for people who want to quit and would like to talk to a decruiter to see if they qualify, in a therapeutic way.
- She created "LineCon," a conference that takes place while waiting in lines. There are talks and activities in the line and nobody needs to to purchase anything at the end.
- She created a Tinder profile for a drone.
- She has a website that recruits people to go to Oracle's annual tech conference dressed up as actual oracles, and pretend it's their conference, and look for sessions on their divination issues, and offer to perform divination for techies in attendance.

All this is cute and funny, right? Sure, but that's just the beginning. Because ... and this is where it gets remarkable ... these aren't just jokes. All of these things really exist. Line-Con really happens, and (prior to the pandemic) has been getting bigger every year.

If you contact The Decruiter website, you can actually get a free consultation and speak to someone – and if you want a second appointment to talk more about leaving your job, you need to pay for the service. And people actually do.

If you match with the drone on Tinder, and chat with it, and aren't too obnoxious, and then try to set up a date? A drone will actually meet you at a bar or restaurant, hover over its chair, and talk with you (Danielle is hidden nearby with a Bluetooth speaker) for as long as the batteries last.

If you sign up to go to Oracle's annual conference as an Oracle? Then you can actually meet with other people, who will spend the day dressed as oracles and infiltrating the conference, and offer to give readings to real conference attendees.

It's real. It all really happens. People actually do this.

And that's what makes it interesting, don't you think? It's all funny in concept, but it's just funny. But when you realize people are actually doing this – that people are paying a decruiter when looking for advice on how to quit their jobs, showing up at a bar to have a first date with a drone? That's interesting. You have so many questions, there's so much to discover, so much to unpack. Now it's the kind of experience that keeps you awake at night, laughing but also wondering: "wait, what?"

Take a look at all the events I've told stories about in this book so far. Every single one has something in common: they were all real. They were non-fiction.

Of the two bars I told you about in the beginning, it was the alchemy bar that was the elaborate fiction: that wasn't really an alchemist's lab, they weren't really serving potions or strange concoctions. It was a bar wearing a LARP costume.

But the other bar? The magical bar? Oh, sure, I may have told a big story about how it was a church – but you know what? I actually believe that. And, more to the point, everything I said would happen actually did. There are no menus there. You order by telling the bartender something that's on your mind or in your heart, and they create a cocktail, never created before or since, as an answer. That's all real. It really happens.

The ritual I created to access Robin's inner asshole? Not playacting – we were doing that for real and she really stabbed me. The ritual she created to summon me in the garden? Not fake in any way. We really broke into the garden, she really couldn't find me, and they really did that to summon me. The Circus Redickuless? It seems like it's something out of a European horror movie, but it was completely real, and people really did run away and join it.

And so on. Across the board.

Sometimes an event will be gussied up a bit, it'll have on a nice costume and a fancy haircut, but the fundamental dynamic in it, the part we really care about, was always true. My surrealist syllabus had a lot of jokes in it ... and look, I didn't really care if students called me "Jedi Master" or not, that was a joke rule. But the important part was that I really wrote it down in a syllabus that I handed out to the class, and used as the class's official paperwork. It wasn't a parody syllabus that I handed out to my friends, or a joke syllabus that I gave to the students and then said "Just kidding! Here's what's really going on." I really did it. And that's the only reason it's actually worth talking about.

It was the bar claiming to be an alchemist's lab, and the tenured professor down the hall who claimed to be a radical pedagogue but whose idea of crossing lines was to arrange the desks in a circle, who were lying. And aren't worth mentioning again.

This is your first design principle. Effective psychomagical events are non-fiction. They can be given a little fantasy trapping, if you like, but the underlying dynamics are at their most powerful when they're real. Whenever you can, design a non-fictional event instead of a fictional one. If you take no other design principles away from this book, take this one: design experiences where people are really doing things, rather than pretending to do things.

Fiction is the enemy of psychomagic. Don't put people in a

position where they have to suspend disbelief: the more disbelief they have to suspend, the less impactful you'll be.

Really cool dance parties where everyone dresses up like their favorite movie characters, Halloween parties where people pretend to be monsters, murder mystery games where everyone pretends to be other people and then pretend to solve a crime ... there's nothing wrong with events like that. If you enjoy them, do them. But they're not numinous. They're psychomagically inert. They do not create the conditions in which the unconscious is stirred and synchronicity happens. They are not so absurdly funny that they are a gateway to awe. You certainly won't remember any of them the way you'll remember just hearing about someone matching with a drone on Tinder, inviting the drone out to a bar, and the drone actually showing up.

People will say: "but wait, what if the costumes we dress up in are REALLY GOOD? And the venue is amazing? And there's a multimedia light show with digital mapping on contoured surfaces, and indoor clouds? Doesn't that do the job?"

Well, you've got something, for sure – especially if you're creating really potent works of art. Art has an important role to play in experience design, and we'll talk about it later. But the rubric still applies: the more fictional your event is, the more it depends on suspension of disbelief or deliberately playing make-believe, the less potent it is likely to be.

Consider Disney World. Imagine the most impressive, impossible, ride that Disney World can create. They're throwing everything they've got at it. They've got actors, they've got sound designers, they've got architects with an unlimited budget. They're going to create a roller coaster that takes you to a beautiful palace filled with secret rooms and holograms telling stories and ... and ... I dunno ... use your imagination. Make it as amazing as you can get.

And this is my bet with you: no matter how amazing Disney World can make that experience, there is no experience Disney World can create that will be as thrilling as breaking into Disney World.

Not "breaking in" like they create a "Breaking into Disney World Experience" – I mean really breaking in. That's the experience you're going to have whose intensity will remain with you for the rest of your life, and will bond you to the people who did it with you.

If they know what they're doing, two guys with bolt cutters can have a more potent experience than all the Imagineers in the world can provide. And that's not a knock on Imagineers, or their skill and their talent, but it's the nature of the beast.

Why is that? Well, to the extent an explanation is needed – and I'm not sure it is, but hey – it's because, as Jodorowsky so keenly observed, the unconscious mind doesn't deal in abstractions. But it does understand action. It speaks the language of doing. Stories are powerful and potent things, but to engage in psychomagic one has to actually do something, preferably something symbolically potent, otherwise the unconscious rarely sits up and takes note. And – this should be axiomatic – the more fictional an experience is, the less you're actually doing. Real is simply more potent to the unconscious.

Make your experiences non-fiction. As real as they can possibly be. Don't ask people to "suspend disbelief" – create an experience where they have to rub their eyes and say "I can't believe this is really happening!" because it really is.

The less fiction is involved, the more the underlying dynamic is real, the more effective the experience is likely to be.

Having learned that the underlying dynamic should be real, what else can we say about such an experience? What other qualities should it have?

Chapter 12:
Engineer Disperfection

Consider this scenario:

It's Christmas season. A child is in a toy store (this was back when that was likely), looking around at all the fun (okay, "fun") items displayed. But his mom won't let him have any of them; they're not here to buy him a toy.

Then Santa walks up and saves the day. "Ho ho ho, little boy! Do you like this! Well, then, okay! It's yours! It's a gift! Merry Christmas!"

But here's the thing: Santa doesn't work for the store. In fact, the store manager has never seen this Santa before in his life.

So what does he do? Does he demand that the kid put the toy back, and disappoint him, ruining the magic of the season that he's just experienced, and creating a scene in front of his other customers? Or does he let the kid keep the toy, because dammit, that's a good thing to do, and take the loss?

There is no right answer to this question, and certainly no easy one. The manager, the mom, even the kid (to a lesser degree) all have to make big choices in that moment about who they are and what they value. They can't just go through this on cruise control. The normal ways the situation might play out have all been broken or blockaded.

Or consider this scenario:

A Saturday night at a pizza chain. People are waiting for tables, and putting their names on the waiting list. The waitress going through the list now has an opening for the group of five people waiting for a table. She's about to read the name on the list, when she sees that somebody's written something down as a joke. "Abraham Lincoln." Oh well.

"Abraham Lincoln?" she calls out. "Table for Abraham Lincoln?"

"That's me!" says a guy wearing a full Abraham Lincoln outfit, walking up to the front of the restaurant.

"That's me!" says another guy, also wearing a full Abraham Lincoln outfit, walking up to the front of the restaurant.

Before she can process what's happening, the two get into a heated argument about whose table this is, and demand that she settle it.

What does she do? How does she figure this out?

Whatever she does, she cannot follow procedure. There is no entry for this in the employee handbook. You cannot logic your way through it.

Here's another great example, which Michael Ryan Garcia created for a Burning Man Regional event in Arizona: he and his collaborators put together a library filled with donated books, and announced that anyone could take as many books as they wanted, to keep. But at the end of the event, all the remaining books would be burned in the structure.

People were outraged at the idea of burning books. They confronted Michael and the organizers. They got angry and in their faces about how: "you can't burn those books!"

"Well," they responded, "you can save them. You can save them all if you want."

Suddenly the conversation shifted. "I don't have room for more books ..."

"Well, neither do we." "But you can't burn them!" "You can save them ..."

What do people do? What's the right choice here?

Or consider this legendary scenario from Chicago, where they wanted to imitate a classic San Francisco Cacophony Society event, the Urban Iditarod, where people get a bunch of shopping carts, have some people ride them and some people push them, and race through the streets.

The police in San Francisco, though not exactly friendly,

are used to this kind of thing by now. Organizers were worried that the police in Chicago were not, and that the whole event – which was impossible to get a permit for – would immediately be shut down and participants arrested.

So what did they do?

On the day of the race, the police did indeed converge on a giant unlawful assembly of people with shopping carts in the street ... and discovered that the entirely illegal event was a drive for a food kitchen in collaboration with a local convent, whose nuns were present, and is presenting awards to local politicians for help with this charitable cause.

If the police break up the event, they shut down a food drive, piss off the nuns, and have to tell the politicians that they're arresting the food drive activists who are giving them an award. If they don't break up the event, they're letting people flagrantly break the law and play with shopping carts in traffic.

Shit comes down on them either way. There's no clear right answer. What do they do?

* * *

The best term for scenarios like these came from Chicken John: he called them "engineered disperfection." To engineer disperfection is to take what are normally routine, even rote, actions and turn them into absurd no-win scenarios. The scenario is so broken that there is no logical or optimal way out.

We normally think of no-win scenarios as bad, devoutly to be avoided. We want "win-win," not "fail-fail." So why would we go out of our way to create conditions like this?

Aside from the fact that, you know, it's hilarious. If you didn't laugh at at least one of those scenarios, you have no soul. Although if you laughed at all three, maybe you're a sociopath. Either way, you have some serious thinking to do.

But I digress.

The problem with "win-win" scenarios is that they're easy to go along with because everybody's winning. Which is great much of the time, but the more you try to "win" in life, the more you tend to habituate yourself to doing whatever seems optimal, rather than what is actually meaningful to you. "Winning," as conventionally defined, is at some level just going along to get along, which eventually becomes going through the motions, which eventually starts to numb you to the conditions of your existence.

The only time you're willing to take a real stand on your values is when you're willing to risk failure. The only time you can really discover who you authentically are is if you're willing to risk failure.

And when you can't win, or at least have no idea how to do it (as my students found out), you are suddenly thrown into an unavoidable choice about who you are and what you really value.

In my book on Burning Man philosophy, I called this "applied existentialism." Being unable to "win," you have to make a choice based on what you truly value – or retreat into yourself and deny your capacity to be authentic.

Engineered disperfection creates situations where applied existentialism has to occur. Not as a hypothetical "trolley problem," but as a genuine moment, that's actually happening (non-fiction) right now. When there is no obvious answer, you're faced with inevitable failure and you have to do something anyway, there is an opportunity to be truly authentic, to do not what is optimized – there is no optimization – but what is most consistent with who you want to be. In such moments, the daimonic is invited to help figure the answer out.

As a result, engineered disperfection is an incredibly potent tool in experience design, enlisting both the conscious and unconscious mind in one of the most fundamental questions of authenticity: what do I truly value here? What do I really want to do, when winning is off the table?

That said ...

Engineering disperfection is one of the most conceptually challenging kinds of experiences to design well, and it can often cross ethical lines. It's rough play, to be sure. It's worth noticing that no one in the examples I gave volunteered for this. The experiences they had were done to them, not with them, which is important – although it's also important to note that their autonomy wasn't being taken away. Just the opposite, in fact: they were being put in no-win situations, but the ultimate decisions about what to do was always in their hands. Once the scenario was set up, they were in charge.

And that, in and of itself, is one of the most important design principles of all. If engineering disperfection is a high level skill, near the top of the pyramid, it has very clear implications for what's at the bottom.

* * *

As it happens, the Chicago police tasked with shutting down the shopping cart race actually turned the situation around. After conferring amongst themselves, the ranking officer finally walked up to the organizers. "You're doing a good thing," he told them, in great frustration, "but you're doing it all wrong!"

The police then called in for more officers and cleared a corridor through traffic along the Urban Iditarod route, not only facilitating the event, but appropriating it – making sure the police were publicly credited as contributors to the food drive, and establishing a relationship with the organizers. The Urban "Chiditarod" is now an annual event, one of Chicago's largest food drives, and a hell of a lot of fun.

For all its difficulty, people often leave moments of engineered disperfection feeling better than when they came in.

Chapter 13:
Encourage Meaningful Choices

Artist Richie Rhombus once wanted to explore the nature of rules and structure. So he threw an event. And in this event were four corners, and you could go to whichever one you wanted, when you wanted.

In the first corner, participants could play a game that had both rules and structure – the structure determined how people took turns, and the rules told you what you could do on your turns.

In the second corner, participants could play a game that had rules, but no structure: the rules told you what you could do and how, but there were no turns, no order to who did what when.

In the third corner, participants could play a game that had structure but no rules. There was a turn system, but you could do whatever you wanted during it.

And then, in the fourth corner, there were neither structures nor rules. Participants had to make everything up themselves as they went.

I went straight for that corner, where a small group of us – the smallest of all the groups – stood looking at one another, wondering "okay, what do we do now?"

This was happening in an art/tech co-op, so naturally they had a costume closet, and we decided to raid it. We came back with a group of props, that included angel wings and devil horns.

Inspired, we decided that one person would wear the angel wings, one person would wear the devil horns, and a third person would name a personal problem they were actually having. Then the devil and the angel would each stand behind one of her shoulders and argue about what to do, and then the person would decide what to do based on that.

It worked beautifully, it was ludicrous and hilarious, and so we traded positions, swapped in the person who hadn't gotten to play, and did it again with a new scenario. It only got better – and it kept getting better until a couple of people, attracted by the obvious fun we were having, asked if they could play too.

Well, obviously – anybody could go to any corner at any time – but the problem was that we only had three roles in this game, and we already had too many people to all play at once. Too many people sitting and waiting wasn't a good idea, so what could we do?

Well ... we had other hats ... so we grabbed a zebra hat and turned the game into "Angel, Devil, Zebra," where now someone would name a real dilemma they had, and would hear from their angel, their devil, and their zebra. And now it was just sublimely silly. Bizarrely, wonderfully, nuts … and yet laced with profundity, as we really were talking about the important issues in people's lives: whether to leave the Bay Area, whether to break up with a significant other, whether to change jobs. It was important for people to know what their inner zebra had to say!

More people wanted to join, and we had more hats, so now we were playing "Angel, Devil, Zebra, Crab." And then "Angel, Devil, Zebra, Crab, Penguin." And then somebody wanted to do some extra fancy costuming, so we played "Angel, Devil, Zebra, Crab, Penguin, 1st Edition AD&D 5th Level Bard." It just kept getting weirder and more wonderful, and we kept growing until we were the largest of all the groups, because we were the ones having the most fun.

That's a very basic illustration of a very important principle. Here's a much more devious, more complicated, example:

You may have seen an advertisement for personal force fields. You may have responded to a flyer looking for test subjects. You may have stumbled across its Yelp page, and been intrigued. You may have heard a strange pirate radio station warning you about a cult. For three years, there were an endless number of ways you could connect to the Jejune Institute. But you had to make the decision to follow them, to notice that there was something strange going on, and track it down. Most of those trails, at least at first, would lead you to a set of offices for the Institute in downtown San Francisco, where you'd register, fill out some paperwork, and then be taken to a small room where you'd watch an increasingly bizarre instructional video.

That video would suddenly be interrupted, hijacked, by "the resistance," which warned you of the Jejune Institute's sinister intentions, and gave you instructions on how to escape the building undetected.

What would you do?

Remember – this wasn't a game you signed up for. Nobody recruited you. To get in this room, you'd stumbled across real events and chosen to follow them to this building, to these offices, where you were put into this strange set of circumstances. What was going on? Who were you going to trust? Would you want to keep pursuing this, as far as it went? And just how far down did it go? The decision was yours, the way it had been the whole time.

We'll leave it there, and talk more about the Jejune Institute later.

* * *

I'm gonna be painfully honest here: from an absolute, disinterested, standpoint, "Angel, Devil, Zebra," or even "Angel, Devil, Zebra, Crab, Penguin, 1st Edition AD&D 5th Level Bard," was not so transcendently good as to be worth the amazing response we had to it – the utterly absurd, wondrous, hilarity of that moment. But we felt it. It was utterly absurd, wondrous, and hilarious, in a way that we all still remember, and occasionally talk about, today. Why? What elevated this incredibly stupid premise, poorly executed, to such extraordinary heights?

A big part of its success was that we created it. Put in a situation where failure was very much an option, and there was no "right" answer, we made choices, and everything that followed came because we had made those decisions, and continued to. We weren't following directions or solving a prefabricated puzzle with just a couple of right answers for us to "figure out" – we were making meaningful choices. And when they worked, it had a far greater impact than it would have if we had gone through the activity at someone else's behest. If Richie had thrown an event in which he took the exact same people into the exact same corner and said, "okay, I have these hats, and we're going to play this game, and when you're wearing the zebra hat ..." we still would have enjoyed it. It would have been funny and entertaining for a little while. But it wouldn't have been transcendently funny. It wouldn't have come close.

The fact that we had made the choices, and events had proceeded on the basis of those decisions, was a crucial factor.

The same factor was at play in the Jejune Institute. There

was so much that was so extraordinary about that experience – three years' worth of surreal mystery playing out across the San Francisco Bay – but one of the most powerful things about it was that it was so self-directed. Everything about your experience in it ... even how you got in it ... was the result of decisions you made in real life. Not "do I want to purchase a ticket to this show?" but, "wait, something strange is going on here. What am I going to do?"

Experiences in which people make meaningful choices, and the experience proceeds from those choices, are always – always – experienced differently, and more powerfully, than experiences in which someone is following a script.

"Choose Your Own Adventure" books weren't so much fun because they were well written. They were so much fun because you *got to make choices*. What makes a game of "Truth or Dare" interesting isn't that all the decisions people make are so good, but that *anything can happen.*

If you want someone's whole psyche engaged in a process, let them make choices that matter. Let them lead. This is our next design principle: create experiences in which people can make meaningful choices.

This is probably the most widely known principle in the field of experience design and also the most misunderstood. And not just misunderstood, but willfully misunderstood: people misunderstand not because it's difficult to grasp, but because it is incredibly inconvenient to actually do.

To understand why, let's go back to our metaphor of creating a garden instead of a mechanism. Why do we even have to have that conversation? Why would someone want to make a mechanistic experience in the first place?

It's because mechanisms are comparatively easy. They're relatively simple to plan. They have fewer variables. You get your venue, decide on your story, and a path by which people will go from point A to point Z (whatever that represents), and can time it out so that everybody knows when it begins and ends. Perhaps most importantly, since it's clear what everybody will be doing, you have to do very little contingency planning for what people *might* do.

Mechanisms are efficient. That makes them convenient.

Gardens, organisms … you never know what the hell they're going to do. You can make educated guesses, you can create incentives and inducements, but you can never predict. And you will often be surprised.

Anyone who has ever tried to produce a live event will tell you: surprises are nothing but stress.

And yet, much of the capacity of a designed experience to reach someone depends upon their ability to make meaningful choices, and for those choices to matter. It's absolutely crucial. People invest in experiences in which they can make meaningful choices. Their whole psyche gets involved. Their unconscious pays attention, their daimonic nature seizes the opportunity. Let's go back to the experiences I've been telling you about, and see how many hinged on the significant choices people in them made:

- It seems weak to say that in the Magical Bar, people could choose their own drinks. At some level that's what happens in every bar. But ordering off of a drink menu isn't the same kind of choice as expressing whatever speaks to your soul. The center of that experience, the key element, was that they could express the wish of their heart and have it specifically responded to. It's the drink equivalent of "make a wish!" and it simply wouldn't have been affecting if their choice wasn't at the heart of it.
- When Robin Ziiro conducted the magical ritual to summon me, the magic experience came from the fact that ultimately (unless there was "real" magic here) I had to choose to engage. Everything hinged on that choice. It would have failed if I'd done literally anything else.
- People chose whether to run away with the Circus Redickuless (pretty much the definition of a life changing choice), and then developed their own acts.
- People chose how to engage with the Burning Man style temples: whether to help build it, whether to visit it, whether to leave something, and what to leave. It was all self-directed.
- Chicken's $20 bill trick entirely depends on the choices

both participants make. They choose to dig themselves deeper, nothing is imposed on them.

- The end of the Funeral Show was completely undirected: people grabbed whatever they wanted, and did whatever they wanted. We never said "grab items labeled for you and we're going to make a parade to the BART station!" We created the conditions, let people do whatever they wanted, and something amazing happened.

- Danielle Baskin's internet pranks entirely depend upon the willingness of the other person to engage. Are you actually going to call a decruiter? What are you going to say when you do? Are you seriously going to swipe right on the drone? Do you invite it out for a drink? What do you do when it shows up? It's all free choice.

- Engineered Disperfection also hinges on the ability of the people involved to make choices. What do you do when two Abraham Lincolns show up at a restaurant to fill one reservation, and both say it's theirs? Without that free choice, it's not an interesting question. At best, you're watching a comedy sketch on TV.

If you do nothing more than give someone an interesting choice to make, and then follow where it leads, there's a decent chance someone will have a meaningful experience as a result.

But looking at that list, you can also see how much harder it is because the experiences depend on someone's open-ended choice. The Circus Redickuless needed to be prepared for zero people to run away and join the circus at any given stop, and it needed to be prepared for 10 people to run away and join the circus at any given stop. David Best has to be prepared to work on building a temple with literally whoever shows up. the Jejune Institute had no idea who was going to walk through those doors, or what they were going to think, or how they were going to react – and there was no way to tell them "oh, wait, no, that's not what we meant."

It's much, much, harder to have this kind of impact if people can't make meaningful choices. It's also much, much, harder to create experiences in which people can.

A mechanistic event is easy to make for small groups of people – you can just play a game of Simon Says, or Hopscotch. And mechanistic events can scale very easily. An organic event is actually pretty difficult to create for a small group of people, and it could fail, and it's excruciatingly difficult to scale. Building a large-scale garden of this kind is stunningly difficult, even for people who are experienced hands.

Event producers often try to square this circle by creating the illusion of choice, letting people make decisions that are obviously trivial and have no actual power to change anything, or letting them select from a very limited number of pre-set options. Letting them have a line of dialogue with characters, but leaving them powerless to change that character's outcome, for example; or asking you to take a letter from one character to another, without any accounting for a decision to not, or to read the letter, or to replace it in the envelope with another letter. I've gone through "immersive theater" performances in which we were basically running errands, from one character to another – and while we were told at every station just how important the work we were doing was, it was obviously busy work: we made no decisions, and so affected nothing. And if they're trying to create a conventional art experience, this is a defensible decision (though it's usually not a good sign): you can still get where you want to go. But if you're attempting to make a psychomagical experience, a numinous one, then this is a deadly decision that will backfire every time.

People who don't see their choices having an impact withdraw from the process. Once they do that, it is exponentially more difficult to reach their unconscious. Their daimonic selves will not see any growth potential in a scenario in which they do not really matter. At this point people are just putting one foot in front of the other until the experience is over and they can go home.

An experience in which you can't make meaningful choices is like a museum that says "okay, you can look at our paintings and statues, but only if you feel what we tell you to feel." It not only doesn't work, it defeats the point.

Fooling people into thinking that their choices are relevant when in fact they are not is a common approach for trying to reconcile the need for people to be making meaningful choices with the fact that it is hard to design experiences around people's ability to make meaningful choices. Maybe you let people pick which character they want to guide them, and each one takes them on a different path, but they all end up in the same place. Maybe the actor is good enough to convince the participants that they're the ones making a decision that has already been made for them. Maybe (this is the best of these options) you create conditions in which there's really only one choice that makes sense for everyone except the most absurdly stubborn participants, but they come to that conclusion themselves, and so believe their autonomy is intact. For The Fallen Cosmos event in 2015, when we needed 300 people to all move from one section of the space to another in short order, despite the fact that they were having a great time where they were and didn't want to do it, we squared this circle by having a musical sound cue. When they heard the cue, all the characters stretched, yawned, and fell asleep. Right where they were. As a result no one was forcing the participants to go into the new area, but they quickly decided that, okay, there's no more fun to be had here because that magical music is playing, so I might as well go to the next place where something interesting is taking place.

It was a cheat that we managed to pull off, which is the best thing you can say about this approach: it works if you can get away with it, but it has a diminishing effect each time. I mean, look at how the language we used changed: suddenly we're talking about "actors" and "characters" ... even if you can get away with it, you're moving in the wrong direction. The more you create the illusion of choice, even successfully, the more you're moving away from an authentic experience. In fact, you're pretty explicitly lying to the participants at that point. You are creating more of a finite game and less of an infinite one.

Again, you'll always have to work with the constraints you're under, but giving participants meaningful choices is at the heart of psychomagical experience design. You can only get so far without it.

The principles of psychomagical experience design we have been looking at so far – making it real, giving people meaningful choices, engineering disperfection – all imply another principle that you may have figured out by now, but that it's time to address specifically.

Chapter 14:
Gardens Aren't Safe

In 2007, Chicken John ran for Mayor of San Francisco. He was hardly alone. A total of 12 candidates, mostly fringe, were running against incumbent Mayor Gavin Newsom. Evidence suggests that the Newsom campaign encouraged so many fringe candidates to enter the race in order to diminish the stature of all the challengers.

Chicken was running for his own reasons, and what they were isn't important for this story. What is important is that, with so many candidates, there was only one debate that Newsom would participate in on stage with everybody. Just one.

It was held at the San Francisco Public Library's main branch, and it had the stupidest format a debate like that can take: the moderators would ask a question to the entire field, and all 12 candidates would have 30 seconds to answer it, with no follow-up or discussion. Then on to the next question.

Useless. No one was expecting anything interesting to happen. But it did.

Every time the question got to Chicken, his answer involved zombies.

A question about education? Well, the problem we

have with education is too many zombies in our schools. A question about public safety? Sure – the reason public safety is a concern is all those zombies running around. A question about pollution? Well, yeah, of course pollution is bad when you've got all these dead zombies in the city.

And the first time he did it, people laughed because it was so stupid. And the second time he did it they laughed a little less. And the third time they thought "oh, God, really? Is THIS what he's going to do?" And it started to get embarrassing and uncomfortable, but he never let up. Zombies, he said over and over again, are the city's number one problem.

Eventually the debate ended and it had all been pointless and everyone slowly walked out of the auditorium and to the exit ...

... where they found a mob of 200 zombies attacking the library.

The street was swarming with them. And as they attacked people on the street, the people became zombies too, and shuffled towards the building. All the candidates, and all their supporters, had to make a snap decision: would they run? Would they fight? Would they try to lecture the zombies about civic participation?

The library soon locked down, lowering its metal screens to keep the horde out, and most of the candidates cowered inside, huddling for safety. And there was Chicken, saying "I TOLD you! I TOLD you zombies are a problem! You wouldn't listen, but I TRIED TO TELL YOU!" Demanding that they now acknowledge the scope of the issue.

* * *

Have you ever looked at a ticket to Burning Man? Seen the fine print? Among the first things it says is that if you do this, you may die.

And people do. Not often, not every year, but it happens. And a lot of people get hurt.

And yet, among the returning Burners and the aficionados of the culture, you won't hear a single voice saying "we really need to focus on safety." On the contrary: the people who keep coming back to Burning Man are concerned that it's getting too safe. They ask themselves, "how can we make it more dangerous?"

That's not cussedness or a lack of compassion, it's a significant point based on a crucial understanding of what makes that culture interesting in the first place. There's a reason the regular attendees at the most significant "transformational experience" on the planet are worried that it's not dangerous enough.

Thus far in this book I've been careful not to use too many

examples from Burning Man, because while there is obviously a relationship between Burning Man and the San Francisco experience design scene – not to mention a lot of back and forth – they are also both distinct cultures which are better understood on their own terms.

Still, it's worth noting certain crucial elements that they have in common, when they're working well.

Burning Man creates magnificent infinite gardens. Participants literally co-create a city together, based on their idiosyncratic passions, and then get to explore it. You never know what's going to happen when you cross the street.

Burning Man is filled with meaningful choices. It is the strongest generator of applied existentialism anywhere. Almost everything you do is a meaningful choice, much in the same way that if you were stranded on a desert island, even the smallest choices you make would have big important consequences.

And Burning Man, as the tickets clearly indicate, is not benign. There is danger baked into it. Not just physical danger – though that's present too – but psychological danger. The choices you make will have significant consequences, good or bad.

Which is our next design principle for psychomagic: you can't make this too safe.

There's a reason why an increased sense of vulnerability is a sign that things are going well: such vulnerability also leads to an increased sense of *capacity*. To learn to love more than you already know you can, to show reserves of empathy you did not know you had, feels vulnerable – feels dangerous. Likewise awe is not an all-positive warm and cuddly feeling, but a lived moment of life's paradoxes – some danger and vulnerability goes with that territory.

This was once an accepted point, almost dogmatically so, in the San Francisco artistic underground. As the experience design community grew and connected more with movements like immersive theater and interactive theater, it has become a much more controversial point. A common argument against keeping experiences dangerous is that roller coasters are both incredibly thrilling and incredibly safe, and they're still thrilling even though everybody knows they're safe, and that experience design should strive for that combination too.

Which is absolutely true. But no one's life was ever changed by riding a roller coaster. They are fun and forgettable. Roller coasters are literally a metaphor for a period of time that will pass and you'll move on from. If that's what you want to design, great, roller coasters are fun, but it's the opposite of what San Francisco's artistic underground achieved.

But, hang on, why shouldn't this be safe? What's wrong with safe?

The problem is that when people are making meaningful choices in real environments, there's only so much you can do to protect them. "Safe" is an optimizable, go-along-to-get-along experience – an authority figure is telling you "don't do that, it's not good for you." Which is a really, really, good idea in many circumstances, but never leads to personal growth. Safety, in its paternal aspects, has nothing to do with authenticity. The more you prioritize safety, the more your garden looks like a kiddie-pool, and the less you are open to wherever the participants are going to lead you.

Molly Vikart, a member of the San Francisco underground art scene since the 90s and, until recently, Burning Man's office manager, fondly remembered the shows of Survival Research Labs (SRL), who created outlandish machine interactions so over-the-top that the San Francisco Fire Department unofficially declared war on them. SRL's tag line has literally been "Producing the most dangerous shows on earth." They're not kidding.

"One of the things I loved about going to Survival Research Lab shows was that they were so confrontational," she told me. "You're not going there just to be entertained. You're not going there to watch. And if you're going there to watch, you're putting yourself in danger in many ways. Either from the physicality of the show itself or from the perception that you're there to be entertained, so what the hell are these people doing? This is not entertaining: this is scary and smelly and loud and crazy, and why the hell would anybody want to do this?"

A few SRL shows still stand out in her memory. In one, the group quite literally took rotting sheep's heads, put them in an industrial shredder, and wheeled the shredder around the space, covering unprepared members of the audience with the remains.

Why? Why? Why? To be sure, that was a horrible thing to experience. But ... well, imagine what that experience was like. It was horrible, but also something more.

"I'm laughing and trying to hide behind a couch because I can see the chipper coming and I'm like 'there's no way I'm going to get hit with the offal!'" Molly remembered. "And this just made my life so much more complete. Because I felt like there was a challenge to the experience that is not entertainment, you know? That we don't just get that much of anymore. The notion that they were really, truly, doing this, and incorporating the audience into it with no expectation that they were going to be lauded for it ... it made me really happy. It was experiential and visceral, and I think people are afraid to push that envelope the way they used to and just put themselves out there with their vision and just let it happen in ways that might not be pleasing to people. People don't always need to be pleased. They need to be scared. They need to feel a little anxiety in their lives that's not related to what's in their heads. Having that kind of experience, I think is really valuable. It may sound ridiculous, but I like confrontation like that. And SRL did that."

A classic SRL show she went to was a funeral for a member of the group. They went to the underside of the 2nd Street freeway, and wrapped ruined pianos around one of the pillars holding the section of freeway up over the street. Then they lit the pianos on fire. Flames roared up on either side of the freeway: unsuspecting cars were passing between them. And then, at the crescendo, the flames exploded a packet of the ashes of their dead friend, and they drifted over the crowd as the cars on the freeway drove through a fiery Viking funeral.

Whoa. Right? I mean ... whoa.

That thing with the rotting sheep carcases? Okay, that's really pushing it just for the sake of saying 'fuck you' to a crowd – although it's worth noting that G.G. Allin and the Murder Junkies did things just as bad in the punk scene. (Which is kind of the point.) But that thing with the pianos and the flames on the freeway? What an incredible, amazing, moment.

And totally unsafe. Absolutely not safe. But the point is that you simply cannot get experiences like that while staying within safety lines.

Which doesn't mean you shouldn't make your experience as safe as you can. Of course you should. The relevant question is: how safe *can* you make it, before you cut people off from the experience you're aiming for?

That question, of course, depends on what you're trying to do. Survival Research Labs has overwhelming safety concerns. Their challenge – when they do this right – is to do incredibly dangerous things without actually hurting anybody. But they don't do it by making the things they do safer, they do it by getting better at managing danger.

Tony "Coyote" Perez, the longtime foreman of Burning Man's Department of Public Works and, hilariously, also its OSHA officer, once explained how much this distinction mattered.

"We did incredibly dangerous, stupidly dangerous, things all the time back in the early days," he said, "and almost nobody got hurt, because these were men and women who *understood danger*. They knew the tools, they'd worked with the chemicals, they were experienced at taking risks that aren't safe for people to take, and knew how to manage them. It worked great. But as we got bigger and more popular, all these people started coming in who didn't understand danger, and had no idea what they were getting into, and they saw people taking all of these big risks and just assumed they could do it too. And that's a serious problem. That's when people get hurt."

There is a way, in other words, to keep people from getting hurt without becoming safe. You get better with danger.

And SRL and Burning Man are very good at it, which is why they're not going to stop doing incredibly dangerous things: the whole point of what they do is to push that envelope. And because they're pushing that envelope, people who experience their events see something amazing and destructive and never before possible, and think "I had no idea it was possible to DO that ..." which opens up the question, "what else is possible?"

Most events have nowhere near the physical safety concerns of SRL. Not even close. To my knowledge, I have only been directly involved in organizing one event where someone actually got hurt. He was sent to the hospital, and was fine.

But physical danger isn't the only kind of danger, and physical safety isn't the only kind of safety. In fact, you've probably noticed by now that the amount of time we've spent talking about physical environments is miniscule compared to the amount of time we've spent talking about psychological environments. About what causes the unconscious to move and act in the moment. Those psychological risks are far, far, more prevalent and often more significant than physical risks, and it is no less important to understand psychological danger, and to get good with it, if you're going to be creating these kinds of experiences.

The most amazing event Molly said she ever saw was not an SRL show, or even all that literally dangerous – no one was going to get hurt. And yet, it was so breathtakingly vulnerable, breathtakingly real, that both physical pain and grave psychological risk were laced through it.

"There was a place called the Sandbox, which was sort of an S&M club ... it wasn't so much a dungeon as a space, and the floor was full of sand, and it was full of all kinds of frameworks and stuff like that," she said. "And my friends put on a show there that combined body manipulation with violin playing. They essentially had a couple of people with flesh hooks in their backs, who were leaning out from frameworks, not so much suspended as they were leaning, held on by metal strings that were hooked into their backs, and a couple of people who were bowing them. They were playing the strings hooked into the people's backs: they were *playing the people.* And the strings were hooked up to mics. And the sound was just incredible. And the feeling in the room was just outrageous. Because that's ... you can't get much more real at that point. That was psychedelic: everybody left there in this highly attuned frame of mind when that was over. And watching someone actually approach what you knew was this taut wire, suspended between someone's flesh and a framework, to create these sounds ... that was fucking incredible. One of the most amazing events I've ever partaken in."

And the truth is that no one was likely to get hurt in this event, even though – and this is also the truth – they were really playing with something dangerous here. And that's because they weren't being safe, but they were very good at danger.

"Getting better with danger" is also a good metaphor for what psychomagical events are trying to achieve: you're tapping into someone's unconscious, and stimulating their urge towards authenticity and growth, and there is no way to become more authentic and to engage in personal growth without taking risks. The more psychologically safe you make your experiences, the more psychologically inert you make the experience. What you want for them as people is also what you want for yourself as an experience designer: to get better at handling psychological danger. The more you can handle danger, the more you have access to the richness, diversity, and possibility of life. These are all things you want to build into your experiences. You never want to do something you know will hurt someone, but you absolutely do not want to create situations in which they can't possibly hurt themselves.

As a result, knowing how to work with people, how to handle something as it's going wrong, is a far better approach than working to ensure that nothing can go wrong. Design for it, and keep pushing yourself.

Chapter 15:
This Could Never Happen Twice

After a four year relationship, performance artists and Dada-fest co-organizers M.I. Blue and Katy Bell invited everyone they knew to watch them break-up live on stage. But strangers were welcome for a $5 cover.

This wasn't a joke. It wasn't a discussion about their breakup. This was the break-up itself. The moment when they had the hard conversation, explained to each other why they felt they had to do this, and exchanged keys.

They broke up to a packed house. Everyone who arrived at Spangaga that night had to wear a nametag on which they wrote their worst trait as a partner: "Emotionally Distant," "Still in Love With the Last One," "Clingy," "Can't Commit," "No Sense of Self-Worth."

On stage, Blue and Bell read emails they'd sent each other over the years, and then messages they'd written to one another just that day, explaining how they felt about this moment. Friends of each partner were called up on stage to defend them to the other, and provide context and insight. Tears were shed.

And then it was over. That was the moment.

They called it "Splitsville."

Even thinking about that show just moves me. Take a moment and imagine what it was like to be there.

Now here's another one.

During the years that I worked with Burning Man, I noticed that people leaving their jobs had a very hard time – either they were walking away from work and a community they were passionate about, and felt a sense of guilt and groundlessness ... or they were let go and felt a sense of loss and fear that they were going to lose their community as well as their work. In both cases, it felt like there was a tear in our social fabric that we had not found an adequate way to acknowledge.

So I designed a ritual to help people transition out of the organization.

The first time we tried it, the alpha test, the grand experiment, was during a cloudy, overcast day while California was on fire. The air was thick and unhealthy. We were in a public park, and it seemed like the world was ending.

We were there for a woman named Kentucky Sunshine.

The ritual had been working: it was moving and affecting and we were all feeling things, together, that were too big to say on our own. A formalized gift-giving process was part of the ritual, and so near the end we all went down the line of attendees, each giving Kentucky something that had personal meaning to us, and spoke to us of her. Eventually, we came to me.

"All right," I said. And I pulled out a thin, beaten down, scorched, uneven metal rectangle out of a bag. "Now, I think you'll like this, but I'm going to need to explain to you what it is ..."

"Oh," she said, without a moment's hesitation. "I know what that is."

"You ... you do?" I was shocked. That couldn't be right. This wasn't actually anything somebody could figure out, out of context.

"That," she said, "is a piece of the copper façade of the 2015 Temple of Promise that was burned with the Temple and recovered from the fire."

I gaped. "How ..."

"I was part of the Temple Crew that year," she said, "and in charge of the Temple's Leave No Trace team, and so me and a couple of other people were out there after it burned, and everyone was walking and dancing around the flaming wreckage, and we were holding them away, and waiting for the sizzling metal to cool down to a temperature where it could be safely removed. No one had ever made a temple with a façade like that before, so nobody really knew how to clean it up after. There was no procedure. We had a plan, but we were also kind of making it up as we went along. It was just me and my small team, all night, fishing those pieces of metal out of fire. I'd know that strip of metal anywhere. I might have been the one who took it out of the inferno."

I was still gaping. "How the hell did you GET that?" she asked.

I hadn't known any of that. It had just seemed like the thing to give her. It's a moment, years later, we still look back on, a surreal connection through which we got to know each other better.

* * *

If you missed Splitsville, you missed it. Obviously it can never happen again.

A moment like the one we had in the transition ritual with Kentucky is never going to happen again.

If Richie were to have tried his experiment in rules and structure a second time, with a different group of people, "Angel, Devil, Zebra" wouldn't happen again. Whatever they did, it would be something completely different. Maybe even if it were the same group of people.

If I were to be in the garden again and hear people singing Hallelujah, it wouldn't be anything like that moment when I was magically summoned. It would be an ironic "Oh, this again?" kind of moment, whatever I decided to do.

No two Burning Mans are ever the same. No two Lost Horizons Night Markets are ever the same. I sure as hell could never possibly repeat that baffling moment when I accidently described a woman's trip to Ecuador to her while falsely claiming to have known her for years.

The Circus Redickuless performed hundreds of shows around the country, but they never knew from show to show who would be getting on and who would be getting off the bus. The real experience, people leaving their lives behind to join the circus, was profoundly different each time.

Are you seeing our next design principle? Tell me you're seeing it.

The more effective a psychomagical experience is, the less repeatable it is. This isn't a flaw, it's a part of what makes it so special: the most powerful experiences are, in fact, once-in-a-lifetime, and if you're trying to make once-in-a-lifetime experiences, you don't plan for extensions and matinees. There is far, far, more potential in designing experiences that are so specific to a moment, a group of people, a threshold that cannot be crossed again, and that's what you want to design for. How can you make this impossible to ever do twice? The more you aim for that, the more something impossible is likely to happen.

And if the synchronicity effect kicks in? Then whatever happens will be one-time-only for sure. On the other hand, if there isn't enough flexibility, enough room, in your design for extraordinary synchronicity to happen, and for people to run with it? Then it won't happen at all, and your experiences will likely all end up resembling each other.

This doesn't mean you can't have a format, that you can't play theme and variations with form. While the most potent experiences really are complete one-offs ... Splitsville, man, that one just kills me ... the Night Market has a format. Burning Man has a format. The ritual I designed for Robin was a true one-off, but the ritual I designed for transitions at Burning Man wasn't specifically for Kentucky, she just ended up being the first person I could offer it to. I have, over the years, designed a number of small art projects with psychomagical properties that follow a clear format, and it repeats for everyone who goes into it.

But formats that are mechanistic drive all the numinous aspects of the experience away, while formats that strive to be an infinite game create a garden. Is your format a non-fiction experience, or a fiction? Does it allow people to make meaningful choices, and let that determine what happens next? Does it carry the potential for danger within it? Does it lead to engineered disperfection?

If the format is answering yes to these questions, then it will also likely produce unique, no-two-moments-alike, experiences. They'll probably still never quite reach the potency of experiences that are entirely unrepeatable, but they can be designed and created at an incredibly high level.

Let's look more closely at a couple of our examples. What you'll see will probably make the "garden" metaphor more apt.

Here are two examples of one approach:

- Burning Man, for all that it has a format, is the closest thing I've ever seen to a true manifestation of an infinite game. They create a space in the desert, and 80,000 people show up to build the city and fill it with their own art, passions, and nonsense. We'll look more closely at some of the elements that make this so effective, but for now the point is that while certain basics return every year – there is a Man that is burned on Saturday, a temple that is burned on Sunday, and so on – the reason each year is unrepeatable is because most of what you experience comes from the participants themselves, tens of thousands of whom are different each year and tens of thousands of whom are upping their game from what they did last year, and tens of thousands of whom are doing something completely different from year to year. The city is never remotely the same twice. You can go back to Black Rock City again, but it will be very different.

- The Lost Horizons Night Market has a clear format, but has a very similar mechanism for keeping each incarnation unique: not only is it literally in a different location each time, but the artists bringing box trucks are different, and what they do with them is different. You never know what you're going to get when you go, and if you miss something, it is gone – probably for good.

The format of these two events is about as open as you can get: it's basically a container for artists and experience designers. There are effective and ineffective ways to do this (more on that soon), but so long as you have new creators and collaborators moving in and out of it every time, each incarnation will be fundamentally different.

Here are two examples of another approach:

- For about five years I co-produced an event with writers Scott Lambridis and Eric Myers (who you may remember founded Burning Man's radio station and met Alejandro Jodorowsky) called "Action Fiction!" For each show, we got short stories from writers we liked, and gave them to actors we liked, and told them to create an original reading of this work. The writers never got to pick who performed their work, and the actors never got to choose what they performed. The actors could get technical help from the theater, but they couldn't rehearse together. Scott, Eric, and I didn't check in on what the performers were doing, only what their technical needs were. The result was a show where literally no one knew what it was going to be like until it finished. You might think, "oh, god, that would be a disaster!" and that's what we worried about too when we started it, but in fact – as long as we picked good writers and good actors – that unpredictability made it electric. The possibility of failure was very real, but most shows came together like lightning and thunder, the energy of pieces carefully rehearsed in secret coming together for the first time leading to an exceptional experience of literary magic.

- For a number of years, Chicken John had a Christmas event for members of the community with no families to spend the holiday with. It was a Christmas potluck feast with a game show. The price of admission was one present. It could be anything, anything at all, janky shit from around your house or something pricy. Get creative. Get weird. It just had to be wrapped. You'd come to his warehouse, show that you had the wrapped present, and then put it under the tree on the stage. The game show went like this: as we feasted, everyone at the party had to get up on stage and answer a trivia question, with Chicken and Dr. Hal as the MCs. If they answered it right, they got to pick a present from under the tree and open it on stage in front of everybody. But if they got the question wrong, they would have to get a present from under the tree and open it on stage in front of everybody. The result was a full Christmas day of camaraderie, hilarious trivia, and the shocking reveals of the weirdest gifts you've ever seen, over and over and over. Honest-to-God, I really miss those parties.

The formats in those two events are much tighter and more directed than Burning Man or a Night Market, but all have elements that make them unrepeatable in important ways.

Action Fiction! was in many ways a fairly conventional literary reading – what made it a lightning rod for numinous moments was the way in which all the pieces were simultaneously rehearsed and planned and collaborative AND thrown together at the last minute on a wing and a song, with no one knowing how it would come together or what was going to happen next. All the individual performances could be repeated, sure, but that energy from having it all come together in the moment of performance, the writers discovering what the actors had done to their work, the actors performing it for an audience for the first and only time, everyone seeing what everyone else had been working on all this time ... that could only happen once with each group.

Chicken's Christmas shows were in some ways just a conventional party with a gift exchange, but combining the sentimentality and loneliness of an orphan's Christmas party with a stupid game show with the absurd "what will happen next?" quality of unwrapping some of the world's most surreal gifts in front of a live audience, created a powerful mix of feelings waiting to erupt when a particularly absurd gift was opened. The specific combinations that resulted were just unique, in all implications of that word.

What we see happening here, as we said in the first chapter of this section, is a dynamic between keeping control and letting it go. Different kinds of experiences call for different levels of control, especially if you're repeating a format, but in every case, if this is going to work you simply have to let go of control over the outcome. Chicken had no idea how long his Christmas game show was going to run, or whether somebody would open up a garbage bag filled with ice and live lobster (yes, that happened). All the punches had to be rolled with, and he encouraged that unpredictability. We simply didn't know how long an Action Fiction! show was going to be or how the pieces would combine together, and the actors had been nervous for weeks before they got their pieces, wondering "what am I going to have to perform?" and the writers were always sitting on the edges of their seats, wondering "what are they going to do to my work?" There was so much creative control given up as part of that process, and it paid tremendous dividends. It opened it up for moments that never would have happened if people had felt we were looking over their shoulders trying to keep them in line.

The Night Market and Burning Man give up even more control. And epic experiences result.

So make unrepeatability a key element of your experience

design. If you can, make it a truly unique, never-to-be-repeated moment from its very concept on up. It's actually easier than you think; life is full of milestones. Someone only turns 40 once, two people can only meet for the first time once, you can only throw a party in a specific building the night before it's torn down once ... the more you think about it this way, the more opportunities you'll see as you look around. And if something can't be a truly unique, never-to-be-repeated moment from its very concept on up, if it's going to follow a format, figure out where you can release control in order to make each incarnation of your format impossible to do over.

Chapter 16:
You're Either in or Out, Except When You're Not

Burning Man, 2011

He's gone deep tonight – as deep as you can before the trash fence suddenly appears in your headlights. The absolute edge of the city.

He's come to be alone. He's come to get away from the thumping techno that still echoes even out here, he's come to get away from the green laser lights that still soar just overhead. If he turns around he'll be able to see all of Black Rock City displayed in the distance like a mirage of heaven and hell, but he doesn't turn around. He looks at the stars. Out here they fill the night sky.

It turns out he can't get away from the music and the lasers and the city: they follow him to the stars. The only thing he can get away from, out here, is people. It will have to do.

He aimed for a spot in the middle of the empty desert, almost dead on 12 o'clock, where there were no red or blinking lights in the distance ... no people visible, no one to be near. Just him and the stars ... or as close as he can get. His lights are all turned off. Darkness is danger, but also privacy.

He opens his mouth and starts to sing.

Usually he starts with soft and lilting Celtic songs ... He's been carrying a song of lost love on his shoulders all week ... but it's a sailor song that comes out. *Goodbye, farewell, I'm bound over the ocean.* His voice carries: it leaps, something in the air is lifting it up into the night. Verse after verse pours out of him, song after song, as though the desert air is drinking the music. He can feel a tickle in the back of his throat ... this dust is terrible on his voice ... and he should stop. But he doesn't. He sings another. And another. He sings the Mingulay Boat Song, an old favorite, a song of struggle towards homecoming ... and something opens up in his throat ...

... and the sound goes big. He's sung this song a hundred times, but never like this. Round, robust, loud and beautiful – the kind of song that could lead a ship over the edge of the earth.

And for a moment it's like he's following the song, sailing through a sea of night, and his voice will carry out to the stars and they will really hear him. One little man's voice, from all the way down here, will carry and be heard across this vast distance. He's never sung this well in his life. It seems ... possible.

What care we, though white the minch is?
What care we for wind and weather?
Heave her round boys, every inch is
Sailing nearer to Mingulay!

But of course it isn't. The earth will keep his song, just

like the playa is sucking the timbre out of his voice – he can feel his throat getting scratchier and scratchier and soon his upper register will disappear. He's giving it his all, and that will be all he's got.

It won't be enough. The truth is it's the stupid, stupid green lasers that will go out into space. It's the stupid, stupid, thumping techno … carried by radio waves … that will travel forever. The very things he came out here to get away from will get where he's trying to go, eventually reaching the stars that he sings to in vain. Even now, at the very best he's ever been, they'll never know he exists.

He sees blinking light at the corner of his eye as he comes to the last chorus. There must be a bicyclist or two here now. They're not moving, they must be standing still and watching him. He tries not to care. If he can just finish this chorus he'll have … he'll have … he doesn't really know what he'll have accomplished. But he'll have sung like it truly mattered. Even if the earth will swallow it whole.

He finishes the last syllables. *"Sailing homeward to Mingulay!"* There's no wind. Above him, the green lasers roam into the horizon. None of the bicyclists move. He doesn't turn. How many are there? None of them speak.

He's not ready to stop. His throat is raw but he's not ready to stop. His upper register is gone, but he's not ready to stop. He picks an easy melody, a ditty, an old religious lullaby – it's all he can offer anymore – and opens his mouth again.

He repeats: *"Allelujah ... Allelujah ... Allelujah ... unworthy I to tend to thee."*

That's all there is to the song. He sings it again. And again.

He sings it again, looking at the stars. *"Unworthy I to tend to thee."*

Eventually he has to stop. He turns back to his bike, grabs his water ... and blinks.

He is surrounded by lights. Red, white, green, blinking, headlights ... a sea of lights stretching out along the trash fence, and in the distance more coming this way. Like comets. Like stars.

Someone he can't see speaks, an old man. "I heard you all the way out from the Bijou," he says, "and I had to come."

* * *

Burning Man events have very clear delineations – strong borders. You're inside the co-created space, where it's important to Leave No Trace and no marketing or commerce is allowed, or you're outside, where a hippie is going to try to sell you a t-shirt with an anti-capitalist meme on it.

It's vitally important to the experience Burning Man creates that these borders be strong. Sometimes jarringly so: crossing from inside to out can be incredibly disconcerting. It is possible, it is absolutely possible, to create Burning Man experiences outside of a specifically designated "Burning Man space," but it is much, much, harder. With a clear, strong, border, it's very easy to say "this is how things work in here": to create an alternate set of social norms and expectations, to create an enhanced sense of trust and shared connection. The first time Burning Man went to the desert, Danger Ranger literally drew a line in the dust and said "across this line, everything will be different," and everyone crossed over it together. (Which, it should be noted, is an amazingly simple and powerful example of a psychomagical act.) That is what strong experience boundaries allow you to do. And of course, the only way in which experiences like the one I wrote above can happen is if there is in fact a boundary, and "edge of the world" that someone can go and stare over and, in this case, sing across.

But there's another approach. Let's consider, once again, the Jejune Institute.

You could discover the Jejune Institute by noticing a weird advertisement for personal force fields in an alternative newspaper; by discovering a strange pirate radio station that could be heard in a public park; by having a friend tell you about a strange experience they had; by observing people doing something strange in front of a building you pass on your commute, and a dozen other ways.

You accessed the Jejune Institute (both the literal thing and the experience) by following up on these things, going to real places, and meeting real people, none of whom sold you a ticket or told you the "rules" or suggested you were in any kind of game at all.

From there, you had to decide who to trust. Do you believe in the Jejune Institute? Are you appalled by the facts the Resistance has put forward? If you kept investigating, you would discover people who were following in the footsteps of a missing girl, hoping to discover what had happened to her. Go with them, and you'd be visiting an ossuary in the day and crawling through the sewers at night, trying to find clues that could unravel the mystery and, perhaps, bring down this sprawling organization that to all appearances is a part of the real world. It rents offices. It has staff. It's holding a conference in a few months, which some people want to crash ...

What are the boundaries of this experience? Where does it begin and end? How do you know you're in or out of it?

You don't. The whole point is that you can't. The whole point is that once you're in it, you no longer know where it begins and ends – rather than having boundaries and borders, it gradually replaces the world you live in.

Now compare both of those experiences with the

Decentralized Dance Party.

It's easy to know where the DDP is and isn't – the big crowd of people dancing is easy to spot. But that misses the most important point about the DDP, which is that it's *mobile*, and takes place in *public spaces*. Do everything a DDP does, but keep it in a dance club for a night, and it would be a slightly-better-than-average dance party, nothing more. The essence of the experience is that it travels to public spaces and takes them over with an open invitation to joy and participation. It doesn't slowly replace the world with a long-term experience, it takes the world over for a brief time.

All three kinds of experiences change the world around you, and each requires a different – but very clear – sense of where its boundaries are, of how you get in and out, to work.

In each case, the moment of entry is at its most potent when it is also a moment of commitment. Because we're creating non-fictions, it's not the moment when they start to suspend disbelief, but the moment when they realize "oh, the world really is this way!" For a Decentralized Dance Party, it's the moment when the party sweeps through the area they're in, taking over the world and changing it - or better yet, when they join in and dance. For Burning Man, it's when they cross a very clear threshold into a world that works entirely differently than the one they left. For the Jejune Institute, it's the moment when they realize "fuck, I'm in this now, and I don't even know what happened, or what this is." Or better yet, the moment when, having realized that, they say "I need to do something!"

The sign of a successful, truly successful, crossing into the experience isn't just an acceptance that the world is different than they thought (though if you can get that, you're doing well), but a commitment to action that rises up from that realization.

The "right" approach to boundaries depends on what kind of experience you want to create. But having a clear sense of how people get in and out, and how they know that (or don't), is crucial in every case. The kiss of death is to do something half-way: Burning Man may have the ultimate ambition of making the whole world more like Burning Man, and adopt an instrumentalist approach to getting there, but when they create Burning Man events they can't have any ambiguity about which spaces are in line with their 10 Principles and which aren't. For best results in a Burning Man space, a critical mass of people have to wholly throw themselves into it, in a way that you can't do if you're also trying to network or are suspicious of people giving you gifts. If the Jejune Institute had created "neutral" spaces where people didn't have to play the game, maybe "no conspiracy Sundays" or "we promise not to fuck with you at home," then the whole impact would have been deflated. And for a Decentralized Dance Party to pull you in to the experience, it has to be "decentralized."

So the next element of psychomagical design is to understand what the boundaries of the experience are; *crossing thresholds should be potent.* How people get in and out of the experience, or don't, plays a significant role in creating a clear sense that the world is different than they thought and gets them to commit to action. Indeed, the very act of establishing those boundaries is often a crucial part of the experience itself. Danger Ranger drew a literal line in the dust and had everyone jump over it together; now, Burning Man has "gates" that represent thresholds that people cross from out to in, and then, greeting stations at which people tell you "welcome home" – not to mention the fact that you're entering a strange, alien environment that is numinous in its own right. This process of entering and exiting is itself extremely potent. Similarly, the most powerful moment in the whole Jejune Institute experience was the realization that you didn't know when you entered and you didn't know how to get out.

Whichever approach you take, go all in. Half-measures will only work against you.

Each approach comes with its own particular challenges. We'll be reviewing the advice of a master on invading public spaces later in the book, so we'll table that discussion for now, and instead look at the challenges you face with the other approaches.

It's worth noting that we've seen many examples so

far of small scale, even personal, seemingly spontaneous psychomagic. This often doesn't have a boundaries problem, because the borders are obvious: this is an experience we're having, together, right now. A personal interaction. But even that can be enhanced, if you're able, by creating a border around what you would do anyway. Circumscribe a ritual space (A magic circle? A pentagram? A side of the room? Anything can hypothetically work, if you can give it symbolic importance). Go to a remote spot in nature, or a place with an amazing view, or in the auspices of an especially interesting work of art. This isn't necessary, but it can definitely enhance. Although don't underestimate the shock of performing a psychomagically potent act in "normal space," the "real world." It's harder to do, but if you can do it well enough, the incongruity between the mundane and the extraordinary can have a long-lasting impact.

But the point here is that for personal-scale experience design, creating boundaries isn't usually crucial, but can definitely enhance. It's when you're dealing with larger scale experiences that a failure to adequately set the boundaries can really screw you up.

The advantages of using a strong perimeter are the opportunities it provides for a clear set of expectations and opportunities to engage participants: you can set the terms of their encounter in your experience, control what information they get, determine what they see and hear at the outset ... you can do an awful lot of things. The problem is that you're trying to set up an infinite psychomagical garden ... and you've just established a perimeter. By saying "this is in" and "this is out" you've actually cut them off from the infinite game. You've gained a number of advantages, and created one significantly big problem. How do you handle it?

There are a couple of ways.

Ramp Up Intensity

The most difficult and, frankly, often less effective approach is to ramp up the intensity until the lack of space created by even a very large perimeter fades into the background. You're effectively betting everything on one big moment. On leading someone blindfolded through a twisting tunnel until suddenly something utterly magnificent is revealed. If it works, it works. But it also has very little margin for error, and not just as a performance moment. (If they think of something funny and get the giggles, you're doomed.) Because to keep ramping up the intensity to that degree, you usually have to keep exerting more and more control – you have less and less flexibility and room for error. Which means you're creating a machine, not a garden. Psychologically, you're giving the daimon an ultimatum: this or nothing. When you're betting everything on one play, you have very little leeway to roll with a counter-offer of "how about this?" Which is not a problem if you're just looking for someone to be impressed. But if you're looking to create a "transformative" experience? Psyches are tricky. They want to work with you, but the conditions have to be right for you to really get their attention. Remember: nobody's life was ever changed by a roller coaster. (At least one working the way it was supposed to). A thrill ride isn't the point.

It can happen, though. Oakland artist (and fellow SFIOP board member) Michelle Bert and her crew have spent ungodly amounts of time putting together an annual haunted house specifically to scare the shit out of their friends. Oh, they open it up to the neighborhood kids and lines go around the block and everybody has a good time, but the real reason they do it is for the "friends and family" nights, when the true sinister design of the thing to make the people they love shit themselves and break down becomes apparent. It is, basically, a series of escalating intense encounters, and it works beautifully.

On the other hand, when escalating intensity goes bad ...

For Chicken's bachelor party, he was kidnapped and put through a series of escalating encounters. Everyone involved has since sworn never to speak of it again. It was wrong. What we did was wrong. We know that now.

Create Super-Abundance

An approach to dealing with strong perimeters that is far more frequently adopted is to create a sense of the infinite by creating depth within the space: to make it super-abundant with unique encounters and discoveries. So long as people are exploring that abundance and constantly surprised, the space will feel infinite, thus making the perimeter boundaries less of an issue.

What does that look like? Well, before we go to exotic counter-cultural examples ... have you ever been to the Louvre? Or the Vatican museum?

They are, of course, limited spaces. Large, to be sure, but limited. However, they are crammed full of so much art and cultural history that you are simply overwhelmed with choices. Even moving at a fast clip, you can't see it all. There will always be something more that you've missed. You'll always think "damn it, I wish I had more time" and be simultaneously so exhausted from the effort of taking in so much art that you feel like even if you had the time, you couldn't do it.

That's super-abundance, in a nutshell.

Let's consider Burning Man again. It has a massive perimeter, but to keep it feeling like an infinite psychomagical garden, it also has a city: an 80,000 person city, in which thousands of theme camps have created unique experiences to be discovered, hundreds of artists have created sculptures and rides and events, hundreds of mutant vehicles are driving along, people are constantly building, and a majority of the people are out in costumes wandering around bumping into each other in strange and synchronistic ways. You literally never know what's going to happen when you cross the street, or where you'll end up when you take a walk in the city. You can go to the perimeter if you want – lots of people like to walk around it and look at the mountains in the distance – but even keeping the perimeter in mind you have the certain knowledge, the whole time you're there, that you couldn't possibly see everything. It has a perimeter, but within that perimeter it seems infinite.

To look at that on a smaller scale, one of the old standby techniques is to get a space with lots of room ... say a hotel, let's say you rent out a hotel ... and then instead of using it to put your guests up you create a unique art experience in every single room. And the stairs. And the elevators. And you just let people go through it in their own way, at their own pace. They'll never run out of things to do ... especially if the experiences in some rooms connect to other rooms in ways that send you back and forth to change the experience.

Or maybe you put an art experience in every single room on every single floor except two. And people aren't supposed to go to either of those floors, but one of them people can access, and they can look around the rooms, with the thrill of knowing they're not supposed to be there, and everything looks normal until one last room. And in that room ...

... I'm not telling. The very fact that you really want to know gets the point across. With that many places to explore in a self-directed fashion, you've created super-abundance.

Oh, at that other floor? The one they really can't go to? When the event is over, you herd everyone up there, for a big finale. After a long night of constant exploration and art experiences and meaningful choices ... that's when you hit them with something truly intense. At that point, when they know that anything can happen, that's when their psyches are ready for it.

Although ... honestly ... however impressive the big finale is, if you've designed this right, it will never mean as much to the people who go through it as some strange and idiosyncratic thing that happened to them as they were exploring, in a self-directed way, through all these rooms. Something somebody said to them, or something they saw, or a choice they made, will have reached them deeply in a way you could have never predicted, and will be what they think about, years after the fact. Oh, the big finale is good too, but it's that small, self-directed, encounter they had that will really have caused their breakthrough.

That's super-abundance.

What about the other approach? The one the Jejune Institute took? Where there is no perimeter and you have no idea where the experience begins and ends, and eventually you're seeing it everywhere?

Then you have the opposite problem, and honestly it's even harder.

Scarcity Requires Depth

Super-abundance is death to an experience like that, because an experience like the Jejune Institute thrives on the question "what is going on?" And if you provide too much access to too many people doing too many things, then there are too many reasonable opportunities for somebody to explain it all. And if nobody is taking up reasonable opportunities to do that, then suddenly it requires the suspension of disbelief to accept that, oh, no, nobody's explaining this to me. At which point you're not having a real experience, you're playing make-believe.

To be clear, of course the Jejune Institute wasn't "real" in one sense. But it was in so many others: it had a real office building under its own name with real staff. It put real advertisements into papers. You really decided to check it out and see what was going on, and you were put in situations where you really didn't know what was and wasn't true. The "lore" of the Jejune Institute was a fraud (except when it wasn't, creators being tricky that way), but it really existed as itself in the world, and all the decisions you were making were real and had real consequences for your life. Compare this to, say, Harry Potter's Wizarding World, where they have absolutely built a castle and let you explore it and give you a magic wand ... but ... it's based on a fictional property, you already know all the back story, you had to buy a ticket to get in, they're trying to sell you merchandise ... Wizarding World constantly requires you to suspend disbelief. The Jejune Institute was really happening in your world.)

In fact, even a regular abundance of experiences is too much to sustain a process like this. When the experience is slowly taking over their real life, it has to be paced and unpredictable. There needs to be a lot of waiting, a lot of hints, a lot of build up, a lot of time for their own mind to do the work for you, rather than constantly being fed. Only then can the sudden burst of activity really capture their psyches and create an experience of the world turning upside-down.

Thus, when you have an experience with no perimeter, you must create and manage punctuated scarcity. You have to create psychomagic in things *not* happening. And don't be fooled – that's much harder than it sounds.

Because, think about it, without a perimeter, without being able to know where the participants are at any moment and what they're doing? You have to both give enough depth to the experience that it does, in fact, turn up at least in small ways in some of the places they look, while having no idea what they're going to try next, while you're waiting ... waiting ... waiting ... to be able to initiate the next big thing.

All those ways to get involved in the Jejune Institute? They had to be ready, week after week after week, month after month, for anybody to just show up off the street. They had to keep a pirate radio station running in Dolores Park, in San Francisco's Mission, without knowing who was listening to it or who was actually going to act on its instructions. Without a centralized authority to take RSVPs, they never knew who the hell was going to join the expedition into the sewer, or the crematorium, or any of the other adventures. Well, actually, they could have spies among the participants ... but that's just something else you have to manage.

The point being, in order to keep from needing people to suspend disbelief, but have them actually be in this world, you have to create a depth to the world that is itself believable – and when there is no perimeter, that means you have to cover a stunning number of eventualities over a prolonged period of time.

That they could keep this going for three years is, frankly, incredibly impressive. We were all kind of stunned.

Does it have to be that hard? Is there a way to do it that doesn't require that extensive a degree of depth?

Oh yes. The All Worlds Fair experimented with that. Then The Fallen Cosmos took it to the next level, essentially creating a much shorter term infinite garden that culminated more quickly into the key experience.

Then the people behind the Jejune Institute tried again, creating the Latitude Society. And that was an incredibly ambitious attempt to innovate through these conundrums and create something sustainable that had everything. It was a work of genius. It also failed spectacularly. Just totally flamed out. But I suspect it pointed the way towards what we'll see coming in years ahead. And we'll talk about that at some length later.

But for now, let's move on to our next design element.

We've got four more to go.

Chapter 17:
The Holy Trinity - Art, Ritual, and Play

In the last chapter, I mentioned how much being in a particularly good museum can itself be a kind of psycho-magical experience. Why is that?

Is it the art?

Yes. Yes, it's the art.

To be surrounded by art, especially art that is very good or very surprising, can have a powerful impact on the psyche. In the best cases, that art actually functions as an Imago – an image that activates one's personal mythology. When someone sees an image like that, their psyche is looking for something to do with its archetypes, some way to engage more deeply, to make something happen.

A truly profound image doesn't replace all the other design elements we've been talking about, but it makes everything you're trying to accomplish so much easier.

There are five statues of Rodin's "Gates of Hell" around the world: in Zurich, Paris, Tokyo, Philadelphia, and on the Stanford University campus in Palo Alto. The sculpture, literally a representation of the entrance to Hell from Dante's *Inferno*, is 6 meters high, 4 meters wide and 1 meter deep, a teeming mass of metal that seems to be moving like liquid, frozen in time, as 180 different figures crawl across it, trying to escape.

It's utterly captivating, and at the Stanford campus it's part of an outdoor sculpture garden, about 45 minutes (depending on traffic) from where I live. One of the simplest events I ever threw was just to have picnics, at midnight, in front of the Gates of Hell. Get a group of friends to all bring supplies, sit on the ground in front of the statue, or at some nearby tables, pour wine, open a basket filled with bread and sausages and cheese, and sit and talk, at midnight, before the Gates of Hell.

Not terribly original. Not terribly involved. But powerful. Eerie and interesting, because the art is just that amazing.

When art is that good, it does much of the work for you – but there was another element involved here. Having a picnic in front of the sculpture was a playful gesture that created a connection to it, even made the art a force in our activity. Not to put too fine a point on it, but the way art galleries are traditionally set up, in which you come and look at art while maintaining a healthy distance, is one of the most psychomagically inert uses of art you'll find.

Having a picnic in front of the Gates of Hell put us into a different relationship with the art, and thus enhanced its ability to reach us.

The Contemporary Jewish Museum in San Francisco

is a very good museum, and it's not a slight to honestly acknowledge that they don't have anything remotely as good as the Gates of Hell in it. But when a friend told me she needed to be taken on an adventure in the city, I brought her to the CJM (which had a touring exhibit I wanted to see), gave her a bag of tiny plastic finger toy monsters, and told her to secretly distribute these monsters throughout the museum.

This was ridiculously fun, with an edge that was absurd for feeling dangerous – but if we'd been caught we would have at least been kicked out, and before we left it was obvious that security had discovered that someone was leaving little plastic monsters all around the exhibits, and was conducting a sweep to find them and put a stop to this nonsense. It was so stupid, and harmless, and transgressive, all at once. It was wonderfully playful.

That playfulness, once again, put us into a different relationship with the art. I don't think we were looking at it any less appreciatively than anyone else – in fact, I bought some of it in the souvenir shop – but now we had a more intimate relationship with it as well. It was a part of an adventure, something that we were directly responding to, and playing with it in this regard opened us up to it in new ways.

There are all kinds of places that we could have monstered where it would have been similarly unwelcome – government offices, libraries, movie theaters, public gardens – but none of them would have had that same charge as doing it in an art museum. Why? Once again: because of the art. Because it was already such a rich psychological environment.

Art on its own can be very psychologically potent; making it part of a playful act, even an adventure, makes it exponentially more so. It doesn't have to be complicated, or intricate. Why? Because it's art. Much of the work has already been done. There's a pretty vital lesson here.

* * *

Art, Ritual, and Play – the person who really cracked their connection open for me is a UCLA anthropologist with whom I once fought a war.

That is not a metaphor.

Back in 2012, Dr. Megan Heller, known as "The Countess," was the leader of the Burning Man Census team. And I, in my guise as Caveat Magister, was the volunteer coordinator of Burning Man's Media team. One of their senior volunteers, Trapper, had wanted to come over to my team, and so I'd made her an offer and we'd gotten her set up ... and then the Census started trying to get her back. They were guilting her like crazy, telling her how important she was and how they couldn't get their work done without her, and Trapper started telling me that maybe she was going to try working shifts on both teams – more than doubling her workload –

because she couldn't let them down.

"Oh no," I said. "No no no. We're gonna handle this. Come with me."

So I got a dangerous looking hook cane and a bottle of Chimay, and I grabbed Trapper and we walked right into the Census camp, where at the top of my lungs I demanded to see The Countess. When the three of us were all together, in the middle of her camp, I issued a dramatic proclamation: I had in my left hand a bottle of beer brewed by monks, and in my right hand a weapon. Trapper was ours, she'd defected to the Media team, and one way or another the Census would have to accept that. They could either accept it gracefully, in which case they could drink the beer with my compliments, or they could accept it in anger, in which case we would go to war, and the streets would run red with blood! What was it to be?

"Oh," the Countess said, without blinking. "War!"

I realized, in that moment, that I had miscalculated. I'd had no idea they were so ready to do this.

Two years later, in her dissertation on adult play, the Countess would describe this incident from her own perspective. In fact she had been just as stunned by my theatrical posturing as I'd expected her to be. But instead of backing down, she'd thought "Oh, geez, I guess this is what the Media team does! Well, in that case ..." and jumped right in.

Thus began a week-long conflict in which we raided each other's camps, "vandalized" one another's stuff, enlisted allies among other camps, and engaged in psychological warfare and dirty tricks. I got the Burning Man radio station to run promotions saying that there was an orgy in the back of the Census camp, and that you could get in by asking for the "long form." So many people showed up demanding to get the "long form" that the Census team eventually created one just because as long as those people were here they might as well provide supplemental data. I also got jumped by three guys in lab coats, which is just a weird and fascinating experience in its own right.

While open hostilities ceased at the end of the week, they simmered for years ... which brought members of both camps further together in common bonds, because we had a very fun game going. Formal peace was declared four years later, after a summit that was somehow even funnier than the war. We exchanged knives. There was an apology mooning. I did a ritual happy dance. People on each team bonded even more closely. But best of all, I became friends with the Countess, who later would talk with me about her work, and give me a key insight into what makes experiences like this tick.

Turns out you can learn from your enemies.

The title of this chapter calls Art, Ritual, and Play the "holy trinity" – and that's not just because they're three things that are important. It's because, in vital respects, they are the *same thing*. They are three, and they are one.

All three are examples of what can be termed "meta-consciousness" – each is an imaginative act that has the potential to significantly reframe the way we look at the world. This connection is particularly clear in rituals and in play: the only difference is that we take one as solemn and important and adult, and the other as frivolous and childish. But at a crucial level, they're doing the same thing.

Think about highly ritualized endeavors: if you "play" a religious "ritual" effectively enough, aren't you really doing a religious ritual? While if you perform a religious ritual in a slapdash manner, aren't you just playing at it? If you "play" soldier hard enough, aren't you in fact being a soldier, while if you are a soldier who screws around at it, aren't you just "playing" soldier? Ritual and play are fungible. The major difference is not that one is good or bad, adult or childish, effective or ineffective – it's that society recognizes one as official and the other not. But they are in fact made up of the same ingredients, and can play much the same roles as one another. The feeling you get when you are deeply enmeshed in play and ritual is the same, as is the feeling you get when you are just going through the motions. In the former cases you are fully present, while in the latter you are forcing yourself to suspend disbelief. When fully lived, both give you a sense that there are new possibilities that you can access – the world works *this* way, not *that* way, while at the same time creating new rules and procedures you need to follow to access it. The Census and the media team would never, under other circumstances, have even considered fighting over a volunteer – but doing so actually made everything better, not only solving the problem but building bridges.

Being moved by a piece of art has much the same effect. It can cause you to see the ordinary in a new way, or imagine something you'd previously never conceived of.

The design element to incorporate here isn't just that art is awesome and play is awesome and ritual is awesome, it's that *they are transitive*: they are at their most potent when they are put next to one another, sequence into one another, and reinforce one another.

Use them. Use them a lot. Have them reference one another, turn into one another, inspire one another.

And when you have multiple rituals going on, and multiple kinds of play, and many pieces of art, all different from one another, and people can choose what to engage with, and how to mix their experience up ... it can become an incredibly potent magical garden.

And when they're all part of a unique and non-benign experience of engineered disperfection in which participants have to make meaningful choices? Pull something like that off, and people who go through it will never be the same again.

On the other hand, and this is an important warning, it's easy to over-rely on them.

"Dance party at the Gates of Hell" is probably about as engaging as "picnic at the Gates of Hell." But if the next thing you do is "movie night at the Gates of Hell," and then "clothing swap at the Gates of Hell," and then another "dance party at the Gates of Hell" … suddenly you've stopped designing experiences and started doing shitty party promotion. Eventually you want to cram more people in the space, because if you're not actually doing anything potent you'll probably try to make it bigger, assuming "more potent" and "bigger" are the same thing, and it's also not technically legal to charge people for access to public art, so you do pop-up events at a club with a giant cardboard cut out of the Gates of Hell. And when that is accidentally lit on fire by a DJ who thought he was good at flame effects, you just start calling your event "the Gates of Hell," and nobody even knows why, except that it's a good name.

Go ahead and laugh, but I've seen it happen.

While art, ritual, and play are in many ways the building blocks of an infinite psychomagical garden, too many people start there and stop there, because the other stuff … creating unique non-fictions and engineered disperfections and encouraging meaningful choices and keeping it non-benign ... is all much harder than slapping some art on a wall and playing Twister.

But the hard stuff is ultimately more important to doing this well, especially at a high level. Art and ritual and whimsy are great at reaching the unconscious, but just being near art is the least effective way to access that capacity, while play and ritual that are neither inspired nor carefully designed (or best of all, inspired through design) generally don't offer the daimonic anything that it thinks is important.

For Robin Ziiro, coming to the art already in a state of ritual and play is a way of both heightening its impact and creating these other important conditions:

"Build a world with your collaborators by connecting and amplifying your own shared schemas, stories and symbol narratives, and then approach the art," she said.

An infinite psychomagical garden is what museums and dance parties dream of becoming, not what they are. It's important not to mistake the building blocks for the final shape.

Chapter 18:
Gary Warne's Chaotic Principles

In 2017, a small group of artistic ne'er-do-wells took over a city block in San Francisco's financial district during the afternoon commute.

Anyone entering the block was greeted by someone wearing a sandwich board with nothing on it, handing out promotional cards with nothing on them. They almost never spoke – only when a direct question couldn't be answered with a shrug or a smile.

An industrial bubble machine had been set up in the middle of the block, creating a robust cloud of bubbles to walk through in the affected area.

As pedestrians passed the blank sandwich boards, holding their blank brochures, they passed signs taped to street lamps and parking meters alerting people that there had been a runaway Roomba, describing it, discussing its temperament, saying what name it answered to, and offering a reward for finding it.

They passed people impatiently waiting at a bus stop that had not been there that morning – the bus was the Infinity route, going from success to prosperity.

They passed a woman standing outside a coffee shop,

holding a coffee. She was drinking the coffee, but somehow the cup was refilling itself. In fact, it was overflowing, coffee cresting over the cup and falling down over her hand, staining her suit, no matter how much she drank. Eventually there was a large puddle at her feet.

They passed people painting sidewalk plants ... and they passed a little "farm" of computer monitors that all had plants emerging out of them.

They passed a woman furiously smashing her cell phone on the ground, then getting out another one and smashing it. And then another. And another ...

They passed people taking surveys asking disturbingly personal information, and municipal workers asking for their help to take bizarre sidewalk measurements.

And more. It just went on. And if they stopped to interact, rather than staring and walking past, then whatever was happening started to include them as a crucial part. They were just what was needed all along!

Eventually, if they kept walking, they exited the field of bubbles, and passed a second person wearing an empty sandwich board, handing out blank promotional cards, and they were back in the city they knew again.

I was one of the people wearing an empty sandwich board,

handing out blank brochures, and it was exhausting: so many people actively try to ignore you when you're handing something out on the street, and there's a kind of fatigue that sets in, an effect of being so visibly not seen. But of course they did see me, and some of them reflexively, automatically, took the brochures ... and at that point, most of them did a double take. Stared. Even stopped. Trying to process that there was nothing on it.

It didn't seem all that unusual to me, honestly, but by that point I'd been doing this kind of thing for a dozen years. It's easy to forget how much people can react to little glitches in reality.

"What is this for?" they asked. I only shrugged.

"What are you selling?" some said again, more insistently.

"What?"

At that point, I would speak. "Nothing." "What, nothing?"

"Nothing."

"Then ... what is this for?" they held the brochure back out to me.

I only shrugged. And then resumed handing the brochures to new people.

Sometimes they kept demanding to know. Eventually, they walked on. Deeper into the glitch.

After sheer confusion and bafflement, a demand to know what we were selling was the most common response. People had a hard time understanding that we weren't selling something. That we weren't promoting anything. Far, far, weirder to them than any of the strange things they saw was the idea that someone would do this without an ulterior motive; that this wasn't part of a marketing campaign or an attempt to collect their data. The idea that they weren't being sold something was a new possibility that they grappled with when they went home: no one had to be selling anything. They needed to wrap their mind around it.

"That's a pretty common experience to the weirdo artist and Burning Man types around here - giving something nice to a stranger creates this little skip in time, and that's a potent moment" said Michael Ryan Garcia, who was the primary organizer of this project. "A lot of the folks involved in this had been going to the Free Buffet events, where artists would gather outside a BART station during the morning commute to give away everything from coffee and donuts to resignation letters and sensual shirt unbuttoning/rebuttoning services."

So there was a lot of confusion. But there was a lot of delight, too, a lot of sudden realizations – spontaneously "getting it" where before there had been only befuddlement. A lot of people asked how they could do this too.

And one woman, right before dark, right before we packed up and went back to our secret lair, walked up to me and gave me one of my blank promotional cards back.

On it, she had written: "Thanks for reminding me that anything's possible."

* * *

That was a flawless experience. Most of us were veterans at this sort of thing, and we all agreed: it went off perfectly. Nobody had a breakdown, nobody got hit by a car, nobody got arrested, nobody had even called the cops. Everyone had fun, all the equipment worked, and far from the apathy we'd feared we were going to encounter, people on the sidewalk had really engaged with us – however confused they'd been.

Many public actions do not go that well. When you create possibility in the world, you invite chaos.

And that can be a good thing. It can be a sign of success. The whole point of psychomagic is to take us out of the world that we are locked into, and make it a playground for the daimonic and our personal mythologies. What happens next is only going to be so predictable, and often will shock the hell out of you. That means it's working.

"Doing weird stuff in public is a moral imperative," DDP's San Francisco organizer Michael Ryan Garcia likes to say. "It demonstrates new ways of interacting with familiar spaces and by extension familiar systems."

But it also means that much in the way you have to learn to understand danger if you're going to effectively introduce it into your experiences, you have to be able to understand, and then manage, the chaos that can follow possibility.

This is hard enough in relatively secure environments where you know whose buttons you're pushing, can control variables, and have resources on hand. It's exponentially more difficult when you're engaging strangers in public places. It is a testament to the skill and expertise of the San Francisco art underground that almost no one died or ended up with a criminal record. At least for doing this stuff.

Different groups have different approaches to handling this, often reflecting their politics and relationship with the larger community. To the extent that a set of common approaches exist, they can be traced to Suicide Club founder Gary Warne, who in the late 1970s developed what he called "12 Chaotic Principles" for how to handle the pushback that can occur when you challenge common perceptions in public. I don't know that anybody has done better since.

"Gary based each one on an event or events where something blew up in his face," his collaborator and protege John Law told me. "'Why did that happen? Oh, well it's because everybody didn't stick together ... or we didn't all agree ...'

We realized early on it was hugely important that everybody who was doing this agreed before they started on what we were doing and how we would respond if things blew up."

The 12 Chaotic Principles were first formally published in the Suicide Club newsletter, then republished in the 2013 book "*Tales of the San Francisco Cacophony Society*," without commentary. This is important, so let's take a look now.

1. Divest Yourself of Expectations.
Make sure the people you're doing something with can dish it out as well as take it. If it isn't funny when it happens to them, then you've got sadists instead of pranksters. Initiate them to make sure they have a sense of humor about themselves. Never preconceive what the reaction to an event will be like; You are sure to be disappointed. Ergo ...

2. You Will Never be Totally in Control.

3. Be a Fool, Not a Sadist. You Should be Able to Take it As Well as Dish it Out.

4. Allow People the Validity of Their Own Emotions (Humor is a Very Serious Thing).
When you are doing what you really want to do, maybe for the first time, allow people the reality of their own emotions and the sincerity of their own responses. Don't be shocked or bummed out if you are ignored, slugged in the mouth, or arrested. People cannot be expected to think your jokes are

funny. Their reactions are no less valid than your own.

NATIONAL CLOWN WEEK Aug 9, 1974 – Twelve clowns went into the B of A at Powell & Market singing "We're in the Money" and tried to deposit fish, flowers, juggling balls, and comics at the tellers' windows. The guards came and they were really MAD; they were definitely going to beat up the ringleader. I was dressed as a Keystone Cop with a giant silver badge, British bobby hat, cane, and long blue trench coat. I ran up, blew my whistle, arrested the lead clown, and dragged him away, rabid as he was, and this was a very scary moment; the other clowns had already run for the door and burst out laughing. We ran. It was scary, but it was their territory, their values, and their job - accept whatever the response is - it's real. The fact that the group broke ranks was really terrifying.

Again remember Principle No. 3.

5. Solidarity is a Necessity.

Every time we changed locations in the course of the evening's bizarity, we lost people. This became a steadfast rule of entropy in future stunts. This is not good. The people need each other for energy and support, plus it is relatively dangerous to go out as a group to do stunts—anything can happen. If you're going to start something, finish it. Corollary: Nothing's Ever Over When You Think It Is.

6. Play it Out to the End.

ANYTHING GOES: A Disaster – It fulfilled its title but the people couldn't trust one another because of the things each of them brought and did for and to each other without knowing one another. A common purpose or focus decided beforehand is the best, even if people still can't go through with it; it will be an inner failing rather than paranoia. Other than initiations, and despite Principle No.II, agree beforehand on what you want to do.

7. The More Extreme the Act, the More Extreme and Varied the Response Will Be.

Voyage to Another Planet – We broke down into three groups and talked about how we imagined life on other planets. Then we blindfolded twenty-five people and took them to two unusual environments, one natural and one synthetic. We told them that when we took off their blindfolds, they could not use proper nouns, names, or earthly references for the sights they would witness. They had to decide what they were, why they were, what they did, as if they had never seen them before. Confused? For example, if we took them to a street and unblindfolded them, they couldn't use the word "concrete," "street," "pavement," "road," etc... We took them to the Judah Street tunnel under the Great Highway and took off the blindfolds in the dark. They had to walk out the seaward side, as if they were just landing on another planet, and "decide" what the ocean was. The descriptions, fantasies, and hallucinations were utterly incredible. I will never think of the ocean in the same way ever again! Then we re-blindfolded them and took them into the belly of the monster, Alcoa Plaza at midnight – to Ripple's, a bar surely from the 21st century. TV sets two feet apart all the way down to the bar with curtains on either side of them like windows – all showing the ocean beating on the shoreline. Eight foot motion picture screens broadcasting a band playing while people danced - the band wasn't there though. Women taking off their clothes in view screens over the urinals—women could enter accompanied by men, but men couldn't see what was going on in the women's bathroom. This place was so way out on a Saturday night that no one could come up with anything farther out.

JOKE CLASSES ARE LISTED ON THE RIGHT SIDE OF THE FRONT PAGE – We ran joke classes in every catalog for two years until our "DEATHSKOOL" catalog, when people got too confused and we stopped for a while. Someone had registered for every joke class we have ever run, no matter how outrageously it was written. When the HARI-KARI class asked them to kill themselves, they politely asked if it was real or not. For DEMONIC POSSESSION we were asked in a whisper if we "had connections." When we ran PARANOIA AS A STATE OF HEIGHTENED AWARENESS, we had to re-evaluate the whole concept of joke classes—a device, as far as we know, that no other alternative university has used. SIXTEEN people signed up for Paranoia. These were the ones either cowardly or fun loving registrars let sign up. Many more were turned away by other registrars. Some people didn't want ANY other class but that one and as you can imagine HATED filling out the skills exchange (a program we run in which participants signing up for the school offer their skills for barter). If you re-read the description a couple of times, I think you might agree that it's pretty horrible. But people wanted it. People in on the joke wanted it to happen but the BIG QUESTION MARK was what kind of people had signed up for it? The joke became too real; everyone who wanted to see what the registrants were like were also afraid to offer their homes to find out! The joke became very real. Eight months later someone was moving out of their house and offered to have the class the night before they gave the keys back to the landlord. We wrote and called people, had the class, and had a very intense and fantastic evening of sharing what we were afraid of. Our first joke had become real. An incredible reversal.

8. Humor is as Relative as Anything Else.

NIGHT OF ADVENTURES, DEATHSKOOL CATALOG SPRING 75 – Description: Bring your ready to live adventures. Leave your pride at home, if we think they're either too dangerous or too boring. Must be in the borders of S.F. Twenty-five people signed up for this class and three came with adventures. After we talked for a while, people started thinking up practical jokes, but I was never sure if they were fantasizing them THEN or they had brought them. There was a practical jokes class in that catalog listed without a teacher, but no one signed up for it (everyone was afraid to sign up first, because then they had to offer THEIR house). We planned two of the three adventures for the first night and the third would be put together later. The first, mine, was to walk through the JUDAH STREET CAR TUNNEL from Duboce Park to Cole & Carl. Half of the group went home right then and never came back. Other people didn't want to go through the tunnel and didn't want to go home either, so they waited for us at the other end.

9. Fear is a State of Mind: The Fear/Risk Ratio is Not Proportional.

Since most fears are about things that have NOT happened to us or that we haven't experienced but have only witnessed through media representation or in our fantasy states, we usually don't know what an experience is like and our fears keep us from finding out.

10. We Have Many Things to Risk Besides Our Lives.

It is also possible, I won't posit a principle here, that our adventures and fantasies are a combination of excitement and fear and other people's adventures are more frightening than our own because THEY have the excitement/motivation and we don't, so we are only left with the fear. To support this, I offer up that one of the people who waited outside of the tunnel was the one who organized the FUR SALE demonstration, which terrified me and which didn't faze him.

11. We Subconsciously Believe We Have Experienced Things When We Have Only Watched Them. We Have Not.

12. When We Test Our Fantasies of Ourselves, We Fall Short – So We Do Not.

This is a very compact way of saying a lot of things, all of which are worthwhile in their own right. But there are some common threads that are worth pulling on.

Fully half of the principles (#1, #2, #3, #4, #7, #8) focus on the issue of the emotions your team and your participants will feel as you create experiences with an unsuspecting public. So far in this book we've talked about deliberately loosening control, and "channeling" what others are experiencing rather than "performing" for them, as necessary elements to create the kind of psychomagical experiences you're trying to design – and they are. But they are also … particularly with people who are involuntary participants … ethical necessities.

Remember how one of the very first experiences I told you about was a ritual I conducted with Robin so that she could access her inner asshole? One of the things I mentioned, which wasn't important then but is now, is that the ritual was preceded by a long discussion about the different kinds of assholes there are in the world, and what it means to be one kind but not another. Robin wanted to access her capacity to be the kind of asshole who is able to be cruel to be kind – to ruffle feathers for a good cause, to not care that she was being impolite while speaking the truth, to administer a shot that makes a child cry because it's a vaccine. She did NOT want to be a sadist.

Someone who always needs to defend their own ego might not start out as a sadist, but if they can't put their need for psychological security aside as they try to create psychomagic, they will probably end up as one. The people going through the experience you've created have every right to be defensive or angry or even to lash out, especially if they're members of the public – *they did not volunteer for this shit.* Chaotic Principle #4 is the one I quote to people most often: you have to allow people the validity of their own emotions.

You, as one of the designers of the experience, do not get to be defensive or angry about what happens. You are the one who has created the conditions in which all this is happening. That doesn't necessarily mean you're responsible for someone's bad behavior, or that you have to put up with people who get abusive – but it absolutely means that you cannot get mad at an audience who didn't volunteer to participate reacting badly to a situation that you set up on purpose knowing it could be psychologically potent.

The only way such experiences can work is if you can match the level of vulnerability you're asking from your participants – which is often true even if they do volunteer and are fully informed. If you cannot put your own urge to perform or spectate aside in the moment and channel instead, and if you cannot be the victim of the kind of experiences you are designing, then the experiences you create aren't going to be nearly as potent as they could be, and will slide surprisingly quickly into the unethical and sadistic.

Much like the way some schools of psychology require people training to become therapists to undergo therapy themselves, people engaging in psychomagical practices really need to be recipients of these experiences as well. And if they can't, they need to bow out. Gary's last, enigmatic, principle speaks to this point: "When We Test Our Fantasies of Ourselves, We Fall Short – So We Do Not." Psychomagical experiences, ironically, are at their safest when you're just seeing what happens: creating them to reinforce your own ego leads to disaster.

Only two Chaotic Principles (#5 and #6) specifically tell you to stick together and that everybody who starts has to see it through – but this is absolutely crucial practice, both generally and especially for public encounters. A lot of the emphasis on that from the Suicide Club days had to do with the rank illegality of much of what they were doing: a crowd of people sticking together together is a lot less likely to get arrested or beaten up than someone alone with no backup. But beyond that there is an important psychological component to this too which has nothing to do with whether you could face jail time. A group of people doing something creates a different set of responses than a person doing the same thing alone. Have a single person stare at a blank wall for an hour, and nothing will happen. Have a group of people standing around staring at a wall for an hour? Other people will stop and stare and act like they see it too. You're effectively leveraging the power of peer pressure: "everyone's doing it" is a shockingly powerful compulsion. And ... this is the real secret ... if everyone doing it looks like they're having a better time than you? Then you really want to try it too, no matter what it is. The most potent weapon that a group of people sticking together have in defusing situations that come up is in their ability *to be visibly having fun*. It goes an incredibly long way.

Four of the Chaotic Principles (9-12), are about the kind of risks you take – why some and not others. One of the reasons psychomagical experiences are so important is precisely that most of us reach a stasis point in our lives where we have taken all the kinds of risks we are able to convince ourselves to take, and are not able to convince ourselves to take the remaining risks that would be good for us. We protect ourselves with complexes, with projections; we cannot see what's standing right in front of us. Deep down we usually know what we need to do. We've just buried the urges under piles of anxiety and dread masquerading as sensible fears and precautions. The urge to psychological integration gets hidden below the toxic manifestations of our inner mythology. Going through psychomagical experiences, even the absurd and silly and pointless (sometimes especially those) puts us in vulnerable positions where we would not put ourselves; it motivates our daimonic impulses to growth and self-healing to take the risks we've been avoiding; and makes sure our unconscious psyches are paying rapt attention.

Past a certain point you can't do that for yourself, but we can do it for one another.

Chapter 19:
The Lazy Man's Guide to Starting a Cult

If the San Francisco experience design scene of the last 30 years had a single origin point, it might very well be considered the Suicide Club, which operated from 1977-1982. Yet much of what the Suicide Club did would not be considered "designed experience" at all, but simply "exploration."

They took illegal trips through the San Francisco sewer system, sometimes in formal wear. They climbed the Golden Gate Bridge, sometimes in formal wear. And then this happened, as told to me by John Law.

The Suicide Club liked to "infiltrate" different groups – secretly showing up to recruiting events for organizations like the American Nazi Party and the Moonies, pretending not to know each other, and seeing what they could discover. It got threatening and weird.

But when they tried to infiltrate the regional chapter of the National Speleological Society (NSS), one of the premier organizations for studying caves in the country, something unexpected happened: Suicide Club members discovered they really liked exploring caves, that these people were in fact really talented, and that they kind of wanted to join for real. Eventually, the Suicide Club gave up the notion of the "infiltration," was honest about who they were, and the two organizations traded members and went on joint expeditions.

So it was that in 1979, several members of the Suicide Club and the NSS went to Central-Northern Mexico, to descend into the deepest free pit cave in the world: Sótano de las Golondrinas - the "Pit of the Swallows."

A "Free Pit" is a hole in the ground where the walls underneath it bell out rather than go (more or less) straight down. So to reach the bottom, you have to descend to the full length of the cave entirely hanging on a rope – there are no walls you can attach anything to as you fall. It's a clear drop.

The Pit of the Swallows is 1,200 feet deep. At the time it was nine miles away from the closest town, accessible by gravel road. Prior to cartographers discovering it just ten years before, in 1969, the indigenous population believed it was the entrance to Hell.

The group, which included Law, then 22, trained for months. They purchased special equipment for the expedition, including two custom-made 1,200 feet ropes for the descent. The ropes, commonly called "static line" as opposed to "dynamic", were a prismatic weave designed especially for caving: 11 millimeters around, designed to hold 5,000 pounds, and only 1.7% stretch on its load. That means that when the rope is under pressure, for every 100 feet of rope it only adds 1.7 feet to the total length when it stretches. You don't want ropes to bounce when you're slowly lowering yourself down into a cave.

Most of northern Mexico is desert, but due to wind currents off the ocean, this region was a lush, 50-mile jungle. "Full-ass Tarzan," John said. "I read Tarzan and all kinds of other shit like that as a kid. I love that kind of thing. So going there was really fun."

After bribing the mayor of the nearest village and hiring two locals to carry the absurdly heavy packs of 1200 foot long rope, their expedition set off across hand-carved stone paths through the jungle into an area with no electricity where no one speaks Spanish, only the local indigenous languages, the canopy above the path so heavy that you couldn't see the sun.

Back then, it was still early enough that only a handful of expeditions had ever made this descent before.

They arrived at the mouth of the pit just before sundown, and began unpacking their supplies to set up camp and carefully lay out the rope. When you're working with a 1200 foot rope, you do not want even the tiniest possibility of a knot developing. They were standing on very hard, very old, volcanic rock: it's easy to cut yourself or a rope on it.

As the sun set they saw a giant dark cloud in the distance, approaching them at high speeds. As it got closer, a strange high-pitched noise covered the forest around them. A moment later they realized it wasn't a cloud: it was a literal mass of swallows, an estimated 250,000, all flying towards them in a giant column. The birds flew down to the height of the jungle canopy in the distance, then over to the pit – the noise so intense that you had to shout to be heard by the person next to you.

Once over the pit, they dove straight down.

Straight down. A quarter of a million of them, all at once, at an estimated 70 miles per hour.

There were so many of them it took a half-hour to complete the run. The pit is their domain, where they nest at night.

Awestruck, the Suicide Club members finished making camp. "Watching these guys, the NSS guys, work with their equipment?" John remembers. "That was an incredible education for me. It's one of the things that encouraged me to become a tradesman later in life. I learned more on this trip about teamwork in dangerous circumstances than I did from anything else in my life."

The next morning, at sunrise, they set up the ropes and descended into the pit.

John's partner for the descent was Henry, who he described as "growing up shithouse poor in the Folsom Army Housing Projects, which at that time was a fucking shithole – dangerous, with common stabbings and killings. He had several brothers, each from a different dad. He was also brilliant, a whip-smart dude," for all that he'd barely made it through high school. "Just incredibly smart, with a sardonic, dry sense of humor. When we'd infiltrated the Moonies, he was the guy who the Moonies kicked out because he couldn't help saying stuff. When his 'shadow' in the organization – they assigned you someone who was always watching you – had asked Henry if he'd had any spiritual revelations, Henry said that yeah, he'd felt the same sense of divine euphoria he did when he strapped someone to the hood of his pickup and drove into a wall – and that was it. Suddenly he was gone."

Henry and John were the least experienced climbers, but the youngest and most energetic of the crew. After the more experienced climbers had gone down, they were the last to descend, going down several hundred feet from one another to keep the long section of rope between the top and bottom anchor points stable.

"The space at the bottom," John remembers, "was mind-boggling." The swallows nested at the very bottom corners where the floor met the bell-shaped walls, creating little mud nests out at the edges, surrounded by 30 foot piles of bird shit.

The center of the cavern, on the other hand, was vast and eerily open, with just enough light making it down from 1,200 feet above to allow low-light plants to grow: moss and miniature banana trees. Occasionally, here and there, was a crack in the floor just big enough to pass through, signs perhaps of a deeper cave system below.

"Henry and I were super jazzed to be there," John said. "This was the most exciting thing we'd ever done. And we didn't want to leave." But the process of getting the 15 person expedition down had taken so long that by the time they reached the bottom, other members of the crew were preparing for the long climb back up: they needed to get out before darkness fell.

John and Henry were too excited to start preparing to go back. Instead, after walking around the massive cavern, they decided to explore some of the cracks in the floor they could get through.

"We aren't the first people in this cave, but we want to push these holes," he said. "Some of the largest caverns in history were found because some crazy nut squeezed his head through a hole in a cave wall barely big enough to fit it. We know this."

But by the time they got back, everyone else on the expedition was gone, and they realized how late it had gotten. They've got to get back. John started his climb, and realized as he did so that even a miniscule 1.7% stretch is massive on a 1200 foot rope: between the section of rope at the bottom and the first anchor point near the middle, it's like a rubber band: "I pulled maybe 20, 30, feet of rope before I got off the ground, and I'm going up and down and up and down on it until I was high enough off the ground to reach the first clip point, where it was more stable."

He kept climbing, Henry-about 50 feet below him. To mask his nervousness, he started telling jokes about getting the shits at just this moment.

Then, at about 600 feet off the ground, hanging over what once was believed to be the entrance to Hell, the sky darkened, the air shrieked, and a quarter of a million swallows made their descent into the cave.

The rope was hanging from a point on the curved ceiling about 50 feet in. They hung there, terrified, as birds by the thousands shot past them at 70 miles an hour. "If we'd been closer to the column, we would have died, beaten to death by the birds. But we were just off to the side and they didn't start spreading out into the cavern until a point below us, thank God. If we'd been lower ..."

Then, suddenly, the rope shook. Something had struck it a few hundred feet above. The shockwave ran through the rope as John and Henry clung on desperately, their hearts pounding. Something's happening to the rope ... and if it goes ... "they won't be able to retrieve our bodies for weeks," John said.

Eventually, when the massive column of birds had passed, they resumed their climb, in nearly pitch dark.

Two hundred feet higher up the rope, John found the body of a swallow with its beak impaled in the rope, its neck broken from the impact. The rope, made of a - diamond weave pattern specifically designed for expedition caving, was mostly intact.

He pulled the limp bird's body out of the rope and tossed it aside, down into the cavern below, and finished his ascent.

The next day, they moved on to another cave. Of course they did: this was the Suicide Club.

That was, unquestionably, a transformative experience. If you'd gone through that, there's a very good chance you would have changed: at the very least, it would define your sense of what is possible for the rest of your life. For many people, it would be psychomagical. I wish I had been there for it. Even though, let's be honest about this, I would have died at least twice.

And yet it was not a designed experience in any meaningful sense, certainly not the way we've been discussing it here. Rather, it was the act of finding a remote and interesting spot in the world, getting some people together, and saying "let's go there!"

Much in the way that experiencing art – either truly great art or any kind of art that is the exact right image at the exact right moment – can be a psychomagical experience, going someplace strange and wonderful, difficult and outside your experience, can be psychomagical. Doing something with people in such a place, even more so.

Often experiences of nature – precisely because they're not designed – don't end up doing anything specific within one's psyche. Just opening one up to a sense of possibility and wonder, which isn't nothing. And in fact can be quite significant. But they're like a cannonball, shot without aiming: undeniably powerful and affecting, but not likely to hit dead on.

Done for their own sake they can be amazing experiences, but they are a lazy form of "experience design." People have been camping since before they knew there was another option. But when you combine these extraordinary places with additional psychomagical components ... then you have one of the most powerful experiences people can ever have.

The San Francisco scene didn't discover this: tribal cultures doing ceremonies in sacred spaces may very well have been the beginning of culture as we know it. And Burning Man founder Larry Harvey liked to point out that there is a reason so many major religions have started in deserts: the vast empty spaces create a sense of overwhelming awe and possibility, while anything you do there takes on an added significance.

Did Burning Man, by far the most famous creation of the San Francisco underground art scene of the last 30 years, take advantage of this? Oh hell yes, they did.

Talk to any of Burning Man's founders and they'll all tell you a story about how, in the early days, they went out to the desert for the first time and that it was the power of the place, as much as anything they were doing there, which overwhelmed them, and changed the trajectory of their lives. You'll hear this over and over again.

If you simply want to have an impact, if you're just going for "that was impressive, and it moved me," the absolute simplest thing to do is take people out into nature. The more remote and unusual the better.

To further heighten the experience, have it be a mix of friends and strangers, and then have them overcome difficulties in pursuit of some common goal, however idiosyncratic.

The impact is potent, almost every time, and it's such a common approach that it's practically Cult Building 101: whether it's Burning Man, military units, messianic churches, corporate "team building," "flow workshops," "intentional communities" – this is your basic, can't fail, people's psyches will be surprised enough to open at least a little and they'll bond over it. It's basic technique.

So much so that, frankly, past a certain point it's just lazy, so lazy that "we're in the wilderness, doing a few team building exercises" becomes a substitute for actual experience design. It becomes what you do when you don't have any real ideas.

It's when you use these environments as a setting for something interesting in its own right that the power of the place begins to really work in your favor, becoming not a lazy design element but a crucial component of something bigger than itself.

Burning Man, after all, didn't rest on the fact that "hey, we're in a desert!" Larry and Michael Mikel ("Danger Ranger") and Crimson Rose, in particular, were absolute geniuses at creating things to do in that environment which heightened and channeled that sense of awe and wonder ... and which targeted it more clearly to the unconscious of the participants. [1] Building, raising, and burning a giant wooden man became the center of the world, something they all did communally. It grew from there.[2]

Many other events in the San Francisco Art Underground were doing versions of the same thing, and would continue to for decades. Most of these events were trying to be far more exclusive than Burning Man, operated under a code of secrecy, and frankly weren't nearly as interesting, so I'm not going to mention them. Of the better recurring events that I'm not going to mention specifically, one still going at least as I write this, insists that people attending refer to it as a "Tupperware party" when they might be around the uninitiated, so that people from outside the community who have not been vetted never even know its name. I can't tell you how obnoxious I found that.

Another, even more secretive organization currently operating– one which once banned people from its events for even vaguely alluding to it cryptically in public – makes a regular practice of infiltrating spaces the way the Suicide Club and the Cacophony Society used to do. A few months before I started writing this they brought people to a lake, "liberated" a bunch of boats, and sent people in boats out into the lake to participate in a series of quests and scavenger hunts until just before dawn. How do you hide items on a lake in a manner that they can still be found? It's an interesting question isn't it, one which I invite you to consider on your own.

Perhaps the largest and most public event of this kind (besides Burning Man) to emerge out of this scene, however – it's been going on for 12 years now – is "Camp Tipsy," the brainchild of the aforementioned Chicken John and later managed by the SFIOP.

The premise of Camp Tipsy is deceptively simple: over a long weekend, it's held on a lake where you can go swimming or boating. The organizers bring almost two metric tons – literally – of junk to the edge of the lake. All kinds of discarded cast-offs from machines, from product packaging, from toys, from vehicles ... anything clean that you can imagine they have in this junk pile. They also bring tools. Lots of tools. And anyone who comes to Camp Tipsy can spend their days building boats out of garbage.

Why would you do that, you ask? Well, clearly you have

never seen a boat built out of garbage, let alone ridden on one. It's amazing: a janky, rickety, impossible thing – like something out of a sci-fi novel - that somehow still manages to float, to carry people impossibly over the water. The best moments, the very best, are when you're actually piloting a boat made of garbage over a river system or the coastline, and you pull it in to a marina: and there you set it next to the massive, multi-million dollar yachts of the elite – giant status-building money pits that are supposed to impress everyone who sees them. Because somehow, when you park a boat built out of garbage alongside the row of yachts – an absolutely unique vessel that could probably never be put together twice even if you have the exact same parts, which you don't, and which cost all of $70 to build while drinking with your friends – it is the boat built out of garbage that no one can take their eyes off of. That gathers all the attention and interest, revealing that the giant floating money pits that are supposed to build up the status of their owners far more than they are supposed to be fun on the water all kind of look alike, and are utterly boring in their conformity.

And yes, if you go to Camp Tipsy, then you will also see – much like at Burning Man – amateurs attempting impossible feats of engineering. Hot tub boats. Ferris wheel boats, day care center boats on which people put their children and send them off into the lake ... these marvels, and more, have all been done. But the essence of the thing, the purest and best form, is not to arrive with a diagram and pre-fab parts in hand, but to walk up to the pile of junk with a bunch of your friends, see what it has to offer, and imagine your boat right then and there with found materials. Then build it.

Sometimes it won't float. Often, in fact. And that is nothing but hilarious too. This is one of those times when failure can be far more spectacular than success.

During the day, you and your friends build boats out of junk – sometimes with the help of complete strangers who have been doing this for years and are remarkably good at it – and sail them on the water. At night, there is a large bonfire, and an impromptu stage, and often baffling musical and variety acts perform until the wee hours of the morning.

On the last day, there is a flotilla of boats, where everything that actually floated is sailed past a lookout point for everyone to see – by far the most bizarre parade you'll see in your life – and stupid prizes are awarded, and everyone can't stop laughing.

Now this is a case where the intrinsic beauty of the spot itself is relatively minor – the lake it's held on is, frankly, nothing all that special – but what they do with the space is so amazing that it takes on a complete life of its own. You can see how it utilizes many of the approaches we've discussed so far:

- It's real, not a fiction – you're really making the boats and really sailing them on the water. This is really happening.

- You make meaningful choices: there's nothing prefab here, it's all an act of imagination, sparked by what happens when you're confronted with a lake, a pile of junk, and tools.
- It is not safe/benign. On the one hand, it has no fatalities in its history. On the other hand, you're using power tools to build a boat out of questionable materials and hoping it will float. The potential for disaster is high.
- For all that Camp Tipsy has a format, it is never the same thing every year, because the garbage is never the same and the people who come are forced to create something new and unique every time, it is filled with moments that can never be repeated.
- It has a clearly delineated space where things happen, both in the campground and – particularly – in the lake. The lake and its shore are where the magic really happens.
- There's not a lot of "art," even in the underground sense, but it's absolutely filled with play and ritual.

... and so on. The result is something truly spectacular and utterly stupid at once. And it would be far less affecting if everyone just gathered around the lake and had a party. Even if it were a much more beautiful lake. Which illustrates the point: remote natural beauty can be psychomagical on its own, but experience design elements like these are often far more impactful on the kind of experience people have.

The same principle can apply to urban environments as well, though those obviously lend themselves to a very different aesthetic than natural beauty. Indeed, while John Law is no longer climbing down thousand foot ropes into caves, he has become a major figure in the global "urban explorer" movement, where people travel to lost urban environments under cover of darkness – vacant hotels, decaying amusement parks, sewer systems, Catskills resorts that have been closed for decades – and see what is otherwise invisible to us. And like awe-inspiring natural beauty, these environments turn the raw materials of the world around us – things we are completely used to in their habitual setting – into strange and compelling vistas to explore.

Exploring new urban landscapes is compelling and even psychomagical on its own. Turning them into designed experiences can be epically so.

A legendary example of this was the Night Heron bar in NYC, which San Franciscans just couldn't stop talking about.

The brainchild of artist N.D. Austin, The Night Heron worked like this: a friend would give you a pocket watch, tell you to report to a certain corner on a certain night, and then call a number on the inside of the watch.

And that was it. That was all you knew.

The right time and place was a street corner near decrepit buildings; if you showed up and called, you would be led by voice instructions and a combination of mysterious figures into one of the abandoned buildings, through it, and eventually over to another one, where you'd climb up to the roof. At the roof was a water tower, and when you arrived, the trap door to the water tower opened – and from it light emerged, along with music, laughter, and clinking glasses.

Squeeze your way up into that small space, the equivalent of a large elevator going up several floors, and you'd discover a gorgeously furnished classic jazz-era style cocktail bar – inside the water tower on the top of a decrepit building – where you could now drink and play for 90 minutes. You had discovered something wondrous, nearly impossible, that almost no one else in New York knew about. On your way out, you were given the opportunity to buy a pocket watch to give to someone else, provided you tell them nothing about the experience that awaited them ...

That's awesome, right? And one of the best parts – one of the things that made it so exceptional – was precisely that it was a genuine act of urban exploration. This wasn't a legal shop, let alone something advertised and zoned: they genuinely invaded a decrepit property with an absentee landlord and set up an illegal speakeasy in its water tower, and you had to follow in their footsteps to reach it. That's a perfect use of an urban environment to create a unique experience – but the experience itself wasn't just "exploration." It's what they used exploration to achieve that made it so exceptional. The ways in which it utilized the other design elements made it a truly unforgettable series of moments.

If you want to start a cult, and you're really lazy, just use these design elements: take a bunch of people, preferably some friends and some strangers, out to a beautiful but remote location; give them a common goal and have them face challenges together. Something will happen.

But the whole point of the last 30 years of the San Francisco underground is that given a beautiful remote location and some people, you can also do so much more, and make it so much better.

Chapter 20:
Honesty is the Best Policy

Without really discussing it, we have been going through examples of two different kinds of experience: those created spontaneously (like my rituals with Robin, and in the magical bar), and those which involve a great deal of planning and forethought (like Camp Tipsy, the Jejune Institute, and The Night Heron).

Spontaneous and planned experiences are indeed very different, but the most important thing is what they have in common. Both involve the exact same design elements discussed here. You're shooting for the same things.

For the design element illustrated in this chapter, I'm going to give two examples of the way experiences can be created: one that was completely spontaneous, the other meticulously planned out. They were extremely different to go through, but both were powerful because at heart they were doing the same thing: asking challenging but honest questions, and going where the answers took them.

Here's the first:

After presenting at an academic symposium in Switzerland, a group of attendees went to Gruyere to tour the H.R. Giger museum. Afterwards, some of us went out to eat, while some of us went to the Giger bar, just across the street.

To sit in the H. R. Giger bar is to sit in the belly of the beast. Named after and designed by the legendary artist, the walls are all the arching spinal columns of some great monstrosity. Some of the chairs are also bones, though it's hard to say of what, while others are some kind of pustule that, were they not made of stone, might burst at any moment. The floors are a strange kind of coded hieroglyphic.

I was sitting alone inside the monstrous bar, writing and drinking the house cocktail – an adequate citrusy gin whose disturbing electric green color caused awe and puzzlement in the lesser souls who only ordered beers.

"Debra" sat down next to me. "Does it taste like it looks?" she asked in her thick accent.

"Not even a little."

I'd met Debra at the symposium, and on the first day she'd decided that she liked me. "You're my favorite," she'd told me. "It's your spirit. The way it comes through in your smile." She'd given me a gift: a piece of flint from the desert where a Regional Burning Man event is held. "With flint, you can make something out of it. Or, if you have another piece, you can strike them together to make fire. But, to get another piece of this flint, you would have to visit us."

Sitting together, I told her that I am taking notes for a series of art pieces that I do, about experiences in bars. I told her that whatever happens next, whatever she says or does, I am going to write about it. And then I asked her to tell me the way in which the museum filled with Giger's surreal and disturbing art had most reached her. What it had most triggered in her?

She nodded. Thought about it. Took a deep breath.

"It made me horny," she said.

I nodded. "Really?" I said, carefully intending to keep any incredulity or judgment out of my voice.

"Yes, it did," she said. "Not all of it. Some of it was not … but some of it, much of it, oh yes. I was really feeling horny in there. I was surprised myself."

I wasn't surprised, because despite the very disturbing nature of Giger's work – life converted into a biomechanical dystopian hellscape – it had seemed like a lot of people were reacting that way. Actually, a lot of women. Enough that, in one particularly elegant room with gorgeous oil paintings of monstrous naked figures engaged in inhuman sex acts and brutal displays involving machines, I had told the assembled group of mostly women, mostly friends, "Okay, let's play 'Hot or Not!'" And after the laughter had faded, some of the girls had jumped into it eagerly. Pointing at some of the terrifying figures and saying "hot!" and treating others to a "not!"

It had gone on for a while, and made everyone a little uncomfortable.

"What do you think that means?" I asked Debra.

"That I have a dark side," she responded. "And that I don't know it so well."

I nodded, thought about it, and leaned forward. "We have just enough time," I said, "that I'm going to make you an offer."

"Yes?"

"Do you want to go back to the Giger museum, find a secluded corner, and make out?"

She started. "Ohhhhhh ..." she said. Her lips pursed. "There are a lot of security cameras ..."

"Yes."

"I ..." she was obviously struggling with this. Fear, interest, uncertainty, repression, curiosity, a lifetime of whatever issues she had around the erotic, and her dark side, all coming up at once, as she debated whether to make the rash choice to explore something she'd felt keenly.

And I'm going to stop the story there, both for privacy

concerns (also because I can be such a tease) and to make a point I've been trying to illustrate before: whatever happened next, either the make-out session or the refusal, isn't the important part. Isn't the experience. Giving her the choice, a choice that was both real and psychologically fraught, was the point. You're not trying to create the ending, to establish the perfect make-out session – you're trying to create the choice she gets to/has to make. (Engineered Disperfection.) Her wrestling with her dark side, and with herself, in a concrete, actionable, way, leading to a choice that could have true consequences, is the heart of the psychomagical experience created.

Whatever she did next, as long as it was honest, would be significant for her. The choice was where the psychomagic was.

(I mean, I like to think I'm a good kisser, but would I call it *magical?* No, no I would not. Although there was this one thing that happened in the Louvre ... you know what? Nevermind, that's for a very different book.)

And it's impossible to prepare for. This was a unique, could only happen here and now moment, never repeatable, that had to be done spontaneously. And it happened because two people were being uncomfortably honest with each other.

Now let's take a look at another, much more complicated, example.

This is going to take a lot of set-up. But you'll see the point.

There was a period in the 1990s when legendary showman and experience impresario Chicken John – a man who will gladly give you the shirt off someone else's back – was living in his truck.

His truck was also the source of his income at the time. He was hauling trash. He'd go to jobs, pick up all their trash, and haul it to the dump. As part of the deal, they also gave him the fees for putting their trash in the dump. Which meant that Chicken would often try to keep the extra money by holding on to the trash until late at night, when he'd circle around San Francisco looking for open dumpsters to put the trash in. Which, of course, is illegal, but if you think that bothered the maestro behind the Circus Redickuless, then you haven't been paying attention.

Once the garbage was in the dumpster, he could sleep in his truck again. No dumpster, no sleep – or sleep in the cab of his truck, not the bed, which is almost as bad as no sleep at all.

One cold and windy San Francisco night, Chicken was desperate. He needed money, badly, and he had taken a big job, so his truck was absolutely full and he really wanted to sleep and he was circling around the San Francisco streets, looking for open dumpsters with enough space for his massive load of garbage.

Then finally, on a side street where no one's watching, he spies his holy grail: three giant dumpsters that are definitely not full. He pulled up, parked his truck, and got ready to go to work.

Now, it is actually quite hard to load big bags of trash into these dumpsters, because they are designed specifically to make it inconvenient for guys like Chicken. So he's got a lot of work ahead of him. There's a lot of lifting and heaving involved. He figures he's going to start with a cigarette. The only trouble is, it's really windy and cold. So, since nothing's sticking out of the dumpsters, he goes in one to light his cigarette and take his smoke. So he climbs up and over and in.

The first thing he realizes, inside, is that this giant dumpster isn't empty. It's got furniture in it. Really nice furniture. Maybe even antique furniture. In perfect condition. It's weird, it's almost like he's in a museum or something. Somebody just took all this really nice furniture and put it in a giant dumpster, and he has no idea why.

Then, in the glow of his cigarette lighter, he spies the book.

A giant leather book. Like a scrapbook. Really thick. The covers far apart.

He's fascinated. Compelled. He opens it up.

The first page contains the birth certificate of a woman

named Margaret Rucker. The last page contains the certificate of her death. In between, in clippings and keepsakes and scraps, is the record of her life.

What happened? How did Margaret, probably her furniture, and this book – her whole life! – end up in a dumpster, waiting to go to the trash heap?

He has no idea, but he knows what he has to do. He spends the rest of the night taking all the furniture out of the dumpster and putting the garbage into it. He's going to sleep in his cab tonight, then sell the furniture tomorrow – he needs the money. But the book he's keeping. He's keeping Margaret out of the trash. She's never going back.

Chicken is obsessed by this book. Margaret, born in 1907, came from a moneyed family out of a town near Seattle. She was a published poet. Her poetry is actually pretty good. She married a military man, became "Margaret Smith," and after WWII he became an admiral. She had two kids. Then, one day, according to a newspaper report meticulously saved in the book, he excused himself from the breakfast table, walked into his room, returned with his service revolver, and blew his own head off.

No one knows why.

Margaret went on, raised her children, and eventually died in a nursing home in 1959. Her death certificate was in the book.

And someone preserved every detail, and somehow she still ended up here.

How can this happen? The question haunts Chicken. He starts showing the book to everyone he knows, and asking them what they think. Then, being Chicken, he turns what obsesses him into a show: he throws events in which he gets on stage and explains what this book is and invites people up to read parts of Margaret's life aloud to the crowd, her poetry, her wedding announcement, the newspaper article about her husband's suicide. And at the end of each show, he opens the question up to the crowd: what do you think happened? What is this? What do we make of it?

The shows are amazing. Unforgettable. But then, working on a job at a place doing a thing, Chicken does something stupid, injures himself, gets really sick, and thinks he's going to die.

He's going through his stuff trying to figure out who to leave it to, and when he reaches the Margaret book he has a problem: he can't think of anyone who will not, eventually, put it back in the trash. Oh, they'll hold on to it for a while, sure, but apartments are small and rent is expensive and eventually someone will move and Margaret won't move with them.

That can't happen. Chicken will not let that happen. But he doesn't know what to do.

So, Chicken being Chicken, he turned his problem into a show. He invites everybody he knows to the final Margaret show before he dies of his internal injuries, and he goes through the book, through the Margaret show, and at the end of the show he invites everyone to come and take a piece of the book. To bring a piece of Margaret's life home with them. This way, he reasons, some part of her will always be preserved by people, even if the book itself is gone.

It's deeply touching and moving and affecting – an event with life and death stakes that could never happen again. The only problem is, Chicken doesn't die. He recovers. And then, of course, he really, really, wishes he hadn't given all the pieces of that book away. Because it's never coming back.

But ... but ... he does have a fallback position. He wanted to keep records of Margaret's life, so he'd had a bunch of the more significant documents digitally scanned, and he still has the images. So he's got that. He has a British woman record voiceovers of all the text, and creates a multimedia slide show. It's not the same as the full book, but he can still tell the story of Margaret's life with visual aids and evidence, and it's still as beautiful as it is puzzling. But time moves on and he gradually does the show less and less often, in part because no answers have been forthcoming.

Then one day Chicken's close friend and occasional collaborator, the Seattle area musician Jason Webly, is in town with his friend Amanda Palmer, and the three of them are on Mission Street, and Jason is explaining to Chicken that he's actually not really from Seattle, he just told people he was, because he's really from a small town outside of Seattle called Everett, and it's much cooler to tell people you're a "Seattle musician" than it is to have to explain where and what Everett is. But he's stopped caring and now he's going to be honest about it.

And Chicken stopped in the middle of Mission street, his jaw agape. "I know someone from Everett that I need you to meet," he told Jason.

Because Margaret was from Everett. That was the small town she grew up in.

So Chicken takes Jason and Amanda back to his place and shows them the Margaret show. And when he's finished, Jason's jaw has dropped.

"Chicken," Jason says, "Amanda and I were just sitting on her tomb less than 24 hours ago!"

Because, you see, the Rucker family didn't just live in Everett, they helped found it. They're that family most places have whose name was on everything. And their family crypt (according to Jason, I haven't seen it - I wasn't there for any of this yet, and am relating it as it was told to me) is a giant pyramid in the middle of the local graveyard, with different levels that are climbable – and obviously the giant climbable pyramid in the graveyard is a place that the local teenagers go at night. Like Jason used to do when he was growing up there.

And so, as he was giving Amanda a tour of his hometown the day before, of course they'd gone to the graveyard and climbed the Rucker family crypt. Like you do.

And here, now, in San Francisco, he'd just met one of its inhabitants. And he had so many questions. What the hell had happened? How HAD Margaret's life been meticulously preserved, then thrown away?

Jason got a copy of the Margaret files from Chicken, and went to the Everett town historian to see if he could clear this up. But it turned out that Chicken had known more about Margaret Rucker's life than the historian did - the guy was thrilled to get this treasure trove of information handed to him. But he didn't have any answers for Jason.

Jason, however, was now as obsessed as Chicken had been - but was a better researcher. Plus the internet had advanced significantly for historical stalking since the late 90s. Even so, new information was slow to come in, and the central question remained unanswered.

But Jason was obsessed, and, Jason being Jason, when he gets obsessed with something, he puts on a show.

Do you see a pattern here? Because this pattern is the point. More on that later.

Jason's "Margaret" show was not like Chicken's. Where Chicken had simply taken the details of his discovery, and the facts of Margaret's life, put them before you, and asked you to speculate, Jason got a bunch of his favorite local musicians together, gave them the information about Margaret's life, and then asked each one to either compose an original song about Margaret or to set one of her poems to music.

The result was a concert of original compositions about Margaret's life, at the end of which everyone in the audience was given a candle, and with their lit candles they walked from the Everett auditorium to the cemetery, and all sat on Margaret's mausoleum, candles alight.

It was an overwhelming success, and it got people asking: "Jason, you've got a whole bunch of original songs here, when are you going to produce an album?" So, eventually, he figured: sure, we'll produce "Margaret" the album. And all the other musicians and composers agreed and got on board.

So Jason Webly produced a "Margaret" CD, and of course if there's an album dropping then there needs to be a release party concert, and – hell – at that point there might as well be a tour, and so Jason and all the musicians set up a "Margaret, the tour," based on "Margaret, the concert," based on "Margaret, the album," which was based on "Margaret, the other concert," which was based on "Margaret, the show," which was based on "Margaret, the person," whose life Chicken found in a dumpster.

And then ... yes, and then ... something happened that everybody should have seen coming, but somehow nobody did.

Members of the Rucker family, which is still an actual family in Everett, Washington, and whose tomb everyone had been climbing on, showed up at the album release concert.

It was a "holy fuck" moment. What were they going to say? Did they bring a lawyer? Have a cease and desist letter in hand?

(I need to emphasize here that this is a conversation I was not present for – and I have not spoken to the Rucker family directly. I am reporting what Chicken, Jason, and other people I knew said about the conversation at the time, and what happened as a matter of public record.)

The Rucker family representative (I am told) came with a story. Margaret had had two sons, with names too generic for Jason to track down. After Margaret died, one of her children finished the scrapbook of his mother's life, took in her things, and moved to San Francisco.

By the 90s, this son of Margaret was dying of AIDS, and his conservative family in Everett, scandalized by his lifestyle, cut him off. When he died they told a local company to simply get rid of everything. All of it.

And so Margaret had ended up in the trash.

Then the Rucker family representative said that the existence of this show, this concert, this album, had forced the family to reckon with that decision, and realize it had been wrong. They were grateful that this secret had been unearthed, and would try to make amends – among other things – by starting a poetry scholarship for women, in honor of Margaret.

There would be no cease and desist letter. Only a quiet, humble, thanks.

The show went on. The tour began.

And here's where my direct involvement picks up. Because when the show got to San Francisco, Chicken needed help. Marketing, people working the doors, ushering the crowds, everything.

I helped with tickets on the night of the show, Dec. 20, 2014, but more significantly, I helped get an article about the whole thing written up in local media. As a result, a man named Rod turned up at the show that night.

I remember the night so clearly. I was deeply depressed, desperately unhappy, all but suicidal – and now I can't remember why, only how painful it was. I plastered a huge phony smile on my face as I did schtick, collecting tickets at the door, trying to get a laugh. Whenever I was let off shift, I slipped into a dark corner and sobbed. God, it kills me that just over four years later I can't even remember why.

Then the show started, and it was a night of heart-staggering beauty. They recounted Margaret's life and performed their music and the whole crowd was swept up in the moment – everyone I've ever met who attended that show talks about it this way – and I realized, as they recounted Margaret's story in song, that art really does have power over death. That realization hit me, and I was no longer depressed, and I was weeping for different reasons.

And then the show stopped. Jason and Chicken stopped the show right in the middle, and called out to Rod in the audience. Rod was Margaret's grandson, and he'd heard about the show through the article I'd arranged, and had come to be part of this experience.

"I hope you like it," Jason told him from the stage. "Because, and I just realized this, we did it all for you."

Art has power over death. It can't be literally true, and yet, somehow, in that moment, I and a thousand other people all experienced it.

* * *

And I wish the story ended there. That's where it should end. That's where it ends for me. But it has a much more complicated coda.

As they learned more about Margaret, as the questions finally began getting answers, Jason and Chicken became convinced that Margaret killed herself: that she stayed alive only as long as she felt her children still needed her, and then immediately left this world. And Chicken further became convinced that Margaret's husband didn't kill himself in front of her – she shot him and claimed it was an inexplicable suicide. To my knowledge Chicken has no actual evidence for any of this: it just seems much more likely to him.

But between suicide and murder it means that Chicken John, the man who found Margaret in the trash, and pulled her out, and revived her life with endless questioning, is done with her now. He no longer even talks about her.

Jason does not seem nearly so disillusioned, and last time I checked was even still on good terms with the Rucker family. But he also came to wonder: was bringing Margaret back to life the right thing to do? Was putting her on stage? Art has power over death, but should we use it? What if Margaret wanted to be forgotten? He composed a song, on the album, in which the chorus is a back and forth: "Leave me in my pyramid/at the bottom of a garbage bin."

There isn't going to be another tour, or another concert, or another show.

But me? I tell this story. I tell it all the time. Chicken has asked me not to, but I refuse. "Let me tell you about Margaret," I say, "and the power that art has over death." And it inspires others to live more deeply.

What, did you think this was going to have an unambiguously happy ending? What have I been telling you about psychomagical experiences not being benign? Being dangerous? You don't get to pick how it ends for someone: we were all changed by this experience, but not the same way. That's what happens. Playing with life and death always involves rolling dice.

But you're getting the real thing here: this is what pure, uncut, 100% honesty looks like.

* * *

It's easy, especially when you're throwing a big massive event, to make things too complicated. To lose sight of where the magic really comes from.

The point of those two stories is that both were the result of paying attention, of listening, and then asking a painfully honest question, and getting an honest answer back, and following it wherever it leads.

Too often, when someone's trying to create an experience, they add flash on top of flash, effect on top of effect, illusion on top of illusion. And sure, that can be very impressive. But the most powerful experiences you have ever had in your life were honest. Were real.

The right – or very wrong – person asking "do you want to kiss me?" can be more affecting than a billion dollars of special effects.

Look at the stories we've talked about: in case after case it worked because someone was asked a very honest question, and got an honest answer. The very first story I told you – about the magical bar – worked because I asked people "what's in your heart," and they told me, and they got it. If I don't ask, or if they lie, it doesn't work. The more honest we are, the better. This dynamic is repeated, over and over again. The Mystic Midway asked people to tell them stories, and the more people reached down deep to reply, the more amazing the experience was for everyone. Everything about the Circus Redickuless was absolutely true, and the question asked at the end "will you run away and join the circus" demanded a radical honesty in response; Splitsville was painfully real. Even in fictional situations, we found a way to make the choices real and honest.

This sounds a lot like one of our first design elements, "create non-fiction," and it is. It's clearly related to that. But this takes it a significant step further: don't just be non-fiction, be *honest*.

When in doubt, when you're struggling to figure out how to make this work: be more honest. Push the truth as far as you can, even into new territory, without ever lying. Turn it into a show, by all means, create engineered disperfection - out of which even more truth comes. Presentation counts. But never lie. Not about anything that matters, and even less than that, if you can help it.

If you simply can't think of what to do when designing an experience, find an interesting question, a genuinely interesting question that opens up other questions and issues, or something that you're honestly grappling with and struggling with, and turn the process of asking it or struggling with it into a show. An open-ended show, because if you prescribe what the ending has to be in advance, then you're already lying. You're not really asking, or struggling – you're performing. Nothing wrong with that as far as it goes, but that's not what this is.

Let the complexity emerge out of honesty, rather than be imposed on top of it. Follow honesty far enough, and things almost always get weird and profound.

And if, in an immediate moment, you want to know how to access psychomagic – be honest. Find the funniest, most artful, most delightful, most inviting, symbolically potent, way to be as honest as you possibly can, and use it to push yourself to be even more honest than that. That's often what it is.

Chapter 21:
Let's Review

One day my friend Elliotte met me for lunch.

"I want to give you something," she said, "but I need your absolute discretion."

"Of course," I said.

"Absolute," she said again, "discretion. Do you trust me? Can I trust you?"

What a strange question for someone who has uprooted her life on my advice to be asking.

"Yes," I said. Perhaps a little too quickly.

"Okay," she said. She reached into her wallet, pulled something out, and handed me ... a blank credit card.

It was a pale white. There was no name on it. All the numbers that a credit card normally has were zeros.

But the back informed me, in elaborate script, that I had received an invitation to visit the "San Francisco House of the Latitude," and offered a web address, and a code.

"What is it?" I asked.

"That's all you get to know," she said. "I'm also bound by absolute discretion."

She was serious, so we went on with our lunch, talking about everything but what had really just happened between us. Which is perhaps the worst kind of lunch that anybody like me can have, even if it's pleasant and fun.

As soon as I got home, I went to the website listed on the card. It was a portal for something called "the Latitude Society" – and I didn't have login credentials. But there was a space where I could enter a code like the one I had on the back of my card. And when I did that, a page appeared on which I could make an appointment to visit a to-be-disclosed location.

I selected a date and time from the available options, and then was given instructions: I was to arrive alone at a Mission district location within a five minute window, and use my card to open the door. If I arrived outside of the five minute window, the door would not open. If I brought anyone, or told anyone, everything would be forfeit. I was not to arrive early and linger outside of the location, waiting for my appointment time, as that would attract unwanted attention. I was to let them know at a particular email address if I had any of a list of infirmities, including: heart problems, knee problems, claustrophobia, and epilepsy. Absolute discretion was required: If I did not demonstrate it, everything else would be forfeit.

The day of my appointment, I arrived early to scout the location. Of course I didn't linger in front of it – but I walked past it on the other side of the street. Then checked out the block around it. Then walked right past it, to get a good look, before settling down at a café a block or two away. There was, it turned out, nothing to see. Just a nondescript building, utterly blank, deep in the Mission – incredibly expensive but not yet gentrified. The door had no sign, just a card reader on the outside.

You need to understand, if you don't have this context already, that space is absurdly expensive in San Francisco. Back when the Suicide Club was active, it was easy to find abandoned buildings and cheap real estate ... and that was a whole different world. When the movie "Milk," a biopic about San Francisco Supervisor Harvey Milk, played in San Francisco in 2008, I saw it in the Castro Theater. And the murder, the homophobia, the police brutality ... none of that shocked the people in the theater. It was old hat. Blasé. But the notion that, back in the 1970s, a guy could move to San Francisco and pay for an apartment with his welfare check? That got gasps. The whole theater gaped at the screen, wondering what strange magic this was.

By this point any organization that wasn't pulling in serious bank was scrambling desperately for space, blowing their budget on leaky broom closets just big enough to fit a desk. So for the Latitude Society – whatever it was – to have an actual building, in one of the most rapidly gentrifying areas of the city, was already making an impression on me and all the other artist-types trying to find wall space on which to hang a painting or an open floor on which to read a poem. In this city real estate is power, and the Latitude Society was flexing its muscles. Who were these people? How the fuck did they do that?

The clock ticked. I got up, and walked back to the building, just in time for my five minute window to open. I ran my card through the scanner. The door unlocked. I stepped in.

Inside was pitch black, except for a throbbing red light overhead. The room the light revealed, in fragments of moments, fading in and out, was also black and featureless, except for a way forward. Through a curtain, into a wall ... and down a hole.

I tried to examine my surroundings, but there was nothing to examine – and the pulsing red light was maddening. I hate to leap before I look, but I wasn't going to find anything here but a headache. I plunged into the hole in the wall ...

... and slid down, down, and around, and down, over and over again. It was a spiral shaped slide, taking me what seemed like two full floors (or more?) below ground.

I landed in a kind of waiting room, in which there was a wall filled with elaborate safe deposit boxes on one side, and a locked door on the other – and a note, informing me that

I needed to trust completely, and it was time to leave all the things of the world above behind. The door would only open when I had put everything in my pockets – phone, wallet, keys, everything – into one of the safe deposit boxes, and locked it shut behind me.

This scared me more than jumping down the slide had. But there was no choice. There was no way back – I'm not John Law, I doubted I could climb back up two floors.

I opened a safe deposit box, and placed everything in my pockets inside. I closed it. It locked, and ... a moment later ... the door opened. I walked through.

I passed a strange scene against a wall, a kind of hologram of a mystic figure walking against a cityscape. I crawled through a passageway into a beautiful library of elaborately bound books – all empty, including one set on a lectern on the floor. But when I approached the lectern, a hidden projector created images on the books, and a woman's voice began to tell me a story about an island, hidden away from the world for all of history: the origin story of the Latitude Society.

From the library, I walked into an elaborate parlor with a bar of crystal decanters, and there I found instructions on what to do when I returned to the outside world: I was to follow certain signs embedded in the street to a secret location, in order to spy the workings of some kind of enemy agents, and report my findings to a number when I was done. A basket had my possessions in it. I took them, walked through a long hallway and … somehow … walked out of an entirely different building than the one I'd entered.

Holy fuck. Who were these people? HOW did they do that? Had there always been a tunnel under these buildings? Had they created one? What was going ON?

That question was far more interesting to me than the need to find secret marks on San Francisco streets – planting those for game purposes is an old and worn-down trick in the art scene – and finding the building to observe, from a great distance away, something strange and supernatural walking through a series of windows.

I reported what I found, and was given instructions to go to a local bar. There, upon identifying myself, I was given a key. Another clue unlocked the address. This building was a multi-use theater and office space. My key opened the outer door, and I explored the various levels until I found another gate I could open, and past that, a room.

A room filled with arcade games.

A token I'd received in an earlier building entitled me to one play of any game. I chose one that I'd loved to play as a kid, and started spinning my character around, shooting things. After a minute of play, the screen froze, then the lines on the screen re-arranged themselves into a face. An angry face, which spoke to me, giving me code words, and warning me of something terrible that was to come.

I left the arcade, leaving my key behind where instructed, left the building, and returned home. I went to the Latitude Society's website, absolutely buzzing from the experience – SUCH an amazing induction into a new world, even if parts of it had felt slightly stretched. I couldn't wait to discover what came next. I typed my code words into the site, and sure enough: I was asked to create a user profile.

I had succeeded. I had cracked the code.

A whole new world awaited me.

I could not wait to begin my new life.

Except ... except ...

Okay, let me walk you through this.

Once you were inside the site, you watched a video about the history of the Latitude Society, and the foundation of the San Francisco chapter, and it was ... okay. It was okay. It would have made a really sharp Kickstarter video. But as a further introduction to the inner workings of a secret society with magic in its deep history? It was ... a Kickstarter video. It claimed to be a message from the Latitude Society, which it religiously maintained was a real thing, but it seemed like somebody playing a game about a secret society would make, rather than a secret society describing itself.

And ... okay ... whatever. Nobody does everything perfectly. But the experience was on shakier ground. The experiences they'd given me were amazing, but the story they were telling about themselves kept missing that high bar. And story is only so important sometimes, but they were the ones who kept pushing it, making it front and center. That seemed like a problem brewing for down the line.

Then I went to my homepage on their site, and my heart just sank. To the pit of my stomach. To the floor. To the basement. Six feet under the earth.

There was a merch section. Full of "Latitude Society" tchotchkes to buy. Which on its own is distressing – but the problem was that they were knick-knacks that violated the whole spirit of the premise: "Absolute Discretion" t-shirts. Latitude Society cufflinks. Hats. Things that no actual organization with its stated history and mission would ever contemplate having. Ever.

The first thing they did after induction – the FIRST thing! - was send you to a shopping page with no connection to the story or mission of the organization at all. Bad enough that it existed: to put it so far forward was untenable.

I couldn't trust them any longer. I'd been willing to

jump down a tunnel into darkness and wander into strange buildings on their behalf; I'd been willing to give up my wallet and leave it in their keeping. But that was when I'd believed they were committed to a higher experience. Now I could never be sure that anything they asked me to do wouldn't end in a souvenir t-shirt.

I looked through the rest of the site, just to see what was there. But I never really came back, and I never engaged with anything they did again.

That's not how everyone felt, however.

The purpose of the Latitude's private social network was not just to notify you about their own events and activities, and to sell you stupid shit: it was to allow people to engage in activities that created the Latitude Society. From their home page, people could contribute recollections of their experiences in the Latitude Society; they could form guilds to "research the history of the Society; and they could create their own events, sometimes using Latitude Society resources as locations.

The reward for these contributions was to be invited deeper into the designed experiences of the Latitude Society, like the induction we'd all gone through to be here.

If enough people got active, the organizers would have created a kind of hybrid organization: active "amateur" members who created much of the basic events and cultural development work, and then were able to experience the exquisitely curated experiences that the "professional" members (paid staff) produced for them.

It was an interesting model, and in other contexts than this it's worth discussing. As an experience itself I was repulsed, but a lot of people – a lot of very good and talented people – were pulled in. They did the work. They had an amazing time. And for a short while, it looked like the Latitude Society was going to be an underground powerhouse, dwarfing anything anyone had done since Burning Man.

Then, suddenly and spectacularly, it all collapsed.

My understanding is that books are being written about this series of events all on their own. And they should be. But here, in a nutshell, is my observation of what happened. (Remember, I was present, and am close friends with several of the people involved, but I was not a part of any of these events: I was watching from the outside, eating popcorn, and having that peculiar sense of delight that comes over you as you see other people's dreams that you have turned your back on collapse. "Yep, I called it," you say to yourself, smirking, as you wince at the loss experienced by people you love. I'm not proud. But I had snacks, booze, and a safe distance.)

The Latitude Society consumed enormous resources to keep up. It could have been done in another city for cheap, or in San Francisco in the 80s. But here and now it was a beast to keep running. The store that had so repulsed me was intended to be a key part of a revenue model that would keep it self-sustaining. People needed to buy shit in order to keep the lights on. And in fact, to invite new people into the Latitude Society – as Elliotte had invited me – required a unique card, and to get those cards you had to pay a fee. So the idea was that members would generate revenues by buying Latitude shit and inviting new members in, who would themselves buy Latitude shit and invite new members in.

Could it have worked? Maybe. Did it? Apparently not even close.

The first problem was that members simply weren't buying enough shit from the store. Even though a lot of people hadn't been as repulsed by it as I was, none of them had actually come in for the t-shirts. None of them were in it for the branding – and in fact the branding ran directly contrary to the story they'd signed up for. I think of this as a huge missed opportunity: I think a lot of people, myself included, would have shelled out cash for items of beauty that actually connected us to the story, rather than served as team flags. But then, it's easy to make claims like that from the outside. What we do know is, it didn't work.

That is at least explicable to me, however. Worse, and far less explicable, is the fact that apparently new membership dropped off a cliff.

A stunning number of people – in San Francisco, cradle of the psychomagical experience design scene – were given a card by a friend, sworn to absolute discretion, and told an adventure awaited ... and did nothing. Just sat on it. Forgot about it. Were too busy.

I've heard (I can't verify) that before the end, almost half of the people offered an induction into the Latitude Society did nothing about it.

I couldn't process that then, and I can't process that now. I do not understand it. But I can tell you this: it wasn't that the people who weren't taking up their invitation were losers. Well after the Latitude Society's collapse, I would realize that several friends – people whose work in the scene I admired - had been among the people who had received a card and ultimately done nothing. So whatever we can say about the dynamic of who did and didn't accept the Latitude Society's invitation, it was definitely not separating the wheat from the chaff.

This was a death knell, however, for the Latitude Society's business model: because once their current members gave out invitations to all the people they wanted to join, and half of those people didn't sign up, and then that smaller cohort offered memberships to the people they wanted to join, and only half of them signed up ... eventually, the flow of new members in turned into a trickle, and then eventually stopped.

The crisis, at least to the management team, was obvious: they were shelling out huge money to set this thing up, and not only were current members not buying enough merch to meet financial projections, but new membership had dried up unexpectedly. Meanwhile the membership was happily going along, using resources and oblivious to the oncoming crisis.

Well, almost happily ... there was one thing they had noticed that bothered a lot of them.

Because of course the Latitude Society's membership model was entirely based on a small group of people who invited their friends, who invited their friends, who invited their friends ... and eventually it became obvious to the famously leftie Bay Area creative that this meant the Latitude Society had all the diversity of a Silicon Valley tech company. Only with artists. And – okay, they've gotta be granted this – a lot more women. But otherwise the problem was eerily similar.

So at the same time that the Latitude's management was wondering "how do we get more money out of our members?" a significant portion of its membership was wondering "how do we get more People of Color and marginalized populations in here?"

So you can imagine how bad the clash was when the Latitude Society management announced that going forward there would be an annual membership fee of several hundred dollars – one that would not only make it much harder to invite marginalized populations in, but which would make it harder for a lot of the current members, many of whom were struggling artists living in the most expensive real estate market in the world on a shoestring budget, and who had spent months creating events for the Latitude for free, to stay in themselves.

The membership rebelled. Management called a "town hall" to discuss it, and was completely unprepared for the response they got. They were accused of being dismissive about diversity concerns, and of exploiting artists. Those are both capital offenses in early 21st century San Francisco, and as it became more controversial management decided to end their experiment. Without any warning, the Latitude Society closed. Its website shut down. All resources were pulled.

Everything was over.

Except ... except ... and this ... THIS ... is the best part of the whole story. The single most amazing thing that happened in this Greek tragedy of underground art. It wasn't over.

Without the Latitude Society as a central hub, a whole lot of people who had met through it didn't know how to contact each other any more. But some of them did. Some of them had formed partnerships, and connections outside of their usual circles, and had created things together ... and decided that they didn't want it to end. Decided that they still really wanted a secret society in their lives, even if the previous one had only been "secret."

And so, before the flames of the Latitude Society's implosion had even cooled, these underground artists reached out to each other, and connected, and vowed to keep going. A dozen real secret societies were born out of the collapse of a fake one.

Or more than that – I can't say for sure. There's probably a lot of them I don't know about. I do know that some of them died, some of them went semi-public, and others are still going. One of them, I do know this, actually gathered wearing black robes and hoods in a place they were not supposed to be and burned Latitude Society materials in the middle of a circle, during a rare and serendipitous lightning storm.

And that ... the emergence of real secret art societies out of the collapse of a fake one ... is the most extraordinary, most psychomagical, part of the whole series of events. The Latitude Society, whatever it intended to be, ended up being a perfect moment of engineered disperfection, and the results were glorious.

As is often the case – almost always the case – the most amazing, life changing moments happen when events take on a life of their own, and choices have to be made with no script to follow.

In the second section, we've looked at the components

of effective psychomagic, the building blocks of these experiences. They are:

1. **Infinite Gardens vs. Finite Robots** - You're not making the thing happen, you're creating the conditions under which something amazing can happen. You're cultivating, but you're not in control.

2. **Create non-fictions** - You want people to understand that *this is really happening.* If someone has to suspend disbelief about something important, then it's not going to work. Ideally, they shouldn't have to suspend disbelief about anything. The more real it is, the more effective it is.

3. **Engineer Disperfection** - Create situations that break conventionality and that cannot be optimized for success. Where there is no "winning" in a conventional sense.

4. **Encourage meaningful choices** - Create moments of "applied existentialism" where people have to decide what's really important to them, and act on it. Where what people choose to do, how they choose to react, has a significant impact on what happens next and the experience they have.

5. **Gardens aren't safe** - Giving people meaningful choices in a non-fictional environment designed to create psychomagic isn't safe. You can't make it safe and get these kinds of impacts. What you can do is get better with danger, physical and psychological, so as to work through risks,

rather than avoid them.

6.   This could never happen twice - Repetition is the hallmark of zzzzzz. The less repeatable a psychomagical experience is, the more impact it is likely to have. Even if you are doing an experience with a format, try to design conditions that are unrepeatable, that could never happen again even if you wanted them to.

7.   You're either in or your out - except when you're not - Unless you're creating a wholly spontaneous act of psychomagic for someone (and maybe even then), it's crucial to either set firm boundaries around an experience (it happens in here, across this line, only) or to try the much harder task of wholly integrating the experience into their world for the long haul. Whichever choice you make, go all in. Going halfway in either direction destroys the impact.

8.   The Holy Trinity - Art, Ritual, and Play - In some ways these are three different things, and in some ways these are all the same thing. The more of each you can incorporate into your experience, and the more you can blur the boundaries between them or shift back and forth, the more likely you are that someone is going to have a profound experience, even if (especially if) it's utterly absurd.

9.   Gary Warne's Chaotic Principles - You must allow people the validity of their own reactions to what you do, otherwise you're a bully and an asshole. Always have a clear agreement with the people in your experience about what you'll do if things go sideways. Always stick together ... lots of important advice here ... but mostly: you're not doing fan service for your self-image, and people have a right to respond however they want to to the weirdness you create.

10. The lazy man's guide to starting a cult - The reason people have been taking each other out into nature and creating challenges for one another as a bonding exercise is that it works. It's psychologically potent. But it's much more potent as one element among many, rather than being the experience itself.

11. Honesty is the best policy - When in doubt, be more honest. Always be more honest. Do it in a theatrical way, do it in an interesting way, do it in an artful way, absolutely - but be more honest, more vulnerable, and more open. That's a royal road to psychomagic.

Once again, it's important to stress that this is a synthesis of everything I've seen people doing over decades of events I was present at and legendary experiences I've only heard of - this is not necessarily how the people themselves would describe what they were doing at the time. Nor is this meant to represent the vast stores of technical knowledge - of scene design and technical fabulation and social engineering - that people and groups in this scene have developed. But I believe that these elements represent the heart of the art form they developed: the elements that set it apart from "art" as we generally think about it, and reality as we generally experience it.

As I hope I've made clear: you can do this. Like all art, it depends on skills that almost all people have, and once they understand it's possible, and practice, they can get very, very, good at it. And when you get a bunch of people who are good at it all in one place, the world changes around them. Impossible things were constantly happening around us as we explored these frontiers.

San Francisco didn't invent psychomagic, and didn't even invent the term. It is a human constant, much like music, mathematics, and religion. But San Francisco became the epicenter of a movement that was never really publicly identified, and developed this art to a level and extent that I have never heard of, let alone seen, in a modern secular society. This had a profound impact on the way people lived, worked, and related to one another.

A few thoughts on that, and the place of psychomagic in society, conclude this book.

But first, a quick interlude to talk about creating psychomagical experiences in a time of plague.

DARK INTERLUDE

Psychomagic During a Pandemic

The first two parts of this book were written prior to a pandemic shutting the world into quarantine. There is every likelihood that, when it is published, the world will still be in quarantine.

If you're wondering: "does being isolated in a pandemic and communicating mostly through the internet make it harder to create psychomagical experiences for people?" That's a very fair question.

And yes, yes it does.

But in a time of mass isolation, when meaningful human contact in its most literal sense is hard to come by, I found these experiences to be even more important.

We were all overwhelmed and so many of us had a sense that we were sinking into a terrible stasis. That we would be drowning if only time were moving. We gasped for something to change, something to happen, as days and weeks and months melted together into less than the sum of their parts. We lost our sense of the future, and eventually we lost our sense of the past, and without that we were reduced. Our sense of self seemed to flatten into this one ongoing misery, and nothing else.

Maybe that was you, too.

So many of us - so many - desperately needed a sense that

we were on a journey rather than spinning in place. That there was forward momentum of some kind in our lives. We needed those parts of ourselves that had gone dormant from shock and suffering to reawaken.

There are other ways to do that, I'm sure. But psychomagic is the one we knew, the one we were good at, so we tried to figure out how to do that over screens.

We're not as good at it as we are doing it in person - we've had less than a year to practice as of the time I'm writing this - but we got there. And when it happened it was like a lightning strike that cleared out all the fog we were walking through: suddenly we were ourselves again. I have spent a lot of time in the pandemic creating psychomagical experiences because I needed them - they kept me on track when nothing else would - but I heard so many beautiful stories of how they had the same effect on others. One of the greatest compliments I received on my events was when a woman told me that they served as a stake pounded into time, clearly orienting her: this event is happening now, and things happened before it and after it. Without these experiences, everything just ran together.

So these experiences can be created online, but a lot of the low-hanging fruit that we rely on in physical experiences is no longer viable. What I've described as the lazy cult practice of taking people to a beautiful remote location and having a group of strangers engage in a dangerous challenge together

... it's just not the same if you're really in your living room and can turn off your camera every time you want to get a beer from the kitchen or check your email. Boundaries are still important ... but how do you create them? How do you create meaningful choices for people when all you can do is stare at each other through screens?

Those are challenging issues, for sure - but even worse is the fact that by now we have over 20 years of very bad habits we've developed being on the internet. Everything we know about "how to use the internet" is an obstacle to creating a psychomagical experience there. The internet experiences that most of us have routinely, every day, are the hallmarks of the "attention economy," where getting likes and clicks is far more important than the quality of the experience you are having. Internet environments are overwhelmingly designed to be frictionless and convenient, to reduce risks, to present idealized and facile versions of ourselves, to present simplified narratives, to dehumanize one another. Most online experiences try to reduce us to consumers of memes. Lab rats that press "like" or click when stimulated. That sort of thing isn't *all* that's on the internet, but those kinds of experiences are so common as to be made habitual ... and we have to break those habits before we can have psychomagical online experiences. To get where we want to go, we have to operate outside the rules and habits of the attention economy.

Undoing those habits - in yourself and others - is pretty hard. But once you've done that, I discovered, designing the actual online experiences to create psychomagic is relatively easy. Here are some of the tweaks I've made to the design elements we've already seen to orient them to an online environment.

Go Beyond Entertainment

There are a few exceptions, but, as a rule, the thing that just doesn't work online is creating experiences with the intention of entertaining one another.

Now, there's nothing wrong with entertainment, or being entertaining. I like being entertained. I like it a lot. But ... if you're only aiming to be entertaining, if that's the entirety of the experience you're designing, then it's probably not going to stand out online, because online entertainment is not hard to come by. The one thing we're not hurting for in this time of global pandemic is on-demand entertainment options. I mean, have you seen Netflix?

More than that, entertainment that asks nothing of the participants (or worse, the spectators) tends to lull the psyche into a dormant state, rather than wake it up. We are drowning in online entertainment, and it's simply not enough to break through that terrible sense of timelessness and despair.

In a time when we have more access to on-demand entertainment than at any point in human history, and less access to one another, it is experiences of authenticity and connection that we what we're desperate to have.

Design for that - for authenticity and connection. It doesn't have to be so dreadfully earnest (though honestly that works a lot better in the pandemic than I had originally thought). By all means, be fun. Be funny. Be weird and wild. But aim through that, and past it. The goal isn't to entertain, it's to connect and develop authentic encounters. Any experience that doesn't achieve those will be largely forgotten before the next meme. Any experience that achieves those can, in a very literal way, save lives.

Start With Immediacy

It's even more important in the digital environment to create non-fiction rather than fiction. I've never seen an effective online psychomagical experience where people pretended to be crazy characters — space aliens or federal judges or magical elves. They've been themselves. And they haven't pretended their living room was an exotic place you were entering or receiving a transmission from. Maybe they decorated their living room, maybe they made it weird and interesting to look at, but they never pretended it was anything other than their living room.

Successful experiences in this context have very little pre-amble. They start with immediacy: where are you, what are you doing, and what are you really experiencing? Come as you are, and acknowledge it.

Cultivate Radical Self-expression

The successful events I've seen so far have begun with

immediacy, and then used that to ask the participants to be radically self-expressive. The idea isn't to be self-expressive at them, but to create opportunities and invitations for them to be self-expressive at you. Or better yet, with you. Success looks like someone expressing themselves in a way, or to a degree, that they wouldn't in their normal life. How can you cultivate that?

Co-create the Experience

The most impactful digital experiences I've been part of or seen have been truly collaborative: participants have been asked to do creative work that develops or shapes the experience everyone has in meaningful ways. Often this means the organizers have no real idea what's going to happen next or how this is going to go. That's okay. That's great, in fact. That's how truly collaborative experiences work.

Find opportunities to co-create experiences with whoever shows up, rather than handing them something already formed. How much control can you give up? If the answer is "none," then - just like psychomagic in the real world - no matter how impressive its technical qualities, what you're doing will probably end up inert.

Make it Hard and Inconvenient, Instead of Easy and Frictionless

This isn't new advice. People have been arguing that we should make Burning Man harder and more inconvenient for years. But even though we didn't, it was still plenty hard, and still plenty inconvenient. And that difficulty level actually worked to make a lot of the things easy once we were there and committed. Because whatever you did in Black Rock City, you had already thrown yourself into Black Rock City. You had taken the time off, gone the likely considerable distance, went inside hauling your own gear, and set up to stay in a place where there isn't really any functional internet. You had to endure the elements and the unpredictability. Then you had to leave again ...

Everything we did in Black Rock City happened as a result of massive effort that everyone had already put into it. That made even ordinary experiences there extraordinary. Somebody's offering you orange slices? THAT'S AMAZING!

Take that uncommon effort that we all had in common away, make it easy and convenient instead, and what you are left with will be memes and videoconferences. It's not the same when you can go into your kitchen, just like you always do, to get an orange.

I've come to call this "The Law of Conservation of Effort" - the amount of effort participants need to put in to have a kind of psychomagical experience is a constant. It can be put into what most people would think of happening ahead of the event (like preparing in creatively challenging ways for it, or getting to a remote and inhospitable location), or during (obviously), or even after (when you undertake a task that causes you to significantly re-interpret an experience you've already had), but the effort has to be put in sometime. Online events often have to be more self-conscious of this, precisely because the internet is designed to minimize all efforts and friction.

Every notable successful psychomagical online activity I've seen so far has gone out of its way to ask the participants to make an inconvenient commitment or sacrifice of some kind. They have:

- created barriers to entry, not to keep people out but to make them work to get in
- asked them to take risks (real ones, not imaginary ones), and to do it with one another, rather than have the organizers take risks while everybody watched
- asked something of the participants — to sacrifice, work, share, do something uncomfortable, and step up in some way
- asked them to stick around and make a real time commitment, rather than to hop in and out when their attention wanders or they think they might have a better offer. You are not "browsing" for experience the way you browse on the internet, but committing to a time spent together.

How do you take risks like that online? Let me tell you about some of the experiences I created, and you'll see for yourself.

From Primal Scream to Primal Song

The event I created that I think of as the most and the least successful at once was called "From Primal Scream to Primal Song," It was incredibly successful because the part that I was able to pull off was one of the most intense experiences of common, shared, humanity that I've ever seen a group of strangers have in less than an hour. Everyone left feeling alive and connected and purposeful in a way that we hadn't during much of the pandemic.

It was much less successful insofar as, you know, I never actually finished the event. After that intense experience of common, shared, humanity, it fell flat on its face and failed.

Let me explain.

The idea behind this event is simple, and happens in two parts. Everyone is fully informed about what's going to happen before we start. In Part 1 you get a small group of people together on a video call, including at least one poet and at least one musician. One by one, everyone except the poet and the musician takes a turn and rants.

Just ... rants. Whatever is on their mind, whatever is bursting to get out. Nothing rehearsed or pre-planned, but anything - everything - else is fair game. Don't worry about oversharing, don't worry about seeming small or petty, don't worry about how it looks at all - no issues too big, no issues too small, no subjects too weird or idiosyncratic - just go.

Rant. Let it out. Get it out. Don't worry about anything - be as honest as you possibly can, and just rant. Go until you're done.

We tried this several months into the pandemic, you can imagine that people had a lot to say.

While they were doing that, the poet (in this case me) was taking notes on each rant.

That's part 1. And it was amazing.

After part 1, the poet turns all the rants into poems, using their exact words whenever possible. Then he turns the poems over to the musician, who sets them to music - so the rants are turned into poems, and then the poems are turned into songs.

So ... from Primal Scream to Primal Song.

The songs are recorded. In part 2, everyone comes back together and hears their songs, and gets a copy of their own.

Unfortunately we never reached that point. The musician I brought in went off the rails. He started changing the poems, and even people's direct words and the themes of what they'd been talking about, because they were "too dark" and he didn't want to put that darkness into the world. We'd be on the phone and I'd be screaming at him "Jeremy!" (let's say his name was Jeremy) "I asked people to open up about whatever they wanted to rant about during a pandemic! Of course it's dark! The whole point is that we're turning their truth into art, it's not their truth anymore if we try to make it happy! We have a responsibility to listen to them and do what we told them we'd do with their intimate truths!"

He couldn't do it. He wanted to start recording his own version of someone's song without their permission ... it became a nightmare. I reached out to some other musicians but they were all in the middle of a pandemic depression, then I got depressed for a while ... it just never happened. I failed. But the half that did happen was so damn good that I really want to try it again ... or somebody else to try it and tell me how it goes.

The Wheel of Zoom!

This one, too, has a very simple premise, but the particulars are crucially important to having it go right.

You get a wheel. Or better yet, you build one - the jankier the better. This wheel should have many spots for numbers or words. My wheel, built by the brilliant Anselm Engle, has 12. You get a bunch of people together on a video call: ideally a group of people that contains a mix of some close friends, some acquaintances you like, and some people who are pretty new to this social group. You make sure everyone knows: you're going the distance tonight. No stopping by just to catch up, no saying hello and then having to go to another meeting. We are hanging out tonight, doing this, for the next few hours. That commitment is crucially important, as is the way in which having the same people doing this over time allows experiences to build upon themselves, becoming greater than the sum of their parts.

Once everyone is ready, you decide, together, what the consequences for landing on each of the 12 spaces on the wheel is. This, too, is crucial. It can't be decided ahead of time by a couple of people: everyone has to decide on it together, in the moments before they start to play.

While the group together can decide what each of the wheel's consequences are, each one should involve a risk of some kind - and ideally they will be balanced out between four different kinds of risks that can be undertaken online in a live environment. The four types are:

- Physical risks: Do something difficult, spontaneous, or intimate with your body in your own surroundings. These have included interpretive dances, exercise routines, and intimate exposure.
- Emotional risks: Take an emotional risk in this moment. Confess a secret, tell someone something you've been holding back, conduct a webcam tour of the private parts of your home, do a show-and-tell with an object that has immense importance for you and explain why.
- Social risks: Do something that helps you learn about and connect with the other participants. Tell someone what

you really think of them. Ask someone something you've always wanted to know, offer someone an experience that you want them to have, or admit something that you really need and ask the group for help. Make someone blush.

- Absurdist risks: A challenge to do something utterly bizarre so that no one can predict what's going to happen next. Examples of that from the past have included "adopt a pet," "strip and weep," "make a friend," "create a work of art." Whatever it is has to be done now, right now, in front of everyone: no promises that you'll do it later. It doesn't matter if it makes sense or not - it's what they have to do.

There are surely more ways to take risks, too - that's just what I've seen so far. A good balance between these different kinds of risks is essential. Also essential is that everyone decides what the risks are going to be together, and that they do it right at the beginning of the experience, rather than the night before.

This matters first because deciding on the wheel's consequences together makes the risks consensual: everyone should be able to say "yes, I accepted this possibility when I signed up, and had a chance to veto it." Obviously that's not something that any given act of psychomagic depends on, but for this experience it's crucial - you're asking for their time, you're asking them to be part of a risky process, this is how you get them to commit to the whole experience. The second reason this matters is that it allows the consequences to be born out of the feelings people are actually having right now... and that is so important. The consequences should reflect where people really are and what they're really experiencing at this moment in time, both individually and collectively: even the same group of people can be in very different headspaces from week to week, or day to day. What's on the wheel should represent *these people* in *this moment*, and speak to what they are feeling and struggling with individually and together.

That's always an ideal in psychomagical experiences, but I think that the conditions of isolation in the pandemic have made it so much more emphatically necessary: whereas before it was something you could draw or coax people into - and in fact was often most potent that way - now it is something that is often much more necessary to make explicit right at the beginning. I'm not entirely sure why, but whereas in normal conditions I've found that surprising people with potent psychomagical experiences is often the most impactful approach, in pandemic conditions I've found that it's far more effective to be explicit: to say "I'm creating this magical experience for you, and we're going to do it right now, and you need to be engaged." I have theories as to why this is, but I doubt they're any better than anyone else's theories so far. It's the observation I'm sure of, not the explanation.

Anyway ... once you have the group assembled and the

consequences of each space on the wheel chosen, you take turns "spinning" it. Since we're talking about a physical wheel, the person in whose home it is becomes the designated spinner, and when each person takes a turn they must offer up instructions about how they want it spun: to the left, to the right, hard, soft, fast, slow ... but more than that, if there's a particular style or idea that one wants it spun with. So, for example: "spin it to the left like you just changed your mind." Or "spin it slowly to the right as though you were meeting your true love for the first time." And then the poor spinner has to try to live up to that command.

The person whose turn it is then does whatever the wheel lands on, until the other players agree that "the wheel is satisfied" - the idea being that they have to go all in, they can't just half-ass it. They may not succeed by any reasonable standard of quality, but they have to *try*. And then, once the wheel is satisfied, they pick the next person to spin. Once everyone has gone, people can be picked for a second time, and so on.

It's fun and funny and weird at first, but the commitment to stay in for several hours is what can make it transcendent: over time, the experiences build on one another in unpredictable ways, the risks people take inspire other people to take bigger risks, and eventually ... something happens. A whole new level of engagement and connection develops.

My favorite moment like that happened late one night:

many rounds in, out of nowhere, one of our players said she was suddenly inspired by what had just happened to share her favorite poem. It wasn't one she had written, and she's not a "poetry" person - but many years ago she had bumped into this piece of short verse and it had absolutely knocked her over with its sense of life's possibilities, and she'd kept a copy of it close by ever since, and she had to - had to - share it with us now.

So she read it out loud ... this had nothing to do with anything on the wheel ... and we were all amazed and moved. And then someone else confessed that she, too, had a poem like that in her life, even though she is also not a person who generally likes poetry, and she got it out and read it. And then someone else said that they also had a poem like that in their life ... until suddenly it just happened that we all went and found the poems in our lives that had never let go of us, and read them to one another, and cried and laughed and were amazed.

It was a moment of pure magic and ... this is what I need you to understand ... it would never have happened if I had created an event in which we were all supposed to bring our favorite poems and read them to one another. That even might have been, 'ya know, nice, but it wouldn't have been this. It wouldn't have been this moment of heartfelt confession and discovery that emerged, for no clear reason, out of a night taking emotional risks and living up to absurd challenges and suddenly feeling so close to one another that we couldn't help but expose our hearts.

That's only happened once, but if you set up the wheel properly and play it for a whole night, something happens.

The Existentialists Anonymous Art Bar

My favorite digital thing to do. The premise is lifted, in part, from the magical bar that I talked about at the very beginning of the book. A group of people gather together on a video conference. One of them is a bartender from that very bar.

To order a drink, you offer the bartender a prompt that is close to your heart. It can be anything: a wish, a desire, a memory, a sense impression, an abstract concept, a fragment of poetry, something you're struggling with (in the pandemic, most people offer up something they're struggling with) ... anything at all, as long as it's close to your heart.

Then the person who ordered the drink uses their webcam to show the bartender their liquor cabinet and kitchen, and the bartender leads them through making an original drink specifically to answer that prompt. The person makes it, while everyone watches and talks and listens.

Everyone, that is, except for me: while the drink is being made I am writing a short story based on the same prompt the drink is being made for. And two visual artists (okay, sometimes one, sometimes more, but usually two) are creating original art pieces. We have until the drink is ready to finish what we're making.

When the drink is ready, the artists stop. The person drinks their cocktail while we share the art: the artists are spotlighted as they show their work, and then I read the story I've written aloud. The person has offered up something from their heart, shared part of their home with everyone at the bar, been led through the creation of an experimental but usually amazing drink, and then been offered art created for them personally as they savor the taste.

It's pretty amazing. Then we do it for the next person who orders. We give everyone who wants a drink a turn before we let people order seconds.

Sometimes other people want to create art too. Drawings or poetry or even dance moves. We always let them. The presentation can't take too long - we have a bar to run and people to serve - but if people want to participate by offering their own art up in response to the drink orders, they are welcome to. We don't want everyone to create art - it's actually a huge benefit that people get to share their spaces with others, and be witnesses to the process of creating that drink. That matters. But everyone who wants to create art to share while the drink is made is welcome to.

This has become one of my very favorite things to do during the pandemic, and like a real bar a small group of regulars keeps coming back, forming an impromptu and entirely organic community.

Reality and Virtual Reality

As of the moment I write this, there's a lot of hope that Virtual Reality can serve as a venue for the kind of experiences we cannot have in person now because of the pandemic.

I hope the people who think that are right. I'm rooting for them. But it hasn't been my experience. That could just be me - certainly some of my favorite people have said they have a grand time in VR experiences. The issue could just be that I don't know how to do it in VR yet: after all, it took time for me to be able to learn how to do this in the real world. These things take time and practice. But to me, thus far, VR is actually an additional level of mediation between us and the reality we are trying to enchant - one more thing we need to work our way through. Virtual Reality adds production value to experiences - and as we've seen, production value has almost nothing to do with psychomagical potency. A simple video feed of someone's real face, their real environment, is so much better for me to work with.

On the other hand, there are so many frontiers of virtual reality, so much you can do ... it's absurd to think that people won't figure out ways to use these tools to create similar effects.

But many of the experiences created offline during the

pandemic have been far more inspiring to me so far.

Scott Levkoff liked to get a bunch of his friends all dressed up in plague doctor outfits and wander through Golden Gate Park together, which was a shocking and otherworldly thing to see. He also created a coin whose instructions, if followed, are designed to facilitate short but intense moments of connection.

"The Goldfire Storycoin offers a simple structure for navigating meaningful conversations and shared stories within a container of trust and safety, mutually upheld by all involved," he said, and by this point in the book I think you can understand what that kind of description might look like in practical terms. As of the moment I'm writing this, he's testing it out in group settings.

Michael Ryan Garcia could no longer do Decentralized Dance Parties the way he had, but he did regularly set up the same distributed boom boxes at a beach at sunrise, where he and others - and anyone who came along - could dance in a socially distanced manner as the sun changed the color of the waves.

In Seattle, a group of people I don't know celebrated the week when Black Rock City would have gone up by turning the second floor kitchen of their house into a pie factory, and creating a chute from the kitchen window down to the ground so that they could safely send free pies down to people passing by.

In San Diego, long time Burning Man camp leader John "Halcyon" Styn found a way to turn the front yard of his home into a socially distanced version of his Burning Man camp - all pink and fluffy and offering cucumber water and refreshments to everyone who happened to pass by. He'd only meant to do it for a week, but the sanctuary he'd created was so popular with the neighborhood that he kept it open for a month.

I've created several socially distanced in-person experiences for people during the Pandemic, in addition to my online experiences above. But the one that really moved me - that changed my own life - also was what I did during Burning Man's traditional week.

I turned my apartment building's small backyard into a visiting area, and made an open invitation to anyone to schedule an appointment to come visit (socially distanced) during that week, and to perform an art ritual I had created just for this moment. When it was all over, a total of 19 people - a combination of deep intimates, friendly acquaintances, and complete strangers - would make the trip and have the experience.

I'm going to be more vague about this than I have with anything else in this book - someday I'll probably talk about it in detail, but right now it's still very fresh and raw. But, broadly, here's what happened:

I instructed everyone to come with a thoughtful gift for whoever the person coming after them in the ritual was - they would never know who. When they arrived, we sat in my backyard, some 8-10 feet apart, with a table between us, on which was sitting self-packed refreshments (small bags of chips, oranges, bottles of wine and beer), instruments for lighting a fire, a pot, a corkscrew, an envelope, and a few other items. I asked them to sit at the table, to make themselves comfortable, and then to pick up the envelope, open it, and read what was inside.

Inside was written:

Through dangers untold and hardships unnumbered, I have fought my way here to the castle beyond the goblin city to take back the child you have stolen. For my will is as strong as yours, and my kingdom as great. You have no power over me.

You have no power over me.

I asked them to tell me what they thought of after they read that. What it brought to mind: any ideas, images, flights of fancy. Some of them recognized it as from the movie *Labyrinth*, some of them didn't, but they all told me what it made them think about. I thanked them, had them put the paper back in the envelope and the envelope back on the table, and told them we'd come back to that later. Then we talked.

We just talked. About anything that was on their mind in this bizarre time in the pandemic when California was on fire. I didn't need to direct the conversation, but I made sure that we kept it deep rather than exchanging pleasantries. We talked and drank together in the sun as the world tried to kill us.

After maybe an hour, maybe more, I told them that it was time to complete the ritual we had started when they arrived. Then I told them a story. A true story. A true and personal and very sad story about something I have struggled with my whole life. I told that story and some of them already knew it because they were among my closest friends and some of them had no idea because they did not know me that well and some of them were complete strangers I had met for the first time just an hour ago. I told them this story about myself, and how it had culminated in someone very important in my life sending me a book early in the pandemic - and that their sending me this book had so encapsulated all the poisonous dynamics of this struggle in my life that I had flown into a rage, and utterly lost control. I had wanted to toss the book out, destroy it utterly, but it had some kind of hold on me, just like the sad struggle I'd been fighting all my life had me in its grip, and so I couldn't do anything about it: and the book just sat there, in my house, day after day, week after week. Something I desperately wanted to do something about, but couldn't.

Eventually the week of Burning Man was in sight, and I knew I wanted to do something - SOMETHING - to mark the occasion. I'd realized by this point that virtual reality wasn't going to do it for me: that while I would certainly hop in and see all the amazing worlds a small army of volunteer artists had created, that if this was all I did for the week that I would end up feeling tremendously sad and lonely. So I'd determined to do something - SOMETHING - with people. To create a ritual - SOME ritual! - that we could do together. But what?

Then I'd remembered that book, sitting in my house all these months, and suddenly I was very glad I hadn't burned it.

Because the truth is that all of the real progress I've made in the last several years of my life has been done with people, in community. I hadn't been able to grow and be better all by myself, because I'd brilliantly thought it through: I'd been able to do it because I'd finally learned how to reach out for help, and ask in ways that people could hear. And they'd helped.

And so how fitting would it be to burn this book communally? Together? And so now ... now (I told them) ... I'm asking you if you will help me burn this book that comes from a kind of relationship I do not want and represents something in my life that I want to be rid of. Will you help me?

They said yes. Of course. Every time.

I brought out the book. The actual book that had been sent to me and been sitting in my house. Take it, I said, and look through it, and find the parts of it that you want to burn with me. It can be whatever you want: I want this book truly gone by the end of the week. Just leave enough for the people who come after you to help, too. I'm going to leave you alone for a few moments, while you look through it, and consider what you want to burn, and then I'll be back.

They had picked out the pages when I returned. Often they had given it a great deal of thought, and wanted to explain to me what it was about these particular pages that they thought had to go.

I had them rip the pages out of the book, fold them up, and put them in the pot. I gave them the lighter. In a moment, I said, you will light it on fire and we will burn it together.

But first I reminded them of the lines in the envelope I'd had them read at the beginning. During the early part of the pandemic, I'd needed a hand washing mnemonic to make sure that I was actually scrubbing them for 30 seconds - and so I'd started reciting that line from the movie, which had always appealed to me. So I ended up saying that whole thing … "from dangers untold and hardships unnumbered" etc. etc. … multiple times a day. And so, inadvertently, it had become a mantra I'd told myself over and over again.

After hearing the story I'd told them, they immediately saw the relevance. Understood what it had meant to me, what these words had become.

When this book is burning, I told them, I'm going to say these words over them.

They lit the flame. The pages burned. I said the words. Sometimes, we said them together.

It had a physical impact on me. Shivers, even shakes, every time. It was extraordinary.

Sometimes, after that, they had things they wanted to tell me. About their own struggles and challenges, or moments they had been liberated. One woman - I'll never forget this - told me the story of the only book she had ever defaced in her life, and it was utterly heartbreaking.

Then I gave them the gift that the person before had left for them, and we discovered what it was. And, I said, I have one more gift for you.

When you first read the words in the envelope, and I asked you what they brought to your mind (I told them) I recorded your answer on my phone, and then I sent the audio file to an artist who spent the hour while we were talking creating an original piece of art based on your response to these words. She sent it back to me, and while you were going through the book finding the pages you wanted to burn, I went into my apartment and printed it out. And here ... here ... is the image, created just for you, of what this invocation brought up. It's yours, your part of this, with my thanks.

That was the ritual. They left their own gift behind for the next person.

I did that nineteen times in a week. It was overwhelming. I was exhausted and spent at the end of each day. I had to cancel a few people's visits because I discovered the hard way that do- ing this more than three times a day was impossible for me.

After it was all over, after I recovered, the experience changed me. In the best way. The book was gone. Everything it represented had no power over me.

You can still do that in a pandemic. I just don't know how to do it in virtual reality yet.

SECTION 3

Psychomagic and Society

Chapter 22:
What Happened to Us?

"What we have loved, others will love, and we will teach them how." - Wordsworth, "The Prelude"

My friend Misa was in town from Prague, and of course we had to see each other. Then she asked if I wanted to hang out with her and our mutual friend Theresa, and of course I did. Then she asked if maybe I could create a little art experience for her, the way she'd heard I had for Kay's 40th birthday party when she'd come down from Seattle.

Of course.

We met in a bar. Hung out there for a while, and I talked about how I might - might - have gotten them access to a rare and precious place, something special in the city, but we'd just have to see. It was up in the air ... you never know with something like this. You have to grab your moment when you can get it.

I got a message on my phone. I excused myself to step out of the bar. If they were looking through the windows - I don't know if they were - they would have seen me accepting a key card from a homeless looking man, and giving him what might (from a distance) have appeared to be a gold coin in return. When I came back, I didn't make any mention of who he was or what had happened. I only held the key card up and said "I got it. We can get in."

It was only a few blocks walk, and on the way I told them about how, not too long ago, there had been a priesthood of underground artists in San Francisco, and that they had achieved remarkable power. Their rituals were lavish and decadent. They grew in both strength and numbers, and for a time their artistic powers threatened to outshine and overwhelm all the other independent artists, who they tried to absorb and claim as their own.

But then, suddenly, the priesthood collapsed. No one really knows why. But their power was gone and all the artists who had rallied to their cause scattered, forming smaller bands of secret cults who still roam the city to this day. That, and the ruins of their temple, is all that is left.

We would be visiting the ruins of their temple tonight. Though the priesthood is gone it is still a strange and uncanny place, and you never know what creatures or landscapes or experiences you will find in what remains. So be careful, be wary, and be prepared, because tonight we explore hidden depths and lost secrets.

"Where is it?" they asked.

"Right here," I said. We had reached an unassuming door in an unassuming building just off Mission street. The door required a key card to access. I used the one I'd been given.

I had embellished the truth, yes, but everything I'd told them had been essentially true: this was the entrance to the Latitude Society's headquarters, the one that I had gone through just a few years before. One of the groups to emerge out of the Latitude Society's collapse - The Rathskeller Club - had taken over the space. They couldn't keep many elements of the experience intact, but much of it was still there - and they paid the astronomical lease by renting it out to the many show producers in San Francisco desperate for a good space in which to create their art. I hadn't lied about not really knowing what was down there, anymore, either. With so many shows passing through, each with their own set designs and physical needs, different rooms in the former Latitude headquarters were often radically transformed: I was just as likely to find an Edwardian drawing room as I was a magical mushroom forest.

So in an important way we really were traipsing through the ruins of the temple of the last attempt to create a major psychomagical experience in San Francisco. The largest single event to follow 2015's Fallen Cosmos. The last major stab at creating a major, region-wide, experience design cohort ... one that had been brilliant for all its tremendous flaws ... and while I knew some of what we'd encounter down there, and had arranged for some of it, I really didn't know just what was happening with the space now.

Hesitantly, they opened the door that my key card accessed, and walked into the dark room with the flashing red light and the hole in the wall ahead. It was all gone and yet, somehow, it was also still here. It was only different to those of us who had been through it the first time, who had seen what it once was. Now it bore a number of resemblances to what had come before, but something new was happening.

One by one, we went into the hole and down the slide in the dark.

To my mind, the arc of San Francisco's pioneering psychomagical experience scene goes from about 1983, give or take, to 2015. The important thing isn't the exact dates. What I'm telling you is: it's over. It ended. It's done. Only the ruins and remnants are left.

What happened?

It would be easy to say that COVID destroyed it, the way it decimated so many arts organizations and scenes across the world. But as my 2015 end date should tell you, COVID was only kicking a corpse.

It would be easier to blame gentrification and economic trends, and this is partly true. Art scenes don't blossom in places where artists can't afford to live. Low rents, the availability of non-exploitative flexible work, easy access to spaces where things can happen, and a lack of constant pressure to monetize have been key conditions for the genesis of just about any major art scene you can think of. John Law, who was a central figure in this scene from beginning to end, once told me that it wouldn't have happened if they'd been facing the same struggles to pay rent in the 70s and 80s that San Franciscans have had in the last 20 years. "We couldn't have done it," he said. "These people never would have even met."

And not just pay rent, but develop spaces in which to make things happen: small theaters, community galleries, cheap venues, and decommissioned buildings have been all but eliminated to make way for commercial spaces where marketing is welcome and artists are forbidden. Gary Warne needed available spaces and low barriers to entry in order to open his bookstore, Circus of the Soul, and his "adult playpen" The Gorilla Grotto, both of which served as key community spaces and incubators early in the scene.

The availability of side work that is related to the arts is also important. As the book *Culture Crash* points out, aspiring directors and producers used to be able to work in video stores, where their expertise was put to good use and they could make industry contacts. Those days are gone. Aspiring writers and poets and musicians used to be able to hop in and out of teaching gigs - take a year, teach college, make some bank, meet interesting people, return to your poetry and performance. But academia has changed, making those jobs much less common, much less lucrative, and much more competitive - so that people primarily working as artists and writers can no longer get them because the competition from people who focus exclusively on academic credentials instead of working primarily as artists is so harsh.

The homogeneity of economically elite spaces is also a problem: scenes thrive when a variety of different kinds of people, from different walks of life, can interact in meaningful ways. The truism about tech start-ups creating apps to solve problems that only tech workers have is exactly the point: art scenes without new blood and ideas coursing through them die in the womb. Or are evicted after the womb goes condo. The more our communities get economically and politically sorted, the harder it is for art scenes to thrive.

Art scenes can exist under these conditions, but they aren't born this way. Even for healthy and strong scenes, enduring these conditions means a constant battle for survival. The minute San Francisco's local geniuses began to say "I can't afford to live here anymore!" the scene was in a struggle for its life.

But while the struggle was real - economic conditions tried to murder us - that wasn't what killed us.

We did.

You may have noticed a trend in the stories of psychomagical experiences that I've been describing in this book - a trend that I mostly missed as I lived through it. Over time, the events became less and less manifestations of non-fictional, authentic, unrepeatable, engineered disperfection ... and instead became big performances through which some of these characteristics also happened to run.

Over time, the design of psychomagical experiences became eclipsed by what is generally referred to as "immersive theater" and "interactive art" and (most recently, with the most technology) "augmented reality games." Shows that try to *give you the feeling* that you are having a psychomagical experience, rather than actually being one. Kind of like the difference between having an actual sword fight with real sabers over real stakes, and going through an intense LARP in which you finally confront a guy playing your "arch enemy" and beat on him with a padded foam broadsword.

LARPing psychomagic is so, SO, much easier and more lucrative to produce, and newcomers loved doing it, so that's what people did. That's what killed us.

When someone points this out, it's often to accuse the people doing the immersive theater of selling out - of watering down this amazing thing we did to create a more popular and accessible version. But I think that's the exact wrong way to understand what happened.

I'm not glad that it happened ... "immersive theater" and "interactive art" and "augmented reality" are frustratingly bland when compared with effective psychomagic. But this transition happened for the right reasons. In fact, it's something that happens to any successful art scene. If it goes on long enough, any successful art scene becomes genteel. It becomes more benign. *Because it's doing something right.*

Nothing Changes Everything Like Success

Think about it: you're in this emerging art scene. You're doing some things that are both amazing and pretty difficult. You can't believe how great it is - you're so damn lucky to be part of it. And of course you want the people you care about to have this experience too. So you start to open it up to more people - and because it's amazing and wonderful they love it too. But because it's so difficult, it's not accessible to all your favorite people. So you make it a little easier to accommodate, and then more of them can participate. And this is good - this is a good thing. Meanwhile these new people coming in also want to participate and create, and they bring new ideas ... and some of these new approaches are right in line with the original intent of the thing, but a lot of them are going to be slightly remixed versions of other existing art forms, which is not a bad thing and sometimes is an awesome thing but also makes the scene more like the things people already know. And a lot of these new ideas are going to bring in even more participation by even more people, which will make it even more accessible.

Then, as it gets more and more accessible, people start to see a payday on the other side of this. And why shouldn't they? Why shouldn't the artists and producers who are making these amazing things make money off of their talents and efforts? That's a good thing! Artists should make a living! Who doesn't want that? Aren't people always telling us to get a job?

It just also happens to be the case that if you're planning to use these events to pay your rent (especially if rents are increasing citywide as part of a massive real estate boom) then you need to make sure that you sell enough tickets to cover it, which means you're even more invested in getting people through the doors. Failure stops being an option (which means it's also no longer a learning experience). Repeatability starts to look really attractive because you can make twice as much from a show that you can do twice, and you can get so much more exposure, and it's easier for the media to cover it because they understand it. And now that you're pulling all these people in to pay your rent money you have significant liability issues, so it really matters that people don't get hurt and sue you, which means you sand down a few more edges. And that's a good thing! Of course you don't want people to get hurt!

It's just that when you do enough of this kind of thing, you're suddenly dealing with a different art form: "immersive theater" instead of "psychomagical experiences." Fictions designed to mimic the non-fictions you used to do. A ride at Disneyland designed to simulate all the fun and excitement of breaking into Disneyland.

And some of the people doing this will be sell-outs, sure.

But most of the people doing it will be doing the right thing for the right reasons, and this is just how it goes - this is a problem of success.

It's exactly the arc that Burning Man followed: it started out as a small group of people doing a thing. It got bigger and bigger because they invited their friends. Some of those friends of friends were really into psychedelic DJ sets, so suddenly there were DJs all over Burning Man. Some of those friends of friends of friends were really into shamanic spirituality workshops and yoga, so suddenly the desert was full of yoga classes with live DJs who hoped you'd stick around for the vision quests that were starting in 15 minutes. Most of these people were not any good at handling danger at all, so for humanitarian reasons the Burning Man organizers started adding a few regulations to make sure that these people didn't kill everyone or damage the natural environment - and that was too bad but, come on, let's stop that humanitarian environmental crisis before it starts, right? I mean, seriously now. And the insurance costs Burning Man needed to cover - it never needed insurance in the old days - meant that it needed to be at least a little more safety oriented, and now it was a whole global event full of new people, and things had to shift at least a little to accommodate them ...

And these were ALL the right decisions! Every one of them made more sense than the alternatives! Unless your position is - as John Law's was - that Burning Man was better off being cancelled than it was changing and letting new people in, then this is what was going to happen. And Burning Man stayed amazing! It still had plenty of psychomagical power coursing through it! That's pretty obvious to anyone who shows up.

But in other ways yeah, it's not like it was. It is more genteel. It is - in some ways - more benign. Success changes things. Not because anybody's sold out, but because the conditions you're dealing with are different.

John's position, by the way, isn't just about Burning Man - it's a statement of how these things always work. Here's what he told me one day, sitting in his strange office at the top of the Oakland Tribune clock tower:

"I've seen, in the ensuing 35 fucking years since (Gary Warne) died, that if you understand this sort of inspiration, creating these magical moments, these apex moments in your life, you can't market it, you can't put the lightning in a bottle. It is a temporary thing. The best you can do, really the best that you can do, is to take the disparate elements that you see that were there that helped, and you can try a new iteration. And sometimes you will hit that note again, and you will recreate that magic. But it's not something you can manufacture. It doesn't work that way. The really really brilliant, the really soul-touching, the real expansive, collaborative stuff that people do, you can't replicate it. I've never seen that work."

John's point isn't that you can save something by refusing

to let new people in and keeping it from changing: it's that it's going to change anyway. So sometimes it's better to move on rather than to hold on.

Indeed, John shocked me by telling me something I didn't know about the Suicide Club: its founder and visionary Gary Warne left it after just two years, precisely "because he felt it was getting too insular. We weren't getting new blood in."

The very same thing that happened to the San Francisco underground art scene at the end happened to The Suicide Club at the beginning: "We were doing more and more elaborate events ... we got better at doing events," John told me. "Really amazing events, but increasingly it was less of a thing we were all doing together and it was more of a 'here's the audience' kind of thing ... even though the audience snuck into the Golden Gate Bridge, which is pretty cool, right? But it was still turning into a set of performances."

One way or another, you're going to lose the magical inspired thing after it peaks. The question is how you want to do that. Let it change, or let it go?

That's part of what happened to the San Francisco scene. It grew. And advanced. And got so good at what it was doing that it changed into something else because the people doing it wanted to see if they could invite more of their friends and start event production companies. I don't like where that took us - I loved the psychomagical experience scene - but many of these people are my friends and I'm rooting for them to succeed.

Each One Teach One

The other thing that killed the psychomagical experience design scene was that - dammit - the old guard was terrible about teaching the newcomers how it worked.

It wasn't always like this. The people who started The Suicide Club were very good at teaching what they did, and they taught The Cacophony Society people very well. The Cacophony Society people were great at teaching what they did - it was part of their mission. Many connoisseurs think that they conveyed their techniques so well that the Los Angeles Cacophony Society, under the leadership of the Reverend Al Ridenour, exceeded their San Francisco forbears in some ways. Cacophony also did very well at transmitting its culture to early Burning Man.

But after that, something shifted. I'm not sure what. Maybe it was a problem of success. Maybe Burning Man and its specific ethos started to overshadow the psychochomagical scene it emerged out of, and so instead of these techniques people learned about Burning Man's 10 Principles.

Here's my best take on what happened: as the scene got bigger and bigger there was less of an opportunity for the kind of "learn by doing with a master craftsman" that had been key to the transmission of knowledge and technique during the early days. Since no relatively consistent body of knowledge was ever synthesized around these approaches, the loss of those apprenticeship opportunities meant the transmission of this tradition became more difficult at just the time that masses of new people were getting bigger and everybody was focusing on Burning Man.

One way or another, it became easier to do "immersive theater" because no one was being taught how to do psychomagic - and without understanding what that is and how that works, it's easy to mistake the costumes and the pageantry for the soul and the psyche. It's so much easier to focus on amazing costumes and a cool storyline that you can use over and over again than it is to engineer a moment so raw and honest that it changes everything and could never happen twice.

Most people, if you tell them "make a cool costume," they'll at least have some idea of what you're talking about. But "create an experience that connects to someone's unconscious in a life changing way which seems like magic?" Not so much - and if they don't know where to look, the odds are they'll end up spouting New Age cliches.

The scene is largely gone, replaced by its more genteel evolution, but there are still significant practitioners and even some notable groups active in the remains. As I said in the introduction to this book, most of them wouldn't appreciate my telling you about them - they're committed to the underground. Others I've already introduced to you: no one tells Danielle Baskin that what she's doing isn't brilliant as both old and new school.

John, by the way, doesn't believe the scene is "over" for just that reason. "I understand the current popular conceit of claiming 'all is over now, OUR TIME was IT!' he told me when I discussed this book with him. "That is bullshit and I do not subscribe to this defeatist attitude. Yes things are different now - harder in some respects, better in others. We find ways to do our thing now - different perhaps than when SF was filled with abandoned buildings, but effective none-the-less!"

He could be right. But it is different. Psychomagical practice is not what it was. It's not really a "scene" anymore. And as each new artist moves away - or, in COVID times, dies - more knowledge and expertise is lost.

This stuff is best taught as a lived experience: you have an experience of it, and it breaks through what you thought were load-bearing walls in your life, and you want to do it yourself, and then you're guided, like an apprentice, through other people's amazing projects and you start to internalize how this works.

But if that's not happening, then I think a book like this is better than nothing. At the very least, it will help people understand: there's something out there that really is possible.

And they'll start to look for it. I hope.

I really hope.

I also think these techniques can be used for tremendous good - they are very much about creating the conditions under which miracles occur. People have used them, very effectively, to address someone's inner demons, solve community problems, and find their way in life.

But we also need to understand: the life of an artist is a strange calling. And it's even weirder if you're diving this deep. We think art is something we can just turn on or off, like a light switch. We think it can be organized and commoditized and kept an orderly and regular part of our lives.

Psychomagic cannot. It's like sex: it refuses to sit in the convenient boxes we try to put it in. You can invoke it, but it has its own agenda. It emerges, sometimes with a roar, sometimes with a whisper, at unexpected times. And this is especially true if you are trying to be a practitioner.

It is not benign. Enter at your own risk..

Chapter 23:
The Difference Between Mystics and Marketing

Just as the psychomagical experience scene in San Francisco was turning into "immersive theater," the idea of "designing immersive experiences" to market corporate intellectual property was taking off.

Theme parks were in the lead, because places like Disneyland have always been about creating "immersive experiences" for customers. But parks were trying to take it to the next level with places like "The Wizarding World of Harry Potter" at Universal Orlando in 2010 and "Star Wars: Galaxy's Edge," which began construction at Disney's American parks in 2016.

It didn't stop there: by 2018 HBO was promoting "Westworld" with an immersive experience at SXSW, and Google was hiring local San Francisco talent to design immersive experiences to highlight the impact of its new products. Around 2017 (dates varied from city to city) AirBnB launched a service in which visitors could get locals to give them experiences. That was also when I started meeting guys in San Francisco bars visiting the city from Ohio who said they worked for marketing companies specifically to create "immersive experiences" for brands. "We do what you do!" they would tell me, excitedly.

And I nodded and smiled.

Companies big and small, in other words, were attempting to do their own version of what San Francisco had developed over 30 years, often directly inspired by it. (If you don't think the tech and marketing worlds have less than six degrees of separation from the San Francisco art underground, then you've never seen them camp together at Burning Man. Sometimes they resent and loathe each other, but they still go to some of the same sex parties.)

These brand-building experiences are a deliberate attempt (knowing or not) to take the techniques developed by the San Francisco art underground, the techniques I've highlighted for you here, and yoke them into the service of product marketing. And many of these marketing experiences have been highly regarded and successful.

So it's worked. Kind of? Hasn't it? Lots of people have enjoyed the hell out of themselves, that's for sure, and arguably (I think?) being marketed to by someone offering you an experience is a much better offer than being forced to watch a commercial. Immersive and interactive experiences are the next frontier in branding and marketing.

And yet … none of these commercial experiences have had the same kind of impact on people that the events created by the San Francisco art underground, from Burning Man on down, have. They do not (at least I've seen no evidence that they do) have the same kind of transformative, life altering, impact. People go, enjoy themselves, and then return to their lives unchanged.

Something is different.

Now before we explore what, we should have a moment of modesty here: it's not like all of the events created by the San Francisco art underground were all so amazing either. I have definitely been cherry picking some of the highlights for you. In figuring out what works, the scene fell flat on its face ... a lot.

"We did a lot of really stupid events," Chicken once told me about the good old days.

John Law was just as blunt: "A lot of what we did was retarded."

And there's nothing wrong with that. That's how people learn, by trying and failing and trying again.

So the point isn't that everything the underground did was good and every experience that the corporate experience designers create is bad. No no - a whole lot of underground experiences were terrible. Some of the marketing and branding experiences are cool.

But ... but ... think about it ... those underground artists had budgets that couldn't pay for shoestrings. They were using decrepit and abandoned spaces ... or sneaking in to new ones and trying to avoid detection. They were working with volunteers, and kids, and obnoxious pranksters and temperamental artists. They could barely afford food, or pay rent, and had to work day jobs. Corporate marketing experiences, on the other hand, are done by seasoned professionals who pull in decent salaries and have sometimes lavish budgets and groups of employees who are paid to show up and do what they're told.

And yet … yet … the underground experiences are far more often the experiences you remember your entire life, rather than one more ride you took and vaguely recall.

Something's going on.

Here's an even more important point: the underground experiences that were mediocre or bland were considered failures. The corporate experiences that are impressively produced but are ultimately just one more entertaining thing you did that day were deemed successes.

That should tell us something. Something we need to pay attention to.

There is no reason - none at all - that companies and marketing consultants and entertainment conglomerates can't use the techniques and approaches listed in this book themselves. Of course they can. And it will probably help them.

But they will never - never - be as good at it as mad artists and psychomagical monks and daimonic shamans who devote themselves to this practice for its own sake.

Remember all the things we went over in the first part of this book, and you'll see that the reason is simple. The essence of psychomagic is *what emerges from within you.* It's the very idiosyncratic and unique ways in which our individual selves, struggling to become, connect with the collective unconscious and create together, because they find a space where they can be seen and engaged. Psychomagical art and experiences are doors that open to wherever you need to be taken, and you ... you personally ... show us where that is through your own projections and inner mythology.

Corporate branding experiences, on the other hand, are about building brands. They cannot afford to go wherever you take them, because they are trying to lead you on a journey to a specific destination that has absolutely nothing to do with you. Harry Potter's Wizarding World cannot and will not go off-brand to accommodate your personal mythology; Star Wars Galaxy's Edge will always put its merchandising ahead of your inner revelations.

The purpose of branding and marketing is to raise product awareness, reinforce brand identity, and sell widgets. The purpose of psychomagic is to give you a breakthrough experience. Brands and marketing are, ultimately, fictions: psychomagic is at its most potent when it is real.

Psychomagical artists go where marketing creatives cannot. Psychomagical artists can make their art about you, personally, in ways that branding creatives cannot. Psychomagical artists can make your real life their subject matter, whereas corporate "experiences" are all about selling you their story.

Oh sure, corporate experience designers could work only with facts and real people - but the moment the story starts to have nothing to do with the product, or questions the brand's legitimacy, they're going to try and drive the experience back "on track." At which point your daimon, your self-actualizing unconscious, realizes there are no meaningful opportunities here, and stops doing its part. It's not an accident that the Latitude Society failed as an experience in the places where it was trying to be a brand.

For dedicated artists, things starting to go off track in unpredictable ways is where things really begin to get interesting. At which point your daimon, perks up and says "let's play!"

Psychomagic is designed to open possibility; branding is designed to limit it.

Corporate brand marketers can productively use all the tricks in this book, but they will never be as good at it as artists.

In her book *Has Modernism Failed?* Suzi Gablick made a very similar point:

"In itself, capitalist society cannot foster a communal spirit or generate the virtues - it can only generate affluence. By now it must be clear that one of the ways in which the adversary culture of modernism has failed was through surrendering its inner independence to the pressures of external, bureaucratic power. The growing dependence on a market-intensive, professionally manipulated art world has resulted in artists losing their power to act autonomously and live creatively. This particular change happened without being instigated. It was non-deliberate. It happened because late capitalism, with its mass-consumption ethic, weakened the capability of art for transmitting patterns of conscious ethical value. And, as we have seen, this was so because often the very same artists who opposed capitalist ideology in their art were not really resistant to it; at the level of personal intention, they had a double standard, and were in complicity. They were unwilling to put their own career interests at stake in the service of convictions they were ready to accept in their art."

If you really want to do it, you have to live it.

Yay for dedicated artists, right? Sure. But truly committing like this ... that is a weird and perilous path. There are good reasons so few people do it. It sounds silly to ask, but it's still worth asking: if marketers won't go there, should you?

How To Ruin Your Life With Art

Doing any particularly intense thing, intensely enough, for long enough, changes you. Makes you comfortable with experiences that are out of the ordinary. There's nothing odd or magical about that. Over time, circus trapeze artists become completely used to flying through the air without a net, which gives them a completely different relationship to gravity and heights and motion than the rest of us. Race car drivers get used to moving at speeds that are hard for the rest of us to contemplate, and makes ordinary traffic seem different. Their reflexes are different, the way they perceive oncoming objects, different. Actors, if they are dedicated enough to their craft, are constantly pretending to be other people - even disappearing into fictional personalities. If you get really good at copy editing, then you can't not edit prose in your head when you read it. Learn a new language well enough and you can't not understand it when you hear it. And so on ... in any field. Expertise changes you.

Psychomagic is no different.

One Halloween night I was at a diner in Rochester, New York, just before midnight. And there was a group of what looked to be teenagers - maybe college freshmen? - sitting together in a big booth next to me.

They were loud - because they're kids - and I couldn't help eavesdropping, and suddenly realized that we knew someone in common. So when their meal was done and they got up to leave, I interrupted their conversation, apologized, and asked after our mutual acquaintance. We talked briefly, and then they started to leave again.

Until I stopped them by asking if they wanted a gift. I just happened to have one of my most successful psychomagical art projects with me in my backpack.

One of the girls said yes. She sat down. Over the next few minutes I passed her a magical book. She looked through it, made a choice, and then I took a page out of the book and gave it to her, along with a quest.

The kids were stunned, and left shouting in excitement about this being the way fantasy adventures begin. And I realized that it was true: I had literally been that fairy tale stranger who gives the hero a magical experience, leading to a quest, at midnight on Halloween. I was now that person. It just kind of happened. I too was stunned.

But that's not actually what I'm talking about: that's more like "if you're a lawyer, you will occasionally give out free legal advice to someone before you think it through." That's not the real change.

No, what happens is that the better you get at working with the unconscious minds of others, the more your own starts to wake up and take charge of your life. This can go several ways, depending on what kind of issues you have and how you react to it, and in the worst-case scenarios you go batshit crazy. If things go better, you just go a little crazy. You lose the sense that you are in charge of your life because you start being led around by synchronicities somehow arranged by your daimonic unconscious; you retain your capacity for rational thought but you find more and more that things go better if you act on the basis of symbolism and serendipity; you make intuitive leaps far more often than you're comfortable with; your private emotional life starts to become visible for everyone to see; the difference between "art" and "life" blurs; and reality gets weird.

And sometimes this is exciting and fun, sure, but do not underestimate how rocky this path is. When Robin Ziiro and I used to talk about forming a club of all the San Francisco psychomagical artists we really respect, we wanted to call it "*The Life Ruiners Guild.*"

"It's not always easy to avoid psychic injury due to improper application of magical thinking," Michael Ryan Garcia told me when we talked about this. "It's very easy to be so earnest and psychomagical in your approach that you get hit by a car, metaphorically or literally."

Marketing and branding companies will never be as good at psychomagic not because marketing and branding are evil (although, sure) but because they have different priorities: they can't really commit. But just "being an artist" isn't commitment enough either. Like anything else in life, if you want to get good at this you have to do a lot of work, and if you do a lot of work then you begin to resemble what you do.

I know I sound crazy. I know this sounds like an almost stereotypical warning from a bad fantasy cartoon, and it pains me. But the things you practice and the things you pay attention to and the habits you cultivate really do change you. That's how this works. So think of me, once again, as being a character from a fairy tale, standing in front of the entrance to strange and wondrous land, warning you: cross this threshold and your life will never be the same.

It doesn't actually work like that, of course. It takes time, and practice, to really ruin your life this way. But the warning is real. You become what you do. And as I've said over and over again: this is not benign.

Chapter 24:
Psychomagic, God, Therapy, and You

"(T)he only way to create significantly political art today is by making the visionary powers central. This widening of the creative field by grounding oneself in transformational vision is the only thing that can eliminate the spiritual sterility of modern life, and possibly save the world from suicide." - Suzi Gablik, Has Modernism Failed?

Art changes lives because it tends to raise the question: "how should we live?" Sometimes it does that in an overt and intellectual way - political agitprop is nothing if not blatant. Sometimes it does that by making us feel things we don't understand but are compelled by, and inviting us to follow those feelings to see where they lead.

In his book *The Use and Abuse of Art*, historian Jacques Barzun suggests that it is better not to talk about "Art," with a capital A, and instead to talk about "the arts" (lowercase) because in fact there are many different kinds of art and they all work in different ways and do different things. I have long thought this is probably the better approach. Or at least the more useful one for most conversations.

But while "Art" with a capital A may not be a real thing, it is a real concept that we have had since at least the period of German Idealism, and it has only become more important over time. Barzun was one of many thinkers - Suzi Gablik,

Philip Rieff, and Camille Paglia are others - who believed that modernity created "Art" because it needed an acceptable substitute for God.

Much of society has secularized, but human nature has not changed - and so the functions performed by religion are still needed. The two places we have ended up putting most of those functions are "art" and "therapy" - artists and therapists are now supposed to be the people who tend to our need for meaning, who hear our confessions, and who offer a sense of transcendence in the world. Together they are supposed to be able to cover all of that holy ground for those who hold nothing sacred.

But art and therapy are not religion. Even if they can do the job adequately (and I'm not at all convinced they can), they're going to do it differently. Different dynamics will emerge. The idea that you could simply slide religion out and put art and therapy in its place and have nothing change is misguided. I don't think secular culture has really reckoned with that dynamic.

Nevertheless, this is in many ways what San Francisco's psychomagical scene was attempting to do.

Art as Therapy as Art

They often didn't see themselves as artists or therapists. In fact, in the early days they were often dismissive of the very notion that they were doing "art."

"It wasn't an art movement," John Law told me.

"It was never conceived of as an art movement at all, so the latter day viewing of it and putting it in that context is interesting, and really needs to be addressed by anybody talking about it seriously, that's not what it was. ... we did not consider what we were doing to be art. Most people in the group - both earlier Suicide Club and later Cacophony - there were some people who were artists who were involved, people with artistic bents. But we did not take ourselves seriously as an art movement."

He added: "I've always identified with the concept of being a prankster. It just seemed like a better, less pretentious thing to do. I always felt that was more of an honest ... if you're going to put yourself in a box, that's a more honest box than art."

But whether or not they were "artists" who were "doing art," there's no question that they were obsessed by art, and by therapy, and that this obsession impacted everything that they did.

John noted that Gary Warne was "hugely influenced by Dada," and loved filmmaking and individual artists - he was informed by them all. And "Gary was always doing, from the very beginning, these really involved, psychologically compelling and confusing sometimes, events, that often incorporated 1970s style group therapy, hippie weird group therapy, along with a more traditional Freudian view of human interaction, Jungian."

"He wasn't a Freudian," John added, "but he read all that shit. It influenced him."

The further away John has gotten from those early events, the more he has seen Gary's work as a kind of therapeutic endeavor:

"(Gary) kept making and creating new mechanisms for exploring his own psyche, really. In retrospect - this is my revisionist view of it - I think that's why he was doing a lot of what he did. He was healing himself. He was trying to heal himself. This horrible fucking childhood. Unbelievable, gothic childhood. Great in some respects, but very lonely, very isolated, childhood."

Larry Harvey was very much a Freudian, and very interested in art, and also had a deeply lonely and isolated childhood.

John ... well, suffice it to say he ran away from home when he was a teenager and has a very deep knowledge of art and anti-art movements and is constantly introducing people to the work of their artistic forebears.

Is it a coincidence that many of the most early and influential figures in what would become the psychomagical experience scene were atheists who were fascinated by art and psychology and looking for ways to break out of their own sense of isolation and connect more deeply, both with others and with something larger?

No, I don't think so.

Viewed from this perspective, it's easy - perhaps too easy - to think of psychomagic as the kind of art that fills the gap in secular society left by religion. Or, if you're a more spiritual person, to think of psychomagic as a spiritual discipline - which is often exactly what it feels like anyway.

Suzi Gablik believed that the next major movement in art would be an explicit connection of the spiritual and the material, the transcendent and the immanent. In Has Modernism Failed? she wrote:

"Trying to make meaningful art in a society that doesn't believe in anything requires breaking down the rigidity of specialization, the segregation of functions and activities, both within the personality and within the community as a whole. It means reintroducing the artist in his role as shaman - a mystical, priestly, and political figure in prehistoric cultures, who, after coming close to death through accident or severe illness, becomes a visionary and a healer. The shaman's function is to balance and center society, integrating many planes of life-experience, and defining the culture's relationship to the cosmos. When these various domains (the human and divine) fall out of balance, it is the shaman's responsibility to restore the lost harmony and reestablish equilibrium. Only an individual who successfully masters his actions in both realms is a master shaman."

That's a book that I know Larry was familiar with, because he introduced me to it after discovering it near the end of his life.

I would love to talk about "the artist as a metamodern shaman," and what that would mean in society. Jodorowsky explicitly talks about psychomagic as a form of shamanic healing. But I can't - not because I think it's incorrect exactly, but because when people in primarily white spiritual communities start using the word "shaman" it pulls in all kinds of other white people who really love to use the word "shaman" a LOT, and are wildly enthusiastic about telling you just what kinds of shaman they are, and suddenly they're asking you if you want an energy healing and are trying to charge you for a somatic vision quest, and you are just filled with regret for ever opening your mouth.

So we're not doing that.

Scott Levkoff, incidentally, wrestled with the same issue years before I would.

"Before I realized the appropriative nature of this term I called what we did: 'Cosplay Shamanism," he told me. "Now

I refer to people in the Mystic Midway as 'facilitators.' We take on the various archetypal roles to facilitate moments of realization. We help uncover that which exists in plain sight for guests but might not have the permission or support to see it."

I have yet to find a word I like better. "Priest" and "sorcerer" and their synonyms just don't cover it, and "art therapist" is already its own well defined thing - so "psychomagical artist" is still my preferred term, until something better comes along. And maybe that's for the best. It's more humble, and so less an attractor of bullshit.

But you see Gablik's point though, right? If we have an art form that:

- Is at its best when it is tailored to specific people;
- Is able to bring out a sense of meaning and authenticity, and;
- Is able to connect that to a feeling of transcendence that
- Is able to heal psychological wounds and provide guidance through life, and;
- Is most potently practiced by people who are taking the profit motive out of it.

... then in a culture that is looking for spiritual substitutes, there's an obvious role for it to play here. One that used to be played almost exclusively by priests and now is often played by therapists.

Right? That just makes sense, right?

It does, and I've always been suspicious of that.

We Can Do This For Each Other

Among the informal circles of psychomagical practitioners in the San Francisco Life Ruiners Guild, we do often serve these roles for one another. I have been asked to create experiences to help people with their grief for lost loved ones, and their suicidal ideations, and communal struggles, as well as for fun and celebration. Though I have never explicitly asked for such support, I've received it - and it worked, and I was profoundly grateful.

Communal events and personal milestones are likewise marked with new psychomagical rituals. Chicken John's bachelor party was filled with bizarre and impossible events which I cannot relate to you because they went horribly off the rails and we all swore that we would never speak of it again and in fact pretend that it never happened. It was bad. But it was the kind of fiasco you have to really tap into something to achieve. At the wedding of Colin Fahrion and Tess Aquarium, on the other hand, they randomly passed out cards to each guest informing them of who they were and the role they would be playing - one person discovered he was the father of the bride, another the best man, another the creepy uncle, and so on. Once you had your part, you were expected to dive in and live it - not for a short, fun, game, but for the entire wedding, from ceremony through reception through afterparty. The stakes were all real: the "father of the bride" really walked her down the aisle, the "family" really gave the toasts ... and at the end Tess and Colin really got married. No one had ever seen anything like it.

We are, in a way, like a religious congregation made up entirely of priests who can never do the same ritual twice, and so have to create new ones for every occasion.

So there is a way in which, yes, it works exactly the way Gablik is talking about.

But it's also way too easy to romanticize. Remember, a lot of these people are all-but-starving artists crashing in corners of America's most superheated real estate market. In practical terms, rent control is our higher power. And for all that we're talking about creating the conditions for miracles to occur, it's not like any of us have superpowers. We don't - and we all know it. A lot of us don't even have our lives together. Not even close.

And Suzi Gablik wants us to restore the lost harmony and balance the equilibrium of our culture? US?

It makes me wonder if she's actually ever met any artists who are doing what she wants us to do.

Beyond the fact that I think she takes us entirely too seriously, I think there are important reasons why psychomagical art is less than ideal to carry the weight of our culture upon its shoulders.

Burning Bushes Don't Scale

As we saw at the beginning of this section, art scenes change. They become different as they grow, not just because people are doing things wrong but because they're doing things right. The longer I've spent in scenes like this, the more suspicious I've become about the idea of "scaling up."

There are many kinds of art it can work for, but I've never seen it work well for this. Up to a point, sure, but we frankly went through heroic efforts - absolutely broke ourselves - to create experiences that would hold potent psychomagic for 2,000 people (and then not even all at once). Michael Garcia had a similar issue with an experience he managed called "The Headlands Gamble," a multiday interactive narrative experience that was also a vacation in scenic west Marin County.

"We would customize the show each week for our clients, asking them to complete a detailed personal questionnaire about their background, relationships, and emotional state," Michael said. "As far as we could tell, we actually managed to create effective psychomagic for a good number of these clients, which is a pretty amazing feat when you think about it, but the customization of the show required a ton of research and thought and empathy and art production, all of which is extremely hard to maintain 'at scale.'"

I'm not saying it can't be done, but "scaling" as a goal is every bit as confounding a variable as "marketing" is. The moment that "scaling up" becomes an important enough goal that you make decisions based on whether it will scale rather than on the kind of experience it is, you start to displace the factors that make truly potent psychomagic possible.

It can scale, but not if scaling is a top priority. So ... paradox.

The one psychomagical experience I have seen ramp up in size and retain potency is Burning Man - and even there, as we discussed, it wasn't the same. When people ask me (as they often do) if "Burning Man has changed," I answer the question they mean to ask: is it still a truly different kind of place where extraordinary and miraculous things happen? And the answer to that is yes. Yes, it is, absolutely.

But what we haven't talked about yet is why it was able to do that. How it was able to grow to 80,000 people at its main event and remain a potent psychomagical force. Because there are reasons, and they matter in this discussion.

It's not - it's absolutely not - that Burning Man began to treat its most potent psychomagical artists as an elite class of priests who were consulted on matters of importance and provided visionary leadership. On the contrary: that's exactly what Burning Man did not do. And it's one of the reasons (just one) why over 30 years most of those most potent psychomagical artists moved on to other things. They'd pop back in and visit sometimes, but on the whole they tended to do their work there for a few years and then step off to other pastures. They're seen as having tremendous moral authority, and are often revered community elders, sure. But successfully demonstrating psychomagical prowess got them exactly nothing in the way of leadership, or money, or influence on Burning Man's decision making processes. It did get them social capital, which as I've written elsewhere is vitally important in Burning Man culture, but it didn't get them any more social capital than people who volunteer to pick up trash or cook meals or tend bars or build camps.

It's ironic for one of the most significant art movements of the late 20th and early 21st centuries, but a good artist at Burning Man is no more revered than is a good floor sweeper, and a great artist at Burning Man is no more revered than a great barista.

And yes, over time this has led many extraordinary artists to move on from Burning Man to other opportunities. And on the one hand, this has absolutely meant that Burning Man has missed out on some of incredible things they've done elsewhere in the world, but on the other hand the refusal to anoint a priestly class of official "artists" has been one of the key elements that has kept Burning Man such a potent psychomagical force.

That's because Burning Man has a participatory ethos instead - everybody contributes. It is an amateur ethos which means that while some people are better at things than others there is no exclusively "professional class" who are the only people allowed to be creative or do certain kinds of work. That doesn't refer just to psychomagic, but it applies there all the same: Burning Man doesn't anoint artists as a priestly class, because it wants everybody to be doing art.

Which means, ironically, that Burning Man culture has done a better job teaching psychomagic by example to new-comers than the San Francisco scene did after the late-90s. Burning Man's language doesn't encompass psychomagic directly ... its 10 Principles are focused on community building and authentic individual engagement ... but it was full of people doing psychomagical things out in public who were happy to let others participate and experience it, and talk about what they were doing.

So Burning Man loses some of its greatest practitioners after a while, but has continued to create an environment in which psychomagic is often (if often accidentally) practiced to a far greater extent.

No Priests, No Kings, No Lords, No Masters
The lesson here isn't that every cultural space should be like Burning Man - oh good lord no - but that if you want a world with more psychomagic in it, that more people have access to, you don't do it by creating a separate priestly class.

You don't make psychomagical art the province of elite

practitioners and say "this is what THEY do." You do it by creating a participatory culture. And yes, a lot of what a participatory culture produces will be mediocre and not really what you want to see, but you'll also be amazed by how many incredible things people create if given a chance. Over time people come to recognize artists and psychomagic as important, and while they'll never give them the same level of individual support they would have given those few priestly artists, there will still be a broader base of support for people who are gifted in this.

For a lot of people - including me - this isn't as temperamentally satisfying as pouring esteem and resources into the very best artists and telling them to go forth and create, and sure there are times when that's exactly what you want to do. But on the whole, I've seen the more participatory, egalitarian approach produce better results over and over again. If you're just trying to get a single, glorious experience created, yeah, go to the elite artists and creators. But if you want to create a scene, a culture, in which more people have access to psychomagic, then create a participatory and open environment without VIP rooms, inner temples, and velvet ropes.

But that still doesn't mean that Burning Man has solved the problem of scaling. If only. No, what they've done very successfully is push this whole thing past the point that many people thought it would be possible to do at all - 80,000 people in one place! - but they're still encountering the same basic problem. Because their solution to scaling requires that new people who enter the culture see models of what to do all around them, and are able to participate and talk to people about what that means. But that works best when you have slow and managed growth, so that the new people who come in all have easy, even unavoidable, access to people who can model the culture for them.

Increasingly, Burning Man has encountered exponential growth spearheaded by people who have no prior experience with Burning Man culture beyond what they've read on the internet, which means it is entirely possible for new people to come in and be mostly surrounded by ... other new people whose only experience with Burning Man culture is what they've read on the internet.

How can they become part of a culture they don't understand? How do you welcome new people in and incorporate them into it while keeping it connected to what made it worth doing in the first place?

Burning Man may figure that out, but they haven't yet. What they have done is that it is possible to *get bigger*, not that it "can scale."

I still have not yet seen any evidence that it is possible for psychomagic to truly scale ... and without that, the kind of social change Gablik envisions cannot be achieved by artists alone. Society should not put that on us, and we should not put that on ourselves.

Which is to say that, just as psychomagic gets less effective when you try to use it for marketing and branding, it also gets less effective when you try to use it to save the world. The whole point of psychomagic is that you're opening the door to whatever comes next. Saving the world may be an altruistic agenda, but it is still an agenda layered on top of the experience you're creating, which will quickly lead to diminishing returns.

"Oh no," you'll say, "your unconscious can't want to go THERE, because that's NOT saving the world!" and suddenly the whole thing doesn't work.

Honestly, I too wish that a league of psychomagical artists could form a priestly class whose wisdom and prowess would lead us to a better future as we shape the psyches of our communities. Then I get over myself. People who are really good at one thing always assume they should be in charge. Psychomagic surely has a role to play in art and culture, but it's not a panacea or a short cut. It's an amazing thing that can change lives and support communities, but then the work still has to be done.

Put another way: psychomagic can *change* the world, but not save it.

But then, that's just like everything, isn't it. Literacy

changed the world but didn't save it. Computers changed the world but didn't save it. Democracy changed the world but didn't save it. And all of these things are at their most impactful when they are at their most accessible. They do what they do best when everyone has access. The only reason to keep people from having access to literacy and computers and democracy, and understanding how they work, is if you want to hold something over them.

A Door To An Infinite Magical Garden
Much like literacy, psychomagic has enriched my life so profoundly that I can't imagine who I would be without it. Like computers, psychomagic has made my life far more complicated than it might otherwise be in ways good and bad. Like democracy, I am frequently terrified of where psychomagic might take me.

What sets psychomagic apart is that it is also anti-utilitarian. It resists being done for any reason other than to be done for its own sake. It can be yoked to another purpose, but the tighter you bind them together the less effective the whole thing becomes.

Which brings us back to you. Inevitably, always, back to you.

Here we have this thing, this kind of experience, present in so many places and cultures but brought to a particular height and shine in a remarkable underground scene in late

20th and early 21st century San Francisco. Now on the decline again because it is hard to hold on to - which makes it more like democracy than literacy or computers. It costs no money, but if you try to do it halfway you're not really doing it at all. It will offer you some of the greatest experiences of your life, but it will change your life in ways you can't imagine. And while it can have a profoundly valuable place in society, it cannot be scaled, it cannot be automated, and for all your good intentions it will often not go where you tell it to go or do what you tell it to do.

Do you want to learn how to do this?

For its own sake?

Because that's really the only way to do it. Yes, these techniques can be used by companies to brand products and museums to make exhibits and theater companies to create different kinds of shows, and communities to create connecting rituals, and all manner of things. And that's great. They can, and should, absolutely do that. We'll all be better off for it.

But this kind of breakthrough experience design, this creation of an infinite magical garden where miracles can occur, this ability to have something that feels exactly like magic flash through people's lives like lightning ... it really only works like this when you do it for its own sake.

And that might ruin your life.

Is it worth it?

I think so. I'd do it all over again, no questions asked.

I feel so blessed, so lucky, to have been part of this, and seen what I've seen. To have lived in a community where this was so plentiful we almost ... almost ... took it for granted.

But it's not for everyone. It's one art form among many, one human endeavor among many.

We're just artists. Of a sort.

There was a time, not so long ago, when I wouldn't have published this book. When I would have printed it up on thick paper, had it bound by hand with a strange hardcover, and left it somewhere for you to find. Perhaps on a rock by a stream, or sitting on a table at an outdoor cafe, or even - if I was feeling especially bold - slipped it through the crack in the window of your car, so that you'd find it on the passenger seat with no explanation.

Finding it like that - a book like this with no provenance, no history, no information at all, just waiting for you - would have been a profound and uncanny invitation. Of course you'd look at it. Of course you'd open it. And then you'd find a description of a surreal and extraordinary art scene and an explanation of the psyche and a course in elements of psychomagic, promising that if you do this ... if you do ... your life will change. There will be miracles, and you will no longer be in charge.

What a moment you would have, deciding whether to keep reading. Deciding what to do.

Oh, I want to do that. I want to give you this book that way.

But I decided to do this instead. To publish it. To root it in time and space, in the belief that more interesting things will ultimately happen if more people read it. To try to correct the mistake the San Francisco underground made of not adequately teaching the next generation. This is, I suppose, my attempt at getting bigger. Not "to scale," but to make sure I reach you. To make sure I didn't miss you.

So it's no longer a book privately and mysteriously found one day at an odd corner of your life.

But it's the same doorway, and the same invitation.

You can be part of this lineage. You can run away and join this circus. You can create an infinite magical garden. You can build a scene.

I would like it if you do that. I would like that very much.

You already know if you want to try. You knew that a hundred pages ago.

Having read everything that came before, now you understand that this moment - this outstretched hand - this choice you make, is really all that matters.

We'll be here, you know where. There is a magical bar where every drink order is a prayer. There are pianos in the park where we can be summoned. I'll be in a diner, just before midnight. The circus leaves at 2 a.m

Acknowledgments

The fact that this book never mentions either the Church of the Subgenius or the Billboard LIberation Front is all the proof you need that it is a "how to" and not a "history of." Over 300 people worked on 2015's "The Fallen Cosmos" alone, all of whom deserve recognition. Over the course of 30 years, thousands of people moved through this scene, doing extraordinary things. Many important, influential members of this lineage have been unjustly left out. In some cases this is because I didn't think they were the right examples to illustrate what I was getting at in what I hoped to be a short book; in some cases it's because so much of their work has been underground and secret that it wasn't really possible to both mention their names and explain why I was doing so without violating their trust; and in some cases, it's because I actually didn't realize they were the people who had done something amazing. During the design process of this book, for example, I briefly lived with a group of mostly strangers and was shocked to discover that they were behind a recent art prank that received international attention. I'd had no idea.

There are absolute geniuses who were not mentioned here, and they should be acknowledged.

Among them are Ms. P Segal (whose role in establishing the scene in the early days was so, so, crucial), Ty Mckenzie, Helena Nolan, Paul Hayes, Naomi Most, Eugene Ashton-

Gonzalez, David Fine, Dori Daniels, Andrew Lowe, Rebecca Power, Uriah Findley, Tracey Feldstein, Donald Bruce, Valerie Leavy, Spy Emerson, Jamie DeWolf, Joshua Marker, Courtney King, Julian Cash, Lynae Zebest, Jeremy Pollock, Cynthia Crews-Pollock, Zoltan DiBartolo, Benja Juster, Joshu DeLeon, Ben Thompson, Brody Scotland, Whitney Deatherage, Harrod Blank, Christopher T. Palmer, Sean Kelley, James Cross (that guy has done SO much work!), Rachel Weidinger, Hillary Andujar, Kate Willett, Mark Krawczuk, Justin Oliphant, Nieves Rathbun, Jim Mason, Mikl Em, Rusty Blazenhoff, Dr. Hal...

And so many more.

I'd also like to particularly thank Stuart Mangrum, both for his long and pivotal involvement in the scene, and for his personal support.

And Andie Grace, who has believed in my capacity to be of use to something she loves, and entrusted it to me, to a degree that still takes my breath away.

About the Author

Caveat Magister is frequently mistaken for a fictional character. He has lived in a Buddhist monastery in India, covered international nightlife for Playboy.com, taught autobiographical writing to high school age students in prison, was a founding member of Burning Man's Philosophical Center, the founding board chair of The San Francisco Institute of Possibility, and covered regional politics for newspapers in upstate New York while he was the bar columnist for the San Francisco Weekly.

He publishes a weekly newsletter and creates exclusive new work for his Patreon, at Patreon.com/BenjaminWachs. His public writing and appearances can also be followed by signing up for his email list at FascinatingStranger.com

Other Books By Caveat Magister (sometimes under the clever pen name of Benjamin Wachs):

The Scene That Became Cities: what Burning Man philosophy can teach us about building better communities

Lamenting Avalon: and other Fairy Tales for Adults

The Deeds of Pounce

A Guide To Bars and Nightlife in the Sacred City